OECD Studies on SMEs and Entrepreneurship

SME and Entrepreneurship Policy in Kazakhstan 2018

OECD

BETTER POLICIES FOR BETTER LIVES

This work is published under the responsibility of the Secretary-General of the OECD. The opinions expressed and arguments employed herein do not necessarily reflect the official views of OECD member countries.

This document, as well as any data and any map included herein, are without prejudice to the status of or sovereignty over any territory, to the delimitation of international frontiers and boundaries and to the name of any territory, city or area.

Please cite this publication as:
OECD (2018), *SME and Entrepreneurship Policy in Kazakhstan 2018*, OECD Studies on SMEs and Entrepreneurship, OECD Publishing, Paris.
https://doi.org/10.1787/9789264301450-en

ISBN 978-92-64-30144-3 (print)
ISBN 978-92-64-30145-0 (PDF)

Series: OECD Studies on SMEs and Entrepreneurship
ISSN 2078-0982 (print)
ISSN 2078-0990 (online)

The statistical data for Israel are supplied by and under the responsibility of the relevant Israeli authorities. The use of such data by the OECD is without prejudice to the status of the Golan Heights, East Jerusalem and Israeli settlements in the West Bank under the terms of international law.

Photo credits: Cover © PhotoAlto/Getty Images, © David Wasserman/Brand X Pictures/Getty Images, © Tim Pannell/Corbis, © Andersen Ross/Photodisc/Getty Images.

Corrigenda to OECD publications may be found on line at: *www.oecd.org/about/publishing/corrigenda.htm*.

Foreword

This publication presents the OECD country review of small and medium-sized enterprise (SME) and entrepreneurship policy in Kazakhstan. The report is part of the series OECD Studies on SMEs and Entrepreneurship undertaken by the OECD Centre for Entrepreneurship, SMEs, Regions and Cities. In addition to Kazakhstan, country reviews have covered Canada, Indonesia, Israel, Italy, Mexico, Poland, the Russian Federation and Thailand.

The series provides a tool for assessing and improving the design and implementation of SME and entrepreneurship policy and for sharing policy experiences among OECD member and partner countries. The reviews are based on a standard methodology, which includes a diagnostic questionnaire completed by national government authorities, a fact-finding mission by an OECD team to hold detailed interviews with policy and business stakeholders, and discussion of a draft report at a peer review session in the OECD Working Party on SMEs and Entrepreneurship (WPSMEE). The final report of the Kazakhstan review of SME and entrepreneurship policy was approved by the WPSMEE through written procedure on 24 August 2018.

Kazakhstan has made great strides in improving its business environment for SMEs and entrepreneurship, generating new start-up enterprises and increasing its stock of SMEs. It has set ambitious targets to take this further and to enable SMEs and entrepreneurship to be a main driver of economic transformation in the country. It has a well-organised policy system for supporting SMEs and entrepreneurship nationally and in the regions. This report shows where this policy system can be strengthened to achieve national SME and entrepreneurship objectives. It recommends that the priority be placed on developing additional targeted policy instruments favouring innovative and growth-oriented entrepreneurship and supporting SMEs to increase their productivity with enhanced measures for business advice, training of SME workforces and business innovation.

This report was undertaken at the request of the Ministry of National Economy of Kazakhstan. It is one of several policy reviews and capacity building projects prepared by the OECD for the government of Kazakhstan on themes including public governance, fiscal affairs, education, competitiveness and business climate, health, employment and social inclusion, statistics and the environment, developed through the Country Programme agreed between the OECD and the government of Kazakhstan for the period 2015-2018.

Acknowledgements

This review was undertaken by the OECD Centre for Entrepreneurship, SMEs, Regions and Cities (CFE) led by Lamia Kamal-Chaoui, Director, in co-operation with the Ministry of National Economy of the Government of Kazakhstan.

The project was led by Jonathan Potter, Head of the Entrepreneurship Policy and Analysis Unit under the responsibility of Miriam Koreen, Deputy Director of the OECD Centre for Entrepreneurship, SMEs, Regions and Cities and Head of the SME and Entrepreneurship Division. The report was drafted by a team involving report co-ordinator Stuart Thompson, Marco Marchese, Jonathan Potter and Kris Boschmans of OECD/CFE with Lois Stevenson and Sirin Elci (consultants). Important local support and inputs were provided by Ilyas Iskakov (consultant).

Within the Ministry of National Economy, project organisation and report development contributions were made by Chingis Akhmetov, Acting Director, Department of Entrepreneurship Development; Dinara Tazhenova, Head of Division, Department of Entrepreneurship Development; and Assel Yegemberdiyeva and Zhanar Darimbetova, Centre for Trade Policy Development JSC.

A Steering Group was formed for this review from among the delegates of the OECD Working Party on SMEs and Entrepreneurship, involving Michiko Enomoto (United Nations Economic Commission for Europe), Piret Triberg (Ministry of Economic Affairs and Communications, Estonia), and Ulrich Oberndorfer (Permanent Mission of the Federal Republic of Germany to the OECD).

The review benefitted from the support of the OECD Global Relations Secretariat and the Eurasia Division responsible for the Kazakhstan Country Programme, notably William Tompson, Head of Division, Jean-François Lengellé, Daniel Quadbeck and Zhanar Darimbetova.

Many individuals and organisations in Kazakhstan provided important information for the review study, including the Ministry of National Economy, the Damu Entrepreneurship Development Fund, the National Chamber of Entrepreneurs, the Forum of Entrepreneurs, KAZKA, the National Bank of Kazakhstan, Tsesna Bank, the State Revenue Committee, the Ministry for Investment and Development, the Socio Entrepreneur Company Astana, the Economic Research Institute, the Ministry of Agriculture, KazAgro, the Fund for Financial Support of Agriculture, the Ministry of Labour and Social Protection of the Population, Nazarbayev University, the Ministry of Education and Science, the Astana regional government authority, National Company "Kazakh Invest" JSC, the National Agency for Technological Development, the Technology Commercialisation Centre, the Kazakhstan Development Bank, Astana Innovations, the National Agency for Development of Local Content, National Managing Holding "Baiterek" JSC, the World Bank and the European Union.

Table of contents

Tables

Figures

Boxes

Abbreviations

BAS	Business Advisory Services
BEEPS	Business Environment and Enterprise Performance Survey
BRM	Business Road Map
CIS	Commonwealth of Independent States
EACU	Eurasian Customs Union
EBRD	European Bank of Reconstruction and Development
ECA	Eastern Europe and Central Asia
EDD	Entrepreneurship Development Department
EGP	Enterprise Growth Programme
ERM	Employment Road Map
ESC	Entrepreneurship Support Centre
FDI	Foreign Direct Investment
GDP	Gross Domestic Product
GEM	Global Entrepreneurship Monitor
GOK	Government of Kazakhstan
HEI	Higher Education Institution
ICAC	Independent Commission Against Corruption (Hong Kong)
ICT	Information and Communication Technology
ISC	Investor Support Centre
JA	Junior Achievement
KAB	Know About Business
KEI	Knowledge Economy Index
KIDI	Kazakhstan Industry Development Institute
KZT	Kazakh Tenge
MES	Ministry of Education and Science
MNE	Ministry of National Economy
NADLoC	National Agency for the Development of Local Content
NATD	National Agency for Technological Development
NBK	National Bank of Kazakhstan
NCE	National Chamber of Entrepreneurs
NGO	Non-Governmental Organisation
NIF	National Innovation Fund
NPL	Non- Performing Loan
OCS	Office of the Chief Scientist (Israel)
OECD	Organisation for Economic Cooperation and Development
R&D	Research and Development
SEC	Social Entrepreneurial Corporation
SME	Small and Medium sized Enterprise
SPAIID	State Programme of Accelerated Industrial Innovative Development
STEM	Science Technology Engineering Mathematics
STEP	Shell Technology Enterprise Programme (UK)
SYB	Start Your Business
SYE	School of Young Entrepreneurs
TCC	Technology Commercialisation Centre
TEA	Total early-stage entrepreneurial activity
TVE	Technical and Vocational Education
VET	Vocational Education and Training
WEF	World Economic Forum

Basic Statistics of Kazakhstan

	KAZ	OECD average		KAZ	OECD average
Population (million) (2016)	17.8		Population density per km² (2016)	6.59	37.5
Under 15 (%)	27.4	18.1	Life expectancy (years, 2015)	72	80.6*
Over 65 (%)	6.8	16.0	Men	67.5	77.9*
Latest 3-year (2012-2014) average population growth (%)	1.44	0.54	Women	76.9	83.1*
ECONOMY					
Gross domestic product (GDP) (volume, 2016)			Value added shares (%) (2016)		
In current prices (billion USD)	137.2		Agriculture	4.83	
In current prices (billion KZT)	46 971		Industry	33.88	
Latest 5-year (2012-2016) average GDP growth (%)	3.46	1.7	Services	61.29	
Per capita (000 USD PPP)	7.71	40.0			
EXTERNAL ACCOUNTS					
Exchange rate (KZT per USD) (2016) (average)	342.16		Main merchandise exports (balance-of-payments basis) (% of total merchandise exports), 2016		
Exports of goods and services (% of GDP, 2016)	31.87	28	Fuel exports	60.74	
Imports of goods and services (% of GDP, 2016)	28.32	28	Manufactures exports	18.42	
Current account balance (% of GDP, 2016)	-6.5	0.2	Ores and metals exports	14.77	
			Main merchandise imports (balance-of- payment basis) (% of total merchandise imports), 2015		
			Manufactures imports	77.83	
			Food imports	11.72	
LABOUR MARKET, SKILLS AND INNOVATION					
Employment rate for 15-64 year-olds (%) (2016)	67.9	66.9	Unemployment rate (age 15 and over, %) (2016)	5	6.3
Men	75.6	74.7	Youth (age 15-24, %) (2016)	4.5	13.0
Women	69.4	59.3	Long-term (1 year and over) (% of total unemployment) (2015)	11.6	30.5
			Tertiary educational attainment 25-64 year-olds (%, 2015)	55	35
			Expenditure on Research and Development (R&D) as a % of GDP (2016)	0.17	2.4

Note: OECD average is the average of the 35 OECD countries.
Source: World Bank Group Country Statistical Profile of Kazakhstan, 2017, https://data.worldbank.org/country/Kazakhstan, OECD Employment Outlook 2017, OECD Labour Force Statistics 2018, Health at a Glance 2017, OECD Factbook 2015-2016, OECD Quarterly International Trade Statistics.

Executive summary

The rate of business creation in Kazakhstan is high and there is a very large base of small businesses. However, small firm productivity is low, there are relatively few high growth firms, and few small businesses reach significant scale. This report analyses the issues and makes concrete proposals on how the government of Kazakhstan can release the untapped potential of small businesses to drive economic growth.

Key findings

Kazakhstan has many SMEs, but their economic contribution is low

Kazakhstan has many small and medium-sized enterprises (SMEs) by international standards, with more than 10 SMEs per 100 working age inhabitants. The rate of new business activity is also high, with nascent and new business owners representing 11.3% of the adult population in 2017. However, just 25% of the value added of the national economy comes from SMEs, which is lower than any OECD country and below several other Commonwealth of Independent States (CIS) countries.

Regulation and tax have become much more business friendly, but there are other business environment challenges

Kazakhstan has made striking improvements in its overall business environment, shifting from 74th in the World Bank Doing Business rankings in 2010 to 36th in 2018. Business surveys nevertheless identify barriers to SME development in the areas of corruption, business informality, an inadequately educated workforce, and inadequate access to finance. Low expenditure on research and development (R&D) also impede SME innovation and innovative start-ups.

The government is committed to SME and entrepreneurship development

The government has made it a priority to strengthen SMEs and entrepreneurship. A dedicated department within the Ministry of National Economy leads and coordinates the policy effort, and the Business Road Map 2020 sets out the main programme interventions. However, it is important to better connect the distribution of policy expenditure by type of programme and target enterprise to the scale of need and expected benefits.

Programme delivery has recently been reorganised. It now rests substantially on four government organisations: the Damu Entrepreneurship Development Fund, which concentrates on financial support; the National Chamber of Entrepreneurs, which provides training and consultancy through a network of Entrepreneurship Support Centres; the National Agency for Technological Development, which supports innovation; and the Autonomous Cluster Fund, which supports high technology start-ups. This system is well constructed. However, there is a need for further professional development and capacity building support to secure high quality business advice from the incubators and Entrepreneurship Support Centres.

Programmes should be boosted for skills, innovation, business advice, finance, and youth and women entrepreneurship

There is a wide range of SME and entrepreneurship development programmes in Kazakhstan but some areas of intervention need strengthening. Numbers of participants and budgets are low in the areas of entrepreneurship training, SME management skills development, SME innovation, SME internationalisation and support for women and youth entrepreneurs. At the same time, new initiatives should support business development needs diagnosis, SME financial literacy development, non-bank financing instruments, and training in SMEs. Success rates of the graduates of entrepreneurship training courses in starting businesses are also low and the approach should be modified.

More could be done to respond to regional diversity

Kazakhstan is very diverse in its regional economic structures and the scale and characteristics of SME and entrepreneurship activity across its regions but the government programmes are largely national. Through their bids and co-funding support, regional governments help adjust the scale of Business Road Map 2020 programme expenditures to the needs, but there are still strong regional differences in the scale of small business support compared with the size of the small business base. Better tailoring of national policies to regional needs could be achieved by developing medium-term regional development strategies linked to new multi-annual regional development budgets, including explicit SME and entrepreneurship actions. Attention is also needed to level up the quality of implementation of business regulations across the regions, making use of the new regional one-stop shops for business support.

Linkages can be strengthened between foreign direct investors and SMEs

Kazakhstan has attracted substantial foreign direct investment (FDI), but the linkages with domestic SME suppliers tend to be limited. There are fledgling initiatives seeking to address this, such as the inclusion of FDI aftercare activities in the remits of the new regional Investor Service Centres and pilot actions to create linkage building teams and demonstration projects with specific FDI ventures in certain regions. These types of actions should be spread more widely across Kazakhstan.

Key recommendations

- Focus policies on SME productivity growth and high-growth potential enterprises rather than simply increasing business numbers.
- Strengthen skills and innovation in the wider economy and promote banking reforms for small business lending.
- Expand and enhance current programmes for entrepreneurship skills, management skills, and SME workforce skills. Increase support for women and youth entrepreneurship. Widen options for access to finance. Boost initiatives for SME innovation and internationalisation.
- Introduce a programme for high-growth potential enterprises in growth pole cities, shift to a multi-annual budget framework for regional SME and entrepreneurship development programmes, and increase the coordination of regional authorities in the implementation of business regulations.
- Create FDI-SME linkage building teams and actions in every region of the country.

Chapter 1. Assessment and recommendations

This chapter summarises the main findings and recommendations of the Kazakhstan SME and entrepreneurship policy review. It covers SME and entrepreneurship characteristics and performance, the business environment for SMEs and entrepreneurship, the strategic framework and delivery arrangements for SME and entrepreneurship policy, national SME and entrepreneurship programmes, the local dimension of SME and entrepreneurship policy, and the promotion of linkages between foreign direct investors and domestic SMEs.

SME and entrepreneurship structure and performance

There are many SMEs, but they are relatively small

The number of SMEs in Kazakhstan is large by international standards, relative to the size of the working age population (Figure 1.1). Moreover, SME activity has been growing. The number of SMEs increased by an average of 12%, employment by 10%, and GDP by 19% per annum between 2002 and 2013 (Figure 1.2).

Figure 1.1. SMEs per 100 working age population

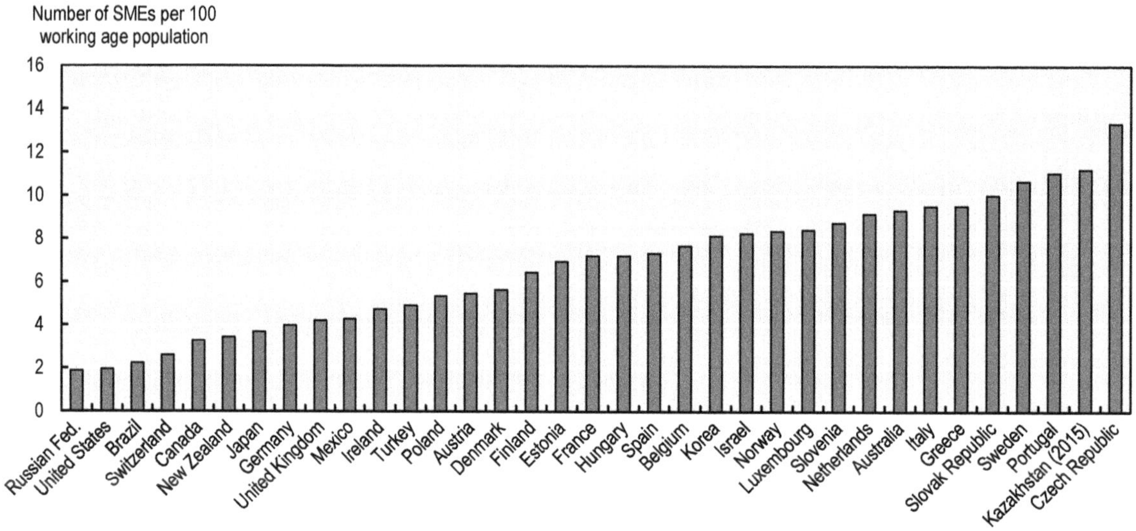

Source: OECD (2016a) Entrepreneurship at a Glance 2016, OECD Publishing, Paris. http://dx.doi.org/10.1787/entrepreneur_aag-2016-en.The Figures are for 2013 or latest available year. The data for Kazakhstan are from the Ministry of National Economy's Committee on Statistics. The figures for Kazakhstan are for 2015.

StatLink http://dx.doi.org/10.1787/888933827669

Figure 1.2. Evolution of numbers, employment and GDP contribution of SMEs in Kazakhstan

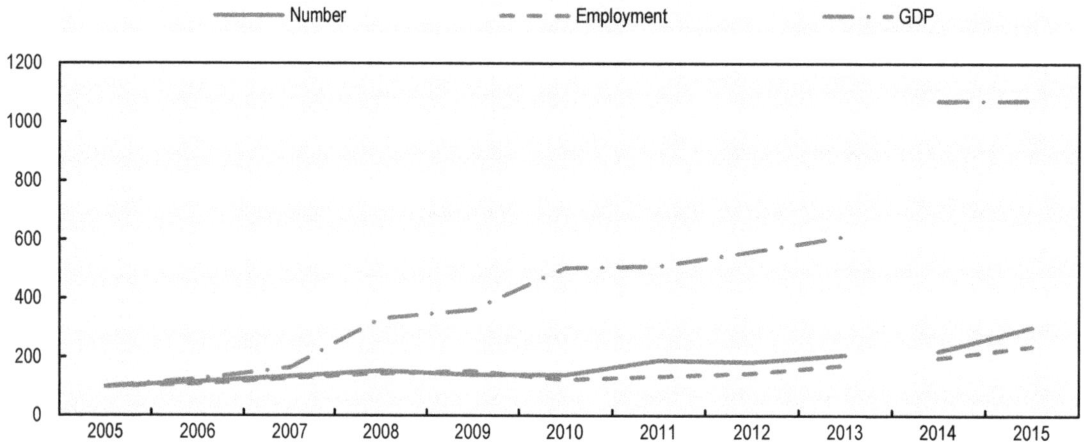

Source: Ministry of National Economy, Committee on Statistics, 2005 =100. Note that owing to changes in definition, figures for 2013 and 2014 are not directly comparable.

StatLink http://dx.doi.org/10.1787/888933827688

However, the SME population includes a large number of very small firms (including those run by independent entrepreneurs). Accordingly, the SME contribution to employment (31%) and value added (25%) is small compared to most Commonwealth of Independent States (CIS) and OECD countries (Figure 1.3). There is also a strong sector weighting of businesses towards the wholesale and retail trade and much more limited numbers of SMEs in manufacturing.

Figure 1.3. Percentage of employment in SMEs, 2013

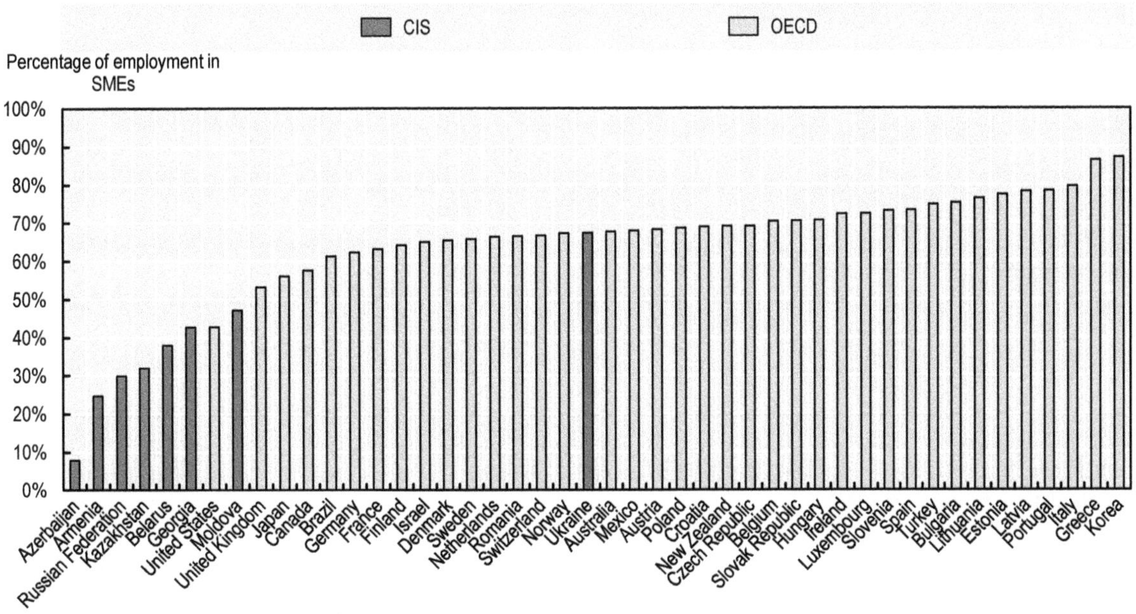

Source: OECD (2016a), Entrepreneurship at a Glance 2016, OECD Publishing, Paris, http://dx.doi.org/10.1787/entrepreneur_aag-2016-en, and OECD/European Union/EBRD/ETF (2015), SME Policy Index: Eastern Partner Countries 2016: Assessing the Implementation of the Small Business Act for Europe, OECD Publishing, Paris. http://dx.doi.org/10.1787/9789264246249-en.
Note: The figures are for 2013 or the latest available year. The figures for Kazakhstan are from the Ministry of National Economy, Committee on Statistics and are for 2015.

StatLink http://dx.doi.org/10.1787/888933827707

Kazakhstan enjoys a healthy entrepreneurial spirit

The Global Entrepreneurship Monitor (GEM) shows that entrepreneurship was seen as a desirable career choice by approximately 60% of the population in Kazakhstan and as high-status by approximately 80% in 2017 (Singer, Herrington and Menipaz, 2018). Furthermore, at 11.3%, the share of total early-stage entrepreneurs in Kazakhstan compares favourably with many other countries, and 50% of the population perceive opportunities for entrepreneurship. These data indicate very positive attitudes to entrepreneurship in Kazakhstan. On the other hand, the established business ownership rate, estimated at 2.4% in 2017, is below the rates observed in most other countries (Table 1.1.), suggesting a need to continue to add businesses to the enterprise population.

Table 1.1.Share of the adult population involved in entrepreneurship activities, 2017

	Nascent entrepreneurship rate	New business ownership rate	Early-stage entrepreneurial activity (TEA)	Established business ownership rate	Discontinuation of businesses
	Percent of the adult population				Percent of TEA
Thailand	10.6	12.1	21.6	15.2	9.2
Qatar	4.7	2.8	7.4	1.3	5.8
Iran	6.8	6.9	13.3	10.6	6.6
China	3.7	6.4	9.9	6.8	2.8
Vietnam	2.5	20.8	23.3	24.7	4.2
Indonesia	3.6	3.9	7.5	10.4	4.8
United States	9.4	4.6	13.6	7.8	4.0
Kazakhstan	8.0	3.8	11.3	2.4	7.5
Australia	6.4	5.9	12.2	9.0	3.8
Canada	11.3	8.1	18.8	6.2	6.9
Taiwan	3.6	5.0	8.6	12.1	4.0
European Union	5.1	3.1	8.1	7.0	2.9
Bosnia and Herzegovina	2.5	1.4	4.0	1.4	1.3
Switzerland	4.7	3.9	8.5	10.5	1.1
India	4.9	4.6	9.3	6.2	3.2
Malaysia	15.4	6.6	21.6	3.8	8.3
Japan	3.2	1.6	4.7	6.3	1.5

Source: Singer, S., Herrington M.,Menipaz Ehud (2018), Global Entrepreneurship Monitor, Global Report 2017/18. Babson College, Universidad del Desarrollo, Universiti Tun Abdul Razak, Korea Entrepreneurship Foundation. Figures for 2017.

The gap between female and male entrepreneurship rates is small in Kazakhstan by international comparison (Khanin et al, 2017; Sange Research Centre, 2013). However, women entrepreneurs are concentrated in the smallest businesses. They also tend to be more involved than male entrepreneurs in trade and hospitality services, and less in construction, farming and manufacturing.

Limited SME exporting and innovation

Only a small proportion of SMEs are exporters, much lower than other upper middle income countries, or countries in Eastern Europe and Central Asia, even though a similar proportion use imported goods.

Table 1.2. Participation of SMEs in trade, 2013

	Kazakhstan	Small Firms (1-19 Employees)	Medium Firms (20-99 Employees)	Large Firms (100+ Employees)	Eastern Europe & Central Asia	Upper middle income
% of Exporter Firms	5.2	2.5	6.8	16.3	22.8	19.1
% of Firms that Use Material Inputs and/or Supplies of Foreign origin	64.0	59.9	65.3	73.7	64.8	67.5

Source: World Bank (2013), Kazakhstan Country Profile 2013: Enterprise Surveys, Washington DC. http://www.enterprisesurveys.org/~/media/GIAWB/EnterpriseSurveys/Documents/Profiles/English/Kazakhstan-2013.pdf\.

SME innovation rates are also limited, as shown for example by a relatively low percentage of sales from new products (Figure 1.4). On the other hand, the European Bank for Reconstruction and Development (EBRD) / World Bank Business Environment and Enterprise Performance Survey (BEEPS) shows that the proportion of companies involved in innovation activities increased steadily from 2.3% in 2004 to 8.1% in 2014.

Figure 1.4. Percentage of sales accounted for by new products, country comparison, 2014

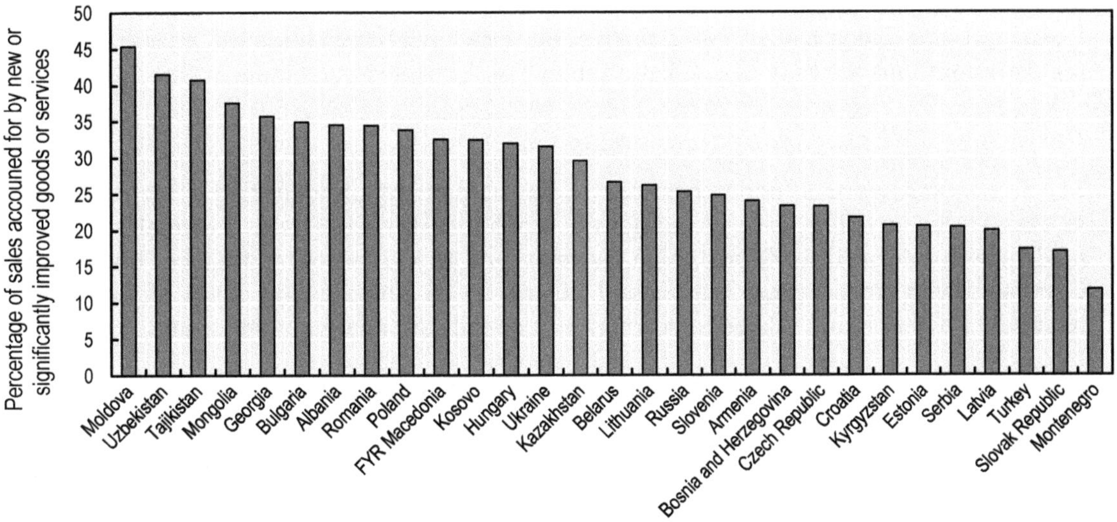

Source: OECD calculations from data from European Bank for Reconstruction and Development (EBRD) / World Bank Business Environment and Economic Performance Survey (BEEPS) V.

StatLink http://dx.doi.org/10.1787/888933827726

Key policy recommendations on SME and entrepreneurship characteristics and performance

- Noting recent healthy business start-up rates and growth in numbers of SMEs, increase the weight of policy attention to encouraging high productivity SMEs, specifically by:
    - Identifying and addressing barriers to high productivity and growth in medium-sized enterprises; and
    - Introducing targeted support to high-growth potential innovative start-ups and SMEs.

Business environment

Long-run macroeconomic conditions are favourable

Economic growth in Kazakhstan has generated 2.3 million jobs since 2000, signalling favourable conditions for SMEs and entrepreneurship (OECD, 2016b). However, Kazakhstan has a relatively narrow economic base, with extractive industries and related activities generating around 30% of GDP and close to two-thirds of exports. Further SME and entrepreneurship development is required to diversify the economy.

Substantial progress has been made in improving business regulation

Kazakhstan has significantly improved its ranking in the World Bank Doing Business survey, from 74th position in 2010 to 36th position in 2018 (World Bank, 2018). Progress has been especially remarkable in improving the ease of starting a new business and offering an effective insolvency regime. These achievements have resulted from major reforms by the Kazakhstan government, such as eliminating registration fees for SMEs, shortening registration time at the public registration centre, and eliminating the obligation to register at the local tax office. It is important that these de jure improvements in legislation are accompanied by effective de facto implementation to ensure that the regulatory reforms are fully enacted and achieve the expected outcomes.

Barriers to SMEs and entrepreneurship

The five most important 'main obstacles' to business operation identified by entrepreneurs in Kazakhstan in 2013 were corruption, competing practices of the informal sector, an inadequately educated workforce, high tax rates, and lack of access to finance (Figure 1.5). Compared with other Eastern Europe and Central Asian countries, the regulatory burden is relatively low but issues related to corruption and skills are relatively important.

Figure 1.5. Major obstacles to business, 2013

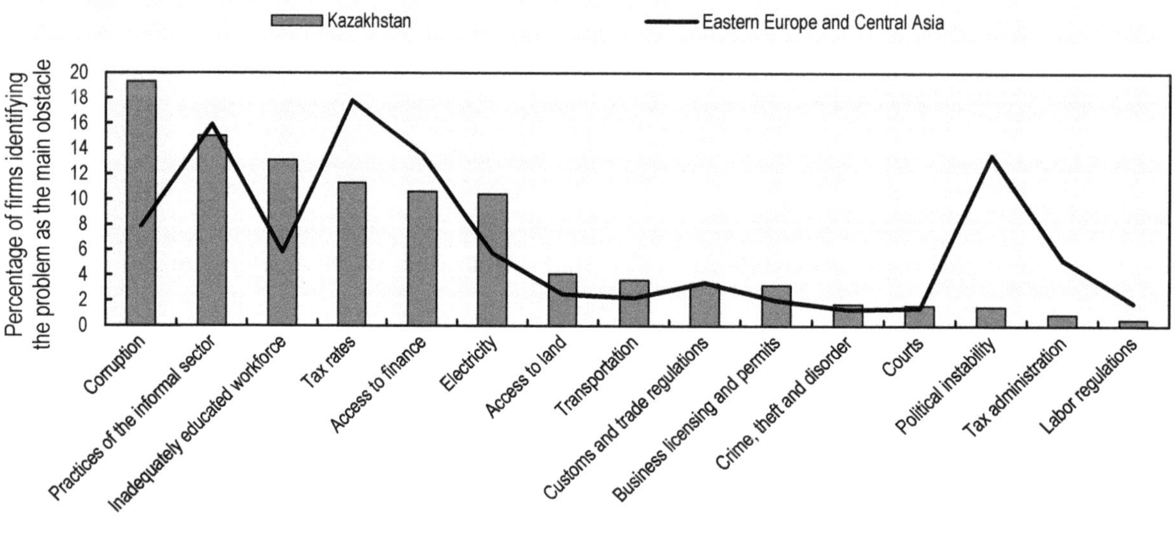

Source: World Bank (2013), Kazakhstan Country Profile 2013: Enterprise Surveys, Washington DC. http://www.enterprisesurveys.org/~/media/GIAWB/EnterpriseSurveys/Documents/Profiles/English/Kazakhstan-2013.pdf\.

StatLink http://dx.doi.org/10.1787/888933827745

The business ombudsman could help reduce corruption

Nineteen percent of Kazakh entrepreneurs identified corruption as a 'main obstacle' in the national business environment according to the World Bank Enterprise Survey, while 14% of business leaders cited corruption as among the five most problematic factors in the World Economic Forum (WEF) Global Competitiveness Report (WEF, 2017). Similarly, Kazakhstan's ranking in the 2016 Corruption Perception Index of Transparency International was 131st out of the 176 countries and territories covered, indicating a significant incidence of corruption.

The creation of a business ombudsman office in Kazakhstan is a welcome development. The business ombudsman is expected to receive complaints by business owners about unfair treatment by government authorities. However, the post needs to be seen to be independent of government.

Advisory councils in government ministries also hold public consultations on regulations. They also strengthen public governance and, indirectly, reduce the risk of loopholes in legislation, which could nurture corruption when a law is implemented. Non-governmental organisations (NGOs) are often members of these councils. However, the requirement that NGOs reapply every three years for approval of their legal status may have a negative impact on their ability to provide independent and critical views (OECD, 2014).

Skills and education levels remain weak

Approximately 12% of the firms surveyed by the World Bank Enterprise Survey point to an 'inadequately educated workforce' as a 'main obstacle' in the business environment of Kazakhstan, a higher share than the average for Eastern European and Central Asian countries. Furthermore, the rate of participation in higher education reduced between 2005 and 2015 and lags behind the OECD average according to World Bank data. The government has committed to increasing investment in education and human capital, which will benefit SME productivity in the long run.

Entrepreneurship education efforts are in their infancy

A first step in developing a stronger culture of entrepreneurship can occur by bringing entrepreneurship teaching and exposure to entrepreneurship into schools and colleges. To date, however, there have been only modest efforts. A non-governmental organisation, Junior Achievement Kazakhstan, is active in providing extra-curricula activities in schools. Furthermore, vocational education now incorporates the study of entrepreneurial activity in economic disciplines. Several higher educational institutions are also seeking to build the entrepreneurial knowledge of students. However, there is no national strategy for entrepreneurship education, nor a shared learning platform for stakeholders involved in delivering entrepreneurship education. In particular, there is a strong opportunity for universities to do more to stimulate innovative entrepreneurship by graduates.

The innovation system needs to be strengthened

Kazakhstan's innovation system is still at an early development stage. Kazakhstan ranked only 78th of 127 countries in 2017 in the Global Innovation Index, conducted annually by Cornell University, INSEAD (a graduate business school), and the World Intellectual Property Organization, behind most other Eastern European and Central Asian countries. Furthermore, at 0.17% of GDP in 2015, R&D spending is very low in Kazakhstan, although the number of R&D researchers increased rapidly between 2011 and 2014 (OECD, 2017a). Innovation and technology policy is a priority of the government of Kazakhstan, but the main targets of the support tend to be large companies and state-owned enterprises rather than SMEs.

Access to finance is a major constraint

Access to finance is a major constraint for SMEs and entrepreneurs in Kazakhstan. Although more than 90% of firms hold a checking or savings account, only 19% hold a bank loan or a credit line, well below other Eastern European and Central Asian countries. Furthermore, a large proportion of Kazakhstan businesses have had a recent loan request rejected (30%). This might be linked to the very low proportion of firms with audited financial statements (23%) and the high collateral requirements applied by local banks (Figure 1.6).

Figure 1.6. Collateral requirements

In per cent, 2013 or most recent

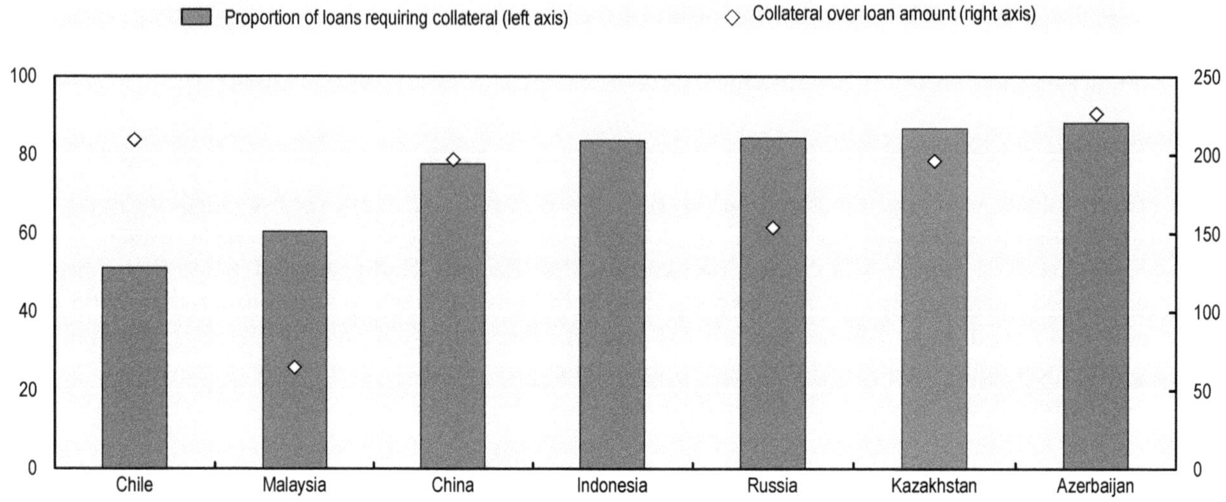

Note: No comparable data on collateral values available for Indonesia. Latest data for Chile (2012), China (2012), Indonesia (2009) and Malaysia (2007).
Source: Authors' calculations based on World Bank Enterprise Surveys (database), http://www.enterprisesurveys.org.

StatLink http://dx.doi.org/10.1787/888933827764

The credit problems reflect the severe impact of the 2008 global financial crisis on Kazakhstan's banking system, which deprived banks of access to foreign capital and increased the costs of servicing their borrowing and resulted in a credit crunch on SMEs. The government intervened by acquiring majority stakes in three large banks and minority stakes in another two. In 2012, it also created a Problem Loan Fund and allowed banks to place non-performing loans in bank-specific special purpose vehicles, and in 2014 it allocated Kazakhstan Tenge (KZT) 250 billion to banks to lend to SMEs at below-market interest rates. Banks were also required to take actions such as write-off /forgiveness of bad loans, restructuring of their loan portfolio, recovery in judicial and extrajudicial procedures, broader acceptance of collateral, and transfer of loans to subsidiaries of banks (that acquired problem assets) or collection agencies. Despite progress, Kazakhstan's banks continue to face difficulties. In 2016, some 6.7% of business loans were non-performing, which is relatively high by international standards and may constrain SME lending (OECD, 2018).

Foreign direct investment offers an opportunity for SME development

Kazakhstan has relatively light foreign direct investment (FDI) restrictions and is one of the top destinations in the world for inward FDI flows. It received 85% of all the inward investment of Central Asia in 2012, suggesting a potential to exploit FDI activity to support the growth and development of the domestic SME sector. On the other hand, more than 70% of FDI inflows are related to the extraction of natural resources, where supply chains tend to be relatively short. The share of inward foreign direct investment in manufacturing was a modest 15% in 2014 (OECD, 2016b).

Key recommendations on business environment

- Continue to take actions in the framework of the government's anti-corruption policy to ensure a change of culture regarding corruption and to reduce the consequences of corruption for SME and entrepreneurship development.
- Increase enrolment rates in tertiary education, for example through increasing the alignment of university degrees with private sector needs and enhancing access to scholarships. Ensure the achievement of minimum tertiary education quality standards throughout the national territory, for example through strengthened faculty training and faster renewal of university resources.
- Strengthen the literacy skills of Kazakh youth at secondary education level, including through better training of teachers and provision of mother-tongue-based instruction, and reduce inequalities in the education system in order to build a broad base of young people with skills for more productive SMEs and entrepreneurship.
- As part of regular surveys of SMEs, identify SME skills needs in Business Road Map 2020 priority sectors. Ensure that these skills are incorporated in the National Qualifications Framework and that appropriate training is provided in vocational education and training programmes. This should include the generic skills as well as the technical skills needed for SME development, for example in business management, marketing and sales, and accounting/finance.
- Expand and strengthen entrepreneurship education in schools and universities, including support facilities for entrepreneurship teachers and encouragement of national and international exchanges of good practice.
- Encourage higher education and vocational education institutions to complement entrepreneurship teaching with extracurricular programmes to support graduate start-ups, such as student business incubators and student entrepreneurship clubs.
- Augment government R&D spending in line with the increase in the size of the R&D workforce in the economy. Increase the emphasis on SMEs in the targeting and management of public R&D spending.
- Ensure access of a wide range of financial institutions to financial information gathered by the State Credit Bureau.
- Continue to reform the banking sector so that in the longer term banks lend to SMEs under normal banking terms without public intervention.

Strategic framework and delivery system for policy

Kazakhstan has a clear strategic vision for SME and entrepreneurship policy

The Entrepreneurial Code produced in 2015 is the key legal document specifying the roles of government bodies in supporting SMEs and entrepreneurship in Kazakhstan. Alongside it, the Kazakhstan 2030 and Kazakhstan 2050 vision statements set out a high-level vision for SME and entrepreneurship policy. The vision statements include targets to increase the contribution of SMEs to GDP from 18% in 2011 to 36% by 2030 and 50% by 2050. Medium-term strategic plans identify priority areas for government action to support the achievement of the vision. One of the most important strategic plans for SME and entrepreneurship development is the State Programme of Accelerated Industrial-Innovative Development of Kazakhstan (SPAIID). This emphasises the development of priority economy sectors and manufacturing and more balanced regional development.

At a more operational level, specific government programme actions and expenditures are detailed in a range of "road map" documents. The most important for SME and entrepreneurship development is the Business Road Map 2020 (BRM 2020), which focuses specifically on business development, but others, such as the Employment Road Map, also include some SME and entrepreneurship related interventions.

Putting together the various documents, the combined SME and entrepreneurship development policy thrusts across government can be summarised in ten priorities:

- Simplification of business regulation;
- Supporting business start-up with advice, counselling and training for entrepreneurs;
- Enhancing the management capability and growth capacity of SMEs;
- Strengthening technologies and management practices in SMEs, particularly in manufacturing;
- Expanding markets for SMEs, including through cluster initiatives and supply chains;
- Improving access to financing for SMEs and entrepreneurs;
- Improving the skills of SME workers;
- Improving availability of and access to business support services;
- Provision of production infrastructure, land and property; and
- Support for innovative start-ups and the innovative activity of SMEs.

The priorities are appropriate for the context and objectives of Kazakhstan, although there is scope for increased emphasis on generating more growth-oriented enterprises and increasing productivity in existing SMEs.

Structures are in place for effective management of SME and entrepreneurship policies

The Entrepreneurship Development Department of the Ministry of National Economy takes the leading role in promoting the SME and entrepreneurship agenda across government and in co-ordinating government ministries and agencies in improving the business environment and delivering programme support to SMEs and entrepreneurs. Significant authority comes from its function as the secretariat to the Prime Minister's Co-ordinating Council on Development of Entrepreneurship. The Entrepreneurship Development Department also supports the design of good policy by consulting with the representative organisations of SMEs and entrepreneurs on their policy concerns. The establishment of the National Chamber of Entrepreneurs in 2013 has played an important role in facilitating the interactions between government and entrepreneurs.

A full analysis of the portfolio of policy expenditures and impacts would support policy decisions

Figure 1.7 shows that there is a strong weighting of expenditure in the government's key SME and entrepreneurship programme support intervention, Business Road Map 2020, towards financial support, including interest rate subsidies, micro loans and loan guarantees. There is also a substantial budget for the development of business sites and premises. On the other hand, non-financial support such as advice, consultancy and training receives relatively little funding. This type of intervention should receive increased emphasis in future, with the aim of increasing growth and productivity in SMEs to meet the vision for a step increase in value added from SMEs.

Figure 1.7. Allocation of total spending projected in the Business Road Map 2020, by type of policy support, 2015-2019

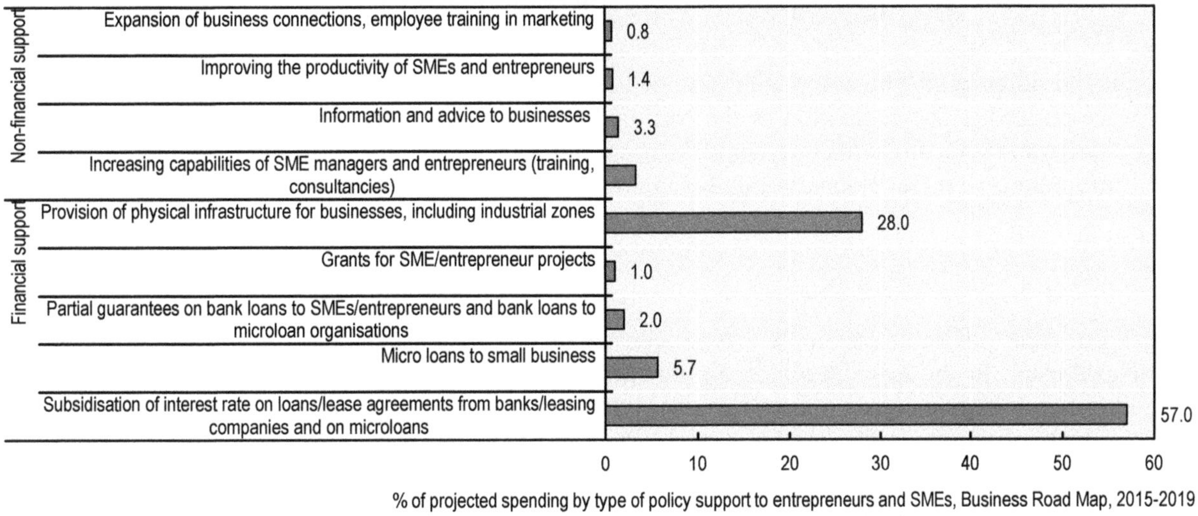

Source: OECD, based on categorisation of budget data in Republic of Kazakhstan (2015), "Resolution No. 168 of the Republic of Kazakhstan dated the 31st of March, 2015 on Approval of a Unified Business Support and Development Programme 'Business Road Map 2020", pp. 53–60.

StatLink http://dx.doi.org/10.1787/888933827783

In order to guide decisions about the best weighting of expenditure across activities, a detailed analysis of the distribution of expenditures should be undertaken in comparison with needs. The analysis should group expenditures by different types of SME and entrepreneurship programme (e.g. access to finance, innovation, workforce training, consultancy, entrepreneurship skills etc.) and different types of target enterprises (e.g. nascent entrepreneurs, micro enterprises, small enterprises, medium-sized enterprises, high-growth potential enterprises, and entrepreneurs and enterprises in under-developed regions etc.). This analysis should include BRM 2020, but also other relevant government programmes. The aim would be to identify expenditure gaps across government by type of programme and type of target enterprise when taking into account different policy objectives.

A few key agencies manage the implementation of programmes

A small set of government agencies are responsible for a large part of government SME and entrepreneurship development programme support, facilitating efficiency and co-ordination of policy. Access to finance support mainly flows through the Damu Entrepreneurship Development Fund. Information, training, and consulting support mainly comes through the National Chamber of Entrepreneurs and its national network of one-window Entrepreneurship Support Centres. Innovation support is predominantly channelled through the National Agency for Technological Development (NATD), which operates several technological business incubators. In addition, the Autonomous Cluster Fund (ACF) implements the Start Up Kazakhstan programme, which attracts high-tech SMEs to Kazakhstan and supports them with incubation and acceleration activities. This provides a clear framework from the delivery of policy.

To strengthen the framework further, measures are underway to increase the co-ordination across the agencies by putting the Damu Entrepreneurship Development Fund, the NATD and eight other state support bodies under the umbrella of the Baiterek Holding Company. This is enabling the testing of a more integrated type of support to SMEs and entrepreneurs through new "package offers" combining financial support and business development services.

On the other hand, the responsibilities of the Damu Entrepreneurship Development Fund were revised with the creation of the National Chamber of Entrepreneurs, which took over responsibility for non-financial support programmes, but the strategic plan for the Damu Entrepreneurship Development Fund was not adjusted in accordance with this change.

Business support structures have been established but need further investment and capacity building support

Significant public investments have been made in business support infrastructures in Kazakhstan in the last decade, enabling the creation of an important support system for SMEs and entrepreneurs. Many elements of this system are still quite new. For example, the technological incubators were established in 2011 and the Entrepreneurship Support Centres in 2013. In this context, efforts are needed to keep building the skills and knowledge of business advisors and consultants in the system and to develop and track performance standards for the centres and incubators over time. Furthermore, the density of business incubators remains low in Kazakhstan and the mix of incubator types (e.g. between technological and non-technological and advanced and basic services) is not necessarily the best match to the opportunities for creating growth oriented enterprises.

More impact evaluation should be undertaken, using robust approaches

Although there are clear arrangements for monitoring the expenditures and outputs of SME and entrepreneurship programmes in Kazakhstan (*e.g.* number of entrepreneurs receiving support, number of loan guarantees issued, participant satisfaction with support etc.), there are relatively few rigorous impact evaluations using control group methodologies. Furthermore, much evaluation is undertaken by ministries and agencies themselves rather than by independent external evaluators. More impact-oriented and rigorous evaluation would be a key support to the future design of SME and entrepreneurship policies.

Key recommendations on strategic framework and delivery system for policy

The policy framework and strategic directions

- Present and review the distribution of expenditures on SME and entrepreneurship support across different types of programme and target enterprise in order to guide decisions on the most appropriate policy mix.
- Review the balance between financial support and non-financial support measures in the Business Road Map 2020 in relation to evidence on policy needs and impacts, noting that although the demand expressed by businesses tends to be for financial subsidies, the greatest needs are often for management development and workforce training.
- Place greater policy emphasis on stimulating high-growth potential enterprises and productivity growth in existing SMEs.

Policy delivery structure

- Fully implement the proposal to deliver the SME and entrepreneurship support tools of the Damu Entrepreneurship Development Fund, the National Agency for Technological Development, the Autonomous Cluster Fund and related state organisations in the form of "packages" that offer SMEs and entrepreneurs access to combinations of financing and competency-building actions that meet their needs in a more holistic manner.
- Continue to invest in the ongoing professional development of the business development advisors and consultants in the network of Entrepreneurship Support Centres and incubators.
- Assess the need for further business incubators and for different types of incubators (e.g. full-service versus partial-service incubators; technological versus non-technological incubators) and offer public support for the development of additional business incubators in function of this analysis.
- Review the strategic plan of the Damu Entrepreneurship Development Fund, noting that it no longer has main responsibilities for non-financial support programmes and that therefore the benchmarks in the current strategy are not appropriate. Create a long-term vision for the future of the Fund based on comparison with the activities of public SME financial institutions in other countries.

Monitoring and evaluation

- Increase the use of robust policy impact evaluations, using independent evaluators and techniques such as control groups, and seek comparability of measures of policy performance across evaluations.

National programmes for SMEs and entrepreneurship

Existing entrepreneurship training schemes are promising but outcomes need to be enhanced

The Business Advisor programme is one of the main publicly funded entrepreneurship training programmes in Kazakhstan. It offers short-term, group-based entrepreneurship training conducted by professional trainers in 209 locations across the country. Business Advisor I targets nascent entrepreneurs with training on entrepreneurship basics. Business Advisor II targets established entrepreneurs with more in-depth knowledge on the functional areas of business and includes on-line mentoring services. Approximately 70 000 potential entrepreneurs received training under Business Advisor I during 2012-2014. However, only 12% reported that taking the course had given them the capabilities they need to start a new business. Only 3 000 participated in Business Advisor II in 2014, signalling a barrier to providing continuing support into the competences needed for successful business creation.

The School for Young Entrepreneurs is another major public entrepreneurship training initiative. It offers a two-week training course on the basics of entrepreneurship and business management run by the National Chamber of Entrepreneurs in partnership with regional universities. However, of the 2014 cohort of trainees, only 57 new enterprises were created, representing only 6% of the individuals trained.

SME management training programmes should be scaled up

There are two main training programmes for existing SME managers – the SME Top Management Training Programme and Business Connections. Both use short-course formats. Monitoring data indicate that they are performing well in increasing SME management competences, helping upgrade SME business and production processes and increasing SME sales and employment. However, currently only approximately 1 000 managers participate annually in these two programmes and increasing the numbers of participants could generate greater impacts. At the same time, an increase in the numbers of trainees could enable a segmentation of the trainees and training offered. For example, separate training streams and tailored materials and approaches could be proposed for medium-sized and small business managers, for highly educated and less educated managers, and perhaps for managers of companies split out on a sector basis.

Business development services capacities should be built up

The National Chamber of Entrepreneurs has recently created a network of 188 Entrepreneurship Support Centres to offer information, advice and consultancy services to SMEs and entrepreneurs and has ambitious targets to increase the number of clients accessing these services both physically and remotely. To achieve this, additional efforts will be required to promote the use of business development services among SMEs and entrepreneurs, increase the number of qualified consultants in the system, and expand the number of service windows at existing centres and open more centres.

The Enterprise Growth Programme of the European Bank for Reconstruction and Development is currently the only business advisory programme with the specific objective of generating and supporting high-growth SMEs. A programme such as this should be operated at larger scale to benefit more high-growth enterprises.

SMEs currently choose their own business advice services from the Entrepreneurship Service Centres. The introduction and systematic use of a business diagnostic tool as an initial stage in the support would help the consultants and clients to better identify their real needs and tailor support accordingly. In addition, if provided online, a version of such a tool could reach out to a lot of firms with generic and basic advice, as well as being a tool to guide SMEs towards further sources of business advice.

A dual training system is being introduced, and should actively integrate SMEs

The government has undertaken considerable recent reform of the vocational education and training system to provide a better match between the training offered and the skills required by businesses. The reforms include introduction of a national qualifications framework, international occupational standards, and sector skills councils. They also include the creation of a new dual training system, combining training in colleges with work placements with employers. To date, most of these employment placements have been with large firms. More deliberate strategies are therefore needed to involve SMEs, both by giving SMEs a role in deciding the design of vocational training programmes, so that they better meet SME employer needs, and in seeking out SME placements for trainees. Furthermore, there is much more scope to offer training to networks of SMEs by organising the creation of local networks of SMEs with related training needs. University graduates could also have a positive impact on SME development with greater efforts to build co-operative education partnerships between universities and SMEs.

Access to finance programmes do not yet reach enough SMEs

The Damu Entrepreneurship Development Fund runs several programmes that are expanding the access of SMEs and entrepreneurs to credit. One of its activities provides lines of credit to second-tier banks for SME lending. In particular, Damu's Stabilisation Programme stimulated some Kazakhstan Tenge (KZT) 1 671 billion of SME lending between 2007 and 2017, benefiting approximately 35 500 projects and 10 000 SMEs, and its Regions Programme provided a further KZT 169 billion to SMEs. Damu also offers interest rate subsidies and loan guarantees to banks for SME lending. In early 2018, the volume of Damu interest rate subsidies for SMEs was KZT 181.7 billion, covering 11 186 projects and loans of KZT 2 068 billion. Its loan guarantees amounted to KZT 56.2 billion, corresponding to 3 662 projects and investments of KZT 129.9 billion.

Although important, these lending support programmes currently reach only limited numbers of SMEs compared to the population of firms experiencing access to credit problems. This lack of penetration to the broad SME market reflects several issues – complicated administration for banks, tight conditions for eligibility, frequent changes in the rules and regulations of the programmes, and limited overall budgets. Furthermore, Damu's range of financial instruments appears to have grown organically based on short-term demands, rather than on research into long-term needs of the sector. Overall, there is therefore a need to streamline the Damu programmes, expand the most effective of them and simplify the administration procedures.

Damu has also been expanding the scope of microfinance, leasing and factoring activity for start-ups and micro businesses in Kazakhstan. Since 2016, it has provided direct credit lines or guarantees to microfinance organisations that have financed approximately 10 000 projects. In addition, Damu places funds in the budgets of short-term banking and microfinance organisations through the State Programme for the Development of Productive Employment and Mass Entrepreneurship, which was launched in 2017. These efforts are making a start in expanding the range of debt financing options for entrepreneurs but these activities are still relatively small.

Attention is also being placed on developing alternatives to debt finance through public support for private equity, venture capital and business angel investments, although few innovative start-ups have been funded in these ways to date. An obstacle is that government investments in equity schemes are expected to make full repayments to public budgets. There are also limited incentives for investors, such as medium-term tax incentives. Furthermore, there remains a lack of awareness of angel investment opportunities. A National Network of Business Angels of Kazakhstan is in existence but its on-the-ground activities have been limited in recent years.

There are therefore a number of measures in place to augment the supply of debt and non-debt finance opportunities for SMEs and entrepreneurs, although the numbers of businesses reached are not yet sufficient. On the other side of the market, relatively few programmes are seeking to build financial literacy skills in SMEs, whereas this type of intervention could have important impacts in increasing access to finance.

Programmes for innovation in SMEs lack scale

The National Agency for Technological Development (NATD) operates many initiatives for technological and business innovation, including providing innovation grants to SMEs, stimulating innovation through technology parks, supporting the development of business incubators under the BRM 2020 programme, developing venture financing, defining technological tasks and finding solutions through international technology transfer networks, and providing technological forecasting information and analytical activities. Its innovation grants to SMEs supported 126 projects in 2015-2017. It has created eight technology parks, five containing business incubators that offer infrastructure and services to 131 companies, 89% of which are SMEs. The NATD also supports two innovation clusters and five regional research commercialisation centres for science-industry knowledge transfer.

In addition, the Autonomous Cluster Fund develops high-tech start-up projects through Start Up Kazakhstan. This initiative makes use of the obligation of multinational enterprises that are sub-soil users to spend 1% of aggregate annual income on local activities such as localisation of production and financing of R&D. In this framework, the Fund uses the competencies, technologies and investments of multinational enterprises to open joint centres for technological development, attracting KZT 3.6 billion and financing 70 projects. The initiative also involves opening joint venture capital funds (notably the GVA Alatau Fund, a joint venture capital fund with GVA of the United States), and the acceleration and incubation of world class export-oriented service companies.

The Ministry of Education and Science is a further significant actor in supporting innovative entrepreneurship and SME innovation. With support from the World Bank, it finances a range of applied research projects in universities and research institutions together with proof of concept and prototype development financing for university spin-off enterprises that help take the ideas to market. Some 43 start-ups were supported in this way in 2018. R&D tax incentives are also available to businesses in Kazakhstan, although there is no specific SME element to this incentive.

These actions show an increasing government commitment to stimulating innovative start-ups and SME innovation in Kazakhstan. This will need to be at the heart of the economic development effort in coming years. Given its importance, the numbers of SMEs and start-ups receiving innovation support should be increased. One of the key tools in this effort can be expanding the innovation support infrastructure for SMEs and start-ups, including growing the business incubator network, but also developing smaller structures such as innovation workshops, fab-labs and co-working centres. It is important to promote innovation in non-technological areas as well as technological innovation, which is currently the focus of the majority of support programmes. Furthermore, there are few measures to develop innovation skills in SMEs (such as innovation consultancy, training and mentoring schemes) or digital technology adoption, and these will need to be developed.

Export programmes could be expanded and made more inclusive of SMEs

Until recently, the main source of exporting support for SMEs was KazNex Invest, the National Export and Investment Agency. It promoted trademarks, business participation in international exhibitions and trade missions abroad, an export directory, export training, development of packaging for export, and internet resources for exporters and buyers. However, between 2010 and 2014, only 31 trade missions were organised and only 170 enterprises participated in foreign exhibitions. In 2017, the export directory had only 1 059 company entries. Since 2018, the National Chamber of Entrepreneurs has taken over export support. This provides an opportunity to strengthen this key area for SME development. Among the priorities are expanding the numbers of businesses reached by the policy and bolstering the infrastructure for SME exporting, for example by increasing the number of centres providing product standards certificates for SMEs and increasing their range of services.

Measures have been taken to secure access to public procurement for SMEs

The government has taken a number of actions to open up public procurement opportunities to SMEs. This includes establishing a "set-aside" share of contracts intended for SMEs, the division of contract lots into smaller sizes, and giving preferences to SMEs in the award of contracts, and SMEs now account for as much as 85% of public contracts awarded. The efforts should nevertheless continue. In particular, more could be done in raising SME awareness of public procurement opportunities and informing SMEs of the improvements they may need to make in terms of their efficiency, quality and timeliness in order to succeed in bidding.

Social target groups receive dedicated support for entrepreneurship, but there are gaps

The BRM 2020 and the Employment Road Map 2020 both include dedicated actions to promote entrepreneurship among women, youth, people with disabilities and the unemployed. Among the key initiatives are the Women's Entrepreneurship Micro-lending Programme, youth entrepreneurship training programmes, an entrepreneurship advice and networking programme for people with disabilities, and entrepreneurship training, finance and advice in employment centres for unemployed people. On the other hand, the programmes tend to be small compared to the scale of the target group. For example, the Women's Entrepreneurship Micro-lending Programme had funded only 1 300 borrowers as of end-2014 and the unemployed microcredit programme granted only 9 000 micro loans in 2014.

In addition, there are some gaps in the scope of support provided to particular groups. For example, there are no women-focused entrepreneurship training courses and the support for disabled entrepreneurs does not include direct financing. In general, the various initiatives do not offer integrated packages of support combining skills development, advice and mentoring, access to financing, and networking, which could increase overall effectiveness. Attention also needs to be paid to ensuring that entrepreneurs and potential entrepreneurs from different social target groups get access to existing mainstream entrepreneurship support, for example by ensuring that frontline staff in Entrepreneurship Service Centres are sensitive to the needs of different social groups and offer them adapted support and advice.

Key recommendations on SME and entrepreneurship programmes

Entrepreneurship training and SME management training

- Identify and address barriers to business creation by graduates of the Business Advisor I and Business Advisor II training programmes as well as barriers to progression between the programmes. This may include making changes to the screening and selection process for applicants, the length of the training, the balance of theoretical versus practical training, the level of guidance and mentoring of the trainees, and the linkages between the training programme and sources of start-up financing.
- Increase the number of trainees supported by the School for Young Entrepreneurs and increase the level of mentoring, coaching, incubation, and post-start-up support services attached to the training.
- Increase the number of participants in the Top SME Managers Training and the Business Connections programmes by increasing the number of delivery partners and locations. Segment the training in order to create more uniform cohorts of SME managers in each training group, grouping trainees on the basis of the size and sector of their firms and their level of existing management expertise and ambitions.

Business advice, consultancy and mentoring

- Develop a business diagnostic tool to enable consultants in the Entrepreneurship Service Centres and other business support infrastructures to assess more systematically the performance of client companies, and to identify strengths, weaknesses, and areas for improvement. Use the diagnostic results to target advice, consultancy and mentoring services to the identified needs. Offer a basic online version of the diagnostic tool to enable SMEs to undertake self-assessments and obtain online guidance.
- Identify and select a group of start-ups and existing SMEs with high-growth potential and offer them a dedicated package of advice and financing aimed at addressing the challenges of high growth.

SME workforce skills development

- As part of regular surveys of SMEs, identify SME skills needs in Business Road Map 2020 priority sectors. Ensure that these skills are incorporated in the National Qualifications Framework and that appropriate training is provided in vocational education and training programmes. This should include the generic skills as well as the technical skills needed for SME development, for example in business management, marketing and sales, and accounting/finance.

- Introduce publicly financed SME training facilitators to support local networks of SMEs that agree to work collectively on training initiatives in co-operation with vocational education and training institutions. The role of these training facilitators should be to: encourage the voluntary formation of the networks of SMEs; help the networks to assess the joint training needs of their SME members; develop joint training plans for the networks; enter into dialogue with colleges to secure training courses tailored to the needs of the networks; encourage the SMEs to offer work placements and apprenticeships to students taking the courses; and monitor the quality of the training plans implemented, according to training standards for the occupations concerned.
- Offer grants to SMEs to cover some of the training costs of hosting apprenticeships and work placements for vocational education and training students and university students, for example by adapting the 'youth practice' component of the Employment Road Map 2020 to finance SME work placements.

Access to finance

- Undertake regular surveys, interviews, focus group discussions and programme evaluations to collect evidence on the range of financing needs and problems of SMEs and entrepreneurs and the performance of financial institutions and financial instruments in supporting access to finance. Use this information to guide development of a more diverse and balanced set of financial instruments, including a wider range of microcredit, factoring and leasing and business angel financing opportunities, in line with the OECD-G20 High-Level Principles on SME and Entrepreneurship Financing.
- Strengthen microfinance provision through the creation of an apex institution to help channel finance to microfinance institutions and support for developing skills and capabilities in microfinance organisations.
- Pilot an initiative to support leasing and factoring mechanisms for SME and entrepreneurship financing.
- Stimulate the development of a venture capital sector that finances innovative start-ups. For this purpose, provide well-designed time-limited public financing for venture capital funds, explore the feasibility of a medium-term tax incentive for investing in venture capital funds and eliminate the requirement for repayment of all public finance invested in funds. Ensure that exit strategies for venture capitalists are in place by developing a secondary market of the Stock Exchange with simplified issuing requirements for SMEs.
- Explore the feasibility and potential of tax incentives to angel investors to stimulate the development of early-stage private finance, and create awareness

of angel investments through media campaigns, seminars, disseminating success stories, and founding an operational business angels' network.

- Develop information, guidance and awareness events and implement training and consultancy programmes for strengthening the financial skills of SME managers and entrepreneurs.

Support for innovative start-ups and SME innovation

- Carry out intensive and targeted actions (such as seminars, innovation fairs, innovation awards, media campaigns, etc.) to raise awareness of the importance and opportunities for innovation and digital technology adoption among SMEs.
- Expand the support infrastructure for innovation in SMEs by expanding the activities of innovation clusters, industrial design bureaus, and incubators as well as smaller structures including innovation workshops, fab-labs and co-working centres.
- Extend training, consultancy and mentoring schemes aimed specifically at developing innovation skills and capabilities among SME managers (including non-technological innovation). Such schemes should be targeted specifically towards innovation and should complement general management support.
- Expand early-stage growth funding for innovative business start-ups from universities and research institutions.

Support for SME internationalisation

- Develop a dedicated internationalisation programme for SMEs targeting the specific problems of SMEs in export readiness. This should identify companies with high export potential and provide targeted consultancy and coaching to improve productivity and quality, as well as giving general information and basic export promotion support to a wider range of SMEs.
- Strengthen the infrastructure for SME export development, including support for product testing, product standardisation and product standards certification.

Public procurement

- Further develop awareness among SMEs of procurement opportunities with public authorities through campaigns and communication strategies and consider introducing a certificate for SMEs that have already performed successfully in government contracts.

Entrepreneurship programmes for special target groups of the population

- Expand existing programmes for women, youth, people with disabilities and the unemployed and offer combined packages of access to finance, training, advice and networking support.
- Establish Women's Enterprise Centres or women's desks in the Entrepreneurship Support Centres in regions where the needs appear to be the greatest. Provide resources to enable the National Chamber of

Entrepreneurship's Council of Businesswomen and its regional branches to provide a comprehensive package of training, consulting, and financial support services to women on a regional level. Implement regional pilot actions to test levels of demand, satisfaction and impact for dedicated women entrepreneur streams of the Business Advisor, Top SME Managers Training, and Business Connections programmes.

- Develop a comprehensive approach to the development of youth entrepreneurship, guided by the OECD principles for youth entrepreneurship policy, involving co-operation between the Ministry of National Economy Entrepreneurship Development Department, the Council for the Development of Youth Entrepreneurship, the National Chamber of Entrepreneurship and other relevant stakeholders.
- Strengthen support for entrepreneurship by people with disabilities by establishing a development fund to provide financing for the launch of businesses including financing for assistance technologies. Provide sensitivity training to staff of the Entrepreneurship Support Centres on how to adapt advisory and other services to better serve entrepreneurs with disabilities. Encourage the National Chamber of Entrepreneurs to facilitate the formation of an "Entrepreneurs with Disabilities Network" to promote mutual support and sharing of experience, using the Entrepreneurship Service Centres as a framework to reach the whole country.

The local dimension

Kazakhstan is a large and heterogeneous country

There is a need for regional differentiation of SME and entrepreneurship policy in Kazakhstan to respond to regional differences in the scale and nature of business activity and in business environment conditions. Regional differences in GDP per head are large across the country, although they have been reducing, and the current pattern of enterprise density reinforces the disparities. In particular, the two major cities of Astana and Almaty have much larger numbers of enterprises per person than the more rural regions (Figure 1.8). Kazakhstan is also host to a number of "mono-industry towns" – cities dominated by a single industry, often suffering economic distress – where entrepreneurship levels are often low.

Figure 1.8. SME density – number of SMEs per 1000 working age population, 2016

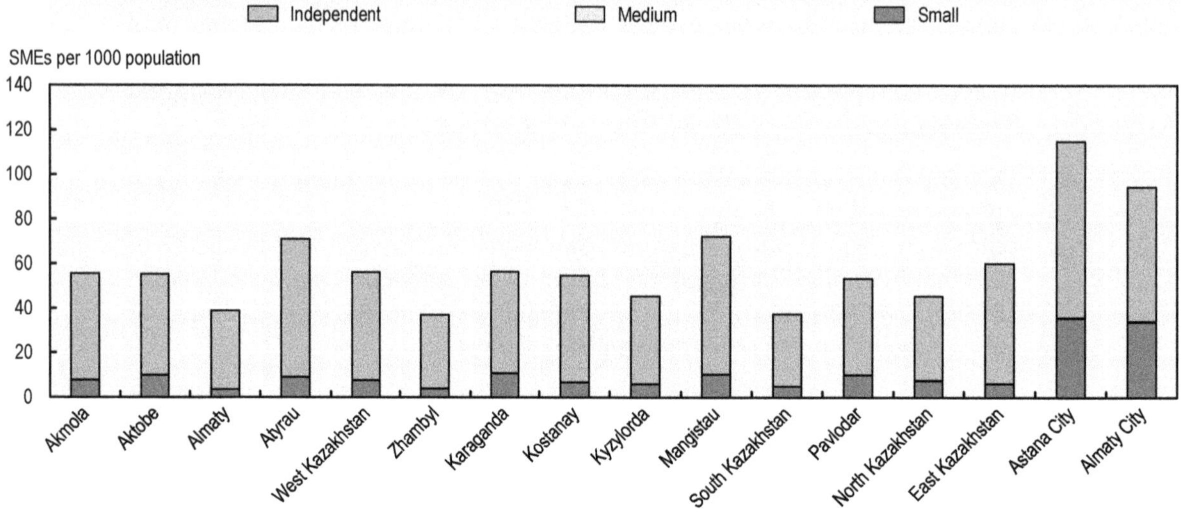

Source: Ministry of National Economy, Committee on Statistics.

StatLink http://dx.doi.org/10.1787/888933827802

There are also regional differences in what businesses perceive to be the main obstacle to their development in the business environment (Table 1.3). While in the Centre, access to finance is seen as the most important single obstacle to business, access to electricity is more important in the East, an inadequately educated workforce in the North, corruption in the South and tax rates in the West.

Table 1.3. Regional variations in major obstacles to business in Kazakhstan, 2014

Per cent of businesses identifying the factor as a major constraint for their business

	All regions	Centre	East	North	South	West
Corruption	16.5	5.5	3.2	7.9	35.2	3.3
Practices of competitors in the informal sector	12.7	3.2	6.1	14.8	14.9	15.3
Inadequately educated workforce	11.2	12.3	14.4	17.3	2.1	19.2
Tax rates	9.4	10.1	14.9	8.1	3.3	24.8
Access to finance	9.4	12.8	6.9	12.3	5.2	12.1
Electricity	8.9	8.1	35.2	11.6	4.1	3.9
Access to land	3.6	3.2	1.1	4.0	5.0	0.9
Business licensing and permits	3.0	5.0	1.0	5.3	1.8	0.4
Transport	3.0	1.4	2.1	2.8	4.1	2.5
Customs and trade regulations	2.8	2.1		1.5	3.9	4.6
Courts	1.4	3.2		2.2	0.8	
Crime, theft and disorder	1.4		2.1	1.8	1.2	1.9
Political instability	1.3				3.2	0.7
Tax administration	0.7	0.4	1.0	0.1	1.5	0.1
Labour regulations	0.5			0.9	0.6	

Source: OECD calculations from data from European Bank of Reconstruction and Development (EBRD)-World Bank Business Environment and Enterprise Performance Survey (BEEPS) V. Centre = Karaganda; East = East Kazakhstan; North = Astana City, Akmola, North Kazakhstan, Kostanay, Pavlodar; South = Almaty City, Kyzylorda, Zhambyl, South Kazakhstan, Almaty Region; West = Mangistau, Atyrau, Aktobe, West Kazakhstan.

Regional adaptation of SME and entrepreneurship policy to the scale and nature of demand could be increased

In principle, all regions of the country have access to the same set of centrally designed BRM 2020 SME and entrepreneurship programme measures, although there are specific measures for rural areas, small settlements and mono-industry towns. Regional government offices can influence the provision of SME and entrepreneurship programmes in their regions by varying the scale and mix of their bids for different elements of national BRM 2020 funding as well as the co-funding contributions they propose to make towards different BRM 2020 measures. This is an important arrangement that can help adapt the mix of SME and entrepreneurship measures to the needs and priorities of different regions.

However, there are some weaknesses in the current arrangements. In particular, there is a mismatch between the number of SMEs receiving BRM 2020 subsidies by region and the size of the region's SME population (Figure 1.9). This contrasts with regional numbers of SMEs receiving business development services from the National Chamber of Entrepreneurs, where there is a close match between the regional distribution of SMEs and the regional distribution of SMEs receiving business advice. In the case of National Chamber of Entrepreneurs services, the provision matches closely to the demand expressed by SMEs to NCE offices. In the case of the BRM 2020 subsidy measures, the numbers of SMEs served reflect national funding decisions based on bids received from the regional government offices (mediated through the Regional Coordinating Councils) and decisions made based on past expenditure levels, which tends to prolong the mismatch.

Figure 1.9. Number of subsidies compared to the SME population

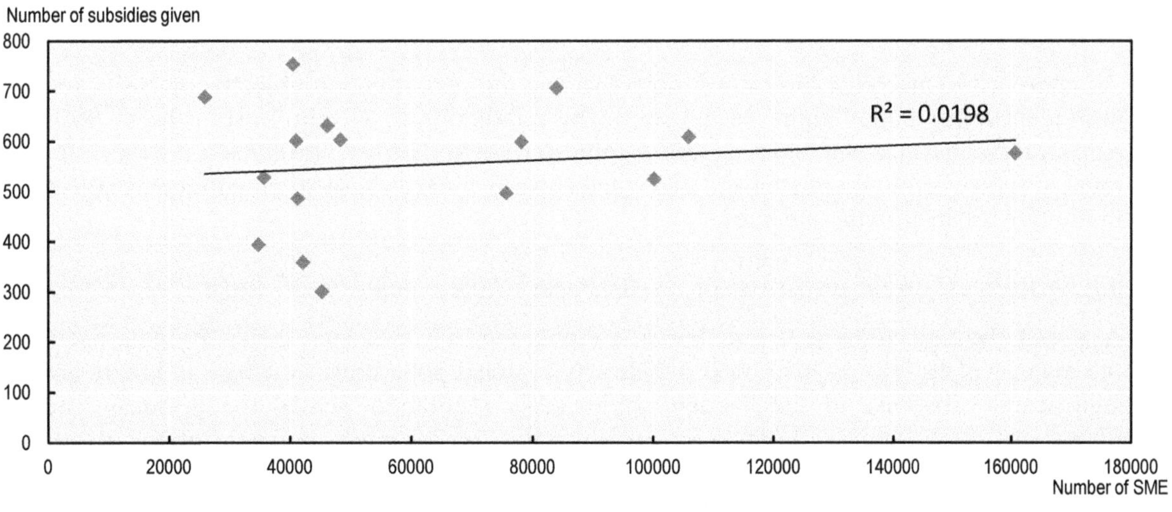

Source: Data provided by Damu Entrepreneurship Development Fund. Figures to January 2017.

StatLink http://dx.doi.org/10.1787/888933827821

Another obstacle to the tailoring of SME and entrepreneurship support to regional needs and priorities is the lack of multi-annual regional budgets for SME and entrepreneurship actions. Annual budgeting makes policy unpredictable for SMEs and entrepreneurs and makes it difficult to develop infrastructure and initiatives that take time to establish. A more transparent multi-annual budgeting system needs to be developed for the allocation of BRM 2020 funding to the regions.

Furthermore, Kazakhstan lacks medium-term economic development strategies for the regions. These would be useful in guiding SME and entrepreneurship support by setting out distinct priorities for SME and entrepreneurship development in each region, together with associated budget distribution and indicators and procedures for regional monitoring and evaluation of SME and entrepreneurship programmes.

Co-ordination between entrepreneurship policy and spatial policy could be strengthened

The spatial planning objectives of the Kazakhstan Government, as set out in the National Strategy for Regional Development, include the development of a limited number of major urban areas as regional growth poles. This would help stimulate under exploited potential for agglomeration economies in Kazakhstan (OECD, 2017b). Meeting this objective implies the need for strong growth of SME and entrepreneurship activities in these urban areas to provide employment within the regional growth poles.

In contrast, the regional development focus of SME and entrepreneurship policy, as set out in the BRM 2020, is on supporting rural towns, small towns and mono-industry towns. While SME and entrepreneurship policy can make an important contribution to the development of low economic potential areas, a regional focus that is only on lagging areas fits poorly with the focus of the national regional development strategy on growth poles. It may also run counter to the objective of reaching the targets for national growth in SME value added set out in the Kazakhstan 2030 and Kazakhstan 2050 vision statements if resources are spread thinly and weighted to low potential areas and insufficient resources are made available for the core, dynamic regions, where the SME growth opportunities may be greatest.

An approach to marrying the growth objective and the redistribution objective in SME and entrepreneurship policy could be developed by continuing to weight existing basic SME and entrepreneurship supports towards lagging territories, whilst introducing a new high-level initiative offering targeted and dedicated support for high-growth potential enterprises in the five urban growth pole hubs.

The quality of implementation of business regulation varies regionally

Although the legislation governing business regulation in Kazakhstan is largely centralised, the manner of its implementation is decided by regional government offices, and there are significant variations in the burden of business regulation across the regions. The divergences in the quality of regulation are illustrated, for example, by the differing degrees to which regulations and corruption are reported to be important constraints by businesses in different regions.

An important achievement in improving the implementation of business regulations in the regions has been the creation of single windows in the Enterprise Support Centres, which provide information and support on business regulations for new entrepreneurs. The linking of the national business ombudsman with the network of the National Chamber of Entrepreneurs will also help to signal and address local difficulties with regulation as information on any local problems is fed up to the ombudsman from via National Chamber of Entrepreneurs offices.

A number of measures can be suggested to further improve the implementation of business regulation at regional level. The single windows in the Enterprise Support Centres for new entrepreneurs could extend their support on regulations to existing businesses. Seamless access could be offered to electronic forms of self-declaration for businesses. Furthermore, information flows on local issues with business regulation could be improved by creating a formal network of business ombudsman representatives in each region. These regional representatives would seek to define ways to improve regulation with each regional government authority and with the region's SMEs and entrepreneurs.

Key recommendations on the local dimension

- Create better alignment between the spatial development priorities of Business Road Map 2020 and those expressed in the national regional development vision by introducing a dedicated Business Road Map 2020 programme for high-potential SMEs and entrepreneurship in the five cities designated as national growth pole hubs.
- Introduce a transparent, multi-annual budget framework for the regional allocation of Business Road Map 2020 resources for SME and entrepreneurship development, based on an assessment of the scale and nature of SME and entrepreneurship support needs in each region, and providing for regional monitoring of key performance indicators on associated SME and entrepreneurship programme activities and impacts.
- Increase the information and support available to existing businesses at regional level on compliance with business regulations. Create a mechanism to consult with regional networks of SMEs and entrepreneurs to identify potential areas for regulatory improvement at regional level.

Promoting FDI-SME linkages

The domestic supply chain linkages of FDI are limited in Kazakhstan but hold strong potential

There are only relatively limited supply linkages between foreign direct investment (FDI) and domestic SMEs in Kazakhstan. This situation reflects the relatively recent inflow of FDI to the country, its concentration in resource extraction industries where supply chains are short and specialised, and relatively weak capabilities of the SME sector, as manifested in low productivity and quality levels. However, stimulating greater local FDI-supplier linkages offers an important potential catalyst for technology, market development and efficiency improvements in SMEs.

FDI policy has focused on attraction rather than supply chain development

To date, FDI policy in Kazakhstan has largely focused on maximising FDI attraction rather than seeking to exploit FDI to develop domestic supply chains, despite some local content regulations for foreign-owned enterprise sub-soil users. It is important where possible to steer the location of FDI within the country towards the regional clusters where there is the greatest potential for local supplier linkages. In addition, much more attention can be paid to offering aftercare to FDI ventures, with a view to building relationships to support the development of supply chain linkages.

Integrated actions should be pursued for linkage building in regional clusters

There is great potential to organise systematic actions at the level of regions to strengthen supply chain linkages involving FDI and local SMEs, which can build on existing work that has been undertaken to identify regional clusters and to pilot regional FDI-SME linkage building activities in pioneer regions.

An initial action required is to undertake matchmaking between FDI operations that are motivated to increase their local supplies and potential local suppliers. The National Chamber of Entrepreneurs and the National Agency for Local Content are creating a database of potential SME suppliers to FDI, including information on their sectors, products and services. This database is a starting point to help broker linkages. In addition, more proactive work to building the capabilities of potential local suppliers to FDI.

The most effective approaches to FDI-SME linkage building involve integrated programmes operating in regional clusters promoted by specific linkage building teams. The approach can combine identifying FDI that is open to developing new local SME supplier linkages, identifying SMEs with strong potential to supply the FDI ventures, brokering supply linkages among these foreign and local firms, and co-ordinating the offer of publicly-supported advice and consultancy and investment and innovation finance to the relevant SMEs to upgrade their supply capacities. The OECD recommended pilot linkage development actions in three regions of Kazakhstan in 2016 as part of the OECD Regional Competitiveness Programme and various regional stakeholders were involved in implementing them. These models and the lessons from them can be spread to other regions of Kazakhstan.

Access to finance for FDI suppliers can be strengthened

SMEs sometimes face constraints in obtaining the working capital and investment finance that they would need to supply FDI, given the gap between investing and delivering products and services and receiving payment from large firms. Kazakhstan does not yet have a strong factoring market that could help overcome this obstacle and initiatives should be considered to address this gap.

Summary of key recommendations on linkages between FDI and SMEs

- Increase the focus of FDI policy on the potential for SME supply chain development by:
  - Seeking to steer appropriate FDI projects to regional clusters in which FDI-SME linkage building has high potential, based on existing regional cluster mapping; and
  - Expanding FDI aftercare activities, including regular contacts between the public sector and FDI establishments already hosted in Kazakhstan, with the aim of building relationships that would support local supply chain development.
- Develop an integrated set of policy measures to support FDI-SME linkages in each region. This should include activities to:
  - Create an easily accessible and usable database of potential SME suppliers to FDI in the regional clusters;
  - Create and develop regional linkage building teams to make contacts with FDI projects and SMEs within regional clusters and broker and support new linkages; and
  - Co-ordinate an integrated package of consultancy, finance, training and innovation support to selected SMEs with strong potential to supply FDI in regional clusters in order to upgrade their capacities to supply FDI and support them in winning supply contracts.
- Introduce supply chain finance initiatives through the Damu Enterprise Development Fund, such as initiatives to stimulate the factoring market.

References

Khanin, D., Subramanian, V., Uvaliyeva, A., Turganbayev, Y., Ospanova, B., Kulbatyrov, N., Tourez, C. (2017) National Report, Global Entrepreneurship Monitor: Kazakhstan 2016/17. Nazarbayez University, Economic Research Institute and National Chamber of Entrepreneurs, Astana.

OECD (2018) *Financing SMEs and Entrepreneurs 2018: An OECD Scoreboard*. OECD Publishing Paris. https://doi.org/10.1787/fin_sme_ent-2018-en.

OECD (2017a), OECD Reviews of Innovation Policy: Kazakhstan 2017, OECD Publishing, Paris, http://dx.doi.org/10.1787/9789264270008-en.

OECD (2017b), OECD Territorial Reviews: Kazakhstan, OECD Publishing, Paris, http://dx.doi.org/10.1787/9789264269439-en.

OECD (2016a), Entrepreneurship at a Glance 2016, OECD Publishing, Paris, http://dx.doi.org/10.1787/entrepreneur_aag-2016-en.

OECD (2016b), Multi-dimensional Review of Kazakhstan: Volume 1. Initial Assessment, OECD Development Pathways, OECD Publishing, Paris, http://dx.doi.org/10.1787/9789264246768-en.

OECD (2014) Regulatory Policy in Kazakhstan, OECD Publishing, Paris, http://dx.doi.org/10.1787/9789264214255-en.

OECD/European Union/EBRD/ETF (2015) SME Policy Index: Eastern Partner Countries 2016: Assessing the Implementation of the Small Business Act for Europe, OECD Publishing, Paris. http://dx.doi.org/10.1787/9789264246249-en

Republic of Kazakhstan (2015), "Resolution No. 168 of the Republic of Kazakhstan dated the 31st of March, 2015 on Approval of a Unified Business Support and Development Programme 'Business Road Map 2020'", Government of Kazakhstan, Astana.

Sange Research Centre (2013), "Kazakhstan: Improving Capacity to Support SME Development - SME Survey – A Needs Assessment", May, Asian Development Bank, Manila.

Singer, S., Herrington M.,Menipaz Ehud (2018), Global Entrepreneurship Monitor, Global Report 2017/18. Babson College, Universidad del Desarrollo, Universiti Tun Abdul Razak, Korea Entrepreneurship Foundation.

WEF (2017) *The Global Competitiveness Report 2017-18*, World Economic Forum, Geneva.

World Bank (2013), *Kazakhstan Country Profile 2013: Enterprise Surveys*, Washington DC. http://www.enterprisesurveys.org/~/media/GIAWB/EnterpriseSurveys/Documents/Profiles/English/Kazakhstan-2013.pdf.

World Bank (2018) *Doing Business 2018: Reforming to Create Jobs*, World Bank, Washington DC.

Chapter 2. SME and Entrepreneurship Characteristics and Performance in Kazakhstan

This chapter examines the state of SME and entrepreneurship characteristics and performance in Kazakhstan. It presents key structural indicators including the SME share in numbers of enterprises, employment and GDP, the sector and size distribution of SME activity, business start-up rates, entrepreneurial intentions, women and youth entrepreneurship, number of high-growth enterprises and the size of the informal economy.

Key messages and policy recommendations

There are large numbers of small and medium-sized enterprises (SMEs) in Kazakhstan. At 11.2 enterprises per 100 working age population, the SME density is substantially above a wide range of other countries. On the other hand, SMEs in Kazakhstan tend to have small average size, and there are few medium-sized enterprises. There is also still a large state-owned sector in Kazakhstan, accounting for approximately one-third of employees.

Kazakhstan has healthy levels of entrepreneurship and business creation. Kazakhstan's total early-stage entrepreneurial activity rate is in line with international benchmarks, and a relatively high proportion of entrepreneurs express intentions to grow their businesses. The entrepreneurial spirit also is healthy – entrepreneurship has good media exposure and is seen as a positive career choice.

Approximately 2.6 million people are self-employed, representing some 30% of the working population. However, a substantial proportion is in low productivity work gaining only subsistence incomes, and up to 44% of self-employment is informal. Some 48% of the self-employed in Kazakhstan are women. However, they are concentrated in independent entrepreneurship and smaller companies. Approximately 30% of youth in work are self-employed, but a large number of them are in low productive activity in the informal sector.

In terms of SME innovation, rates of introduction of new products in SMEs in Kazakhstan are in line with comparable countries. However, the World Economic Forum index identifies a number of problems affecting SME innovation, including availability of the latest technologies and firm-level technology absorption. SME usage of the internet is also low by international standards. Only a small proportion of SMEs in Kazakhstan are exporters.

The nature of SMEs and entrepreneurship activity in Kazakhstan, in terms of large numbers of businesses and start-ups but low average productivity levels, imply a need for policy to concentrate on supporting enterprise growth. This could be achieved by targeting enterprises with high growth potential and providing intensive support to overcome barriers to growth among existing medium-sized SMEs, including support for innovation and internationalisation.

The key recommendations of the report on improving SME and entrepreneurship characteristics and performance in Kazakhstan are set out below.

Key policy recommendations on SME and entrepreneurship characteristics and performance

- Noting recent healthy business start-up rates and growth in numbers of SMEs, increase the weight of policy attention to encouraging high productivity SMEs, specifically by:
  - Identifying and addressing barriers to high productivity and growth in medium-sized enterprises; and
  - Introducing targeted support to high-growth potential innovative start-ups and SMEs.

Numbers and share of SMEs

Numbers of SMEs are high and increasing

The Committee on Statistics of the Kazakhstan Government currently produces only limited data on SMEs, in particular with regard to their size distribution. Until 2014, only two size bands were defined (small and medium) on the basis of number of employees and some additional financial criteria. In 2015, the definition of "small" was adjusted from up to 50 employees to 15-100 employees, and a new category of microenterprises (up to 15 people) was introduced, although as yet there are limited statistics regarding the latter category. In addition to SME businesses, the Committee on Statistics produces statistics for individual entrepreneurs. These statistics are not broken down by size category based on number of employees, but they have very small average size.

Comparison with OECD countries shows that the number of SMEs relative to the working age population (including individual entrepreneurs) is relatively high in Kazakhstan. The SME density at 11.2 per 100 working age population is substantially above a wide range of other countries, including the Russian Federation (1.9), Brazil (2.2), Germany (4.0), Mexico (4.3), and Turkey (4.9) (Figure 2.1).

Figure 2.1. SMEs per 100 working age population

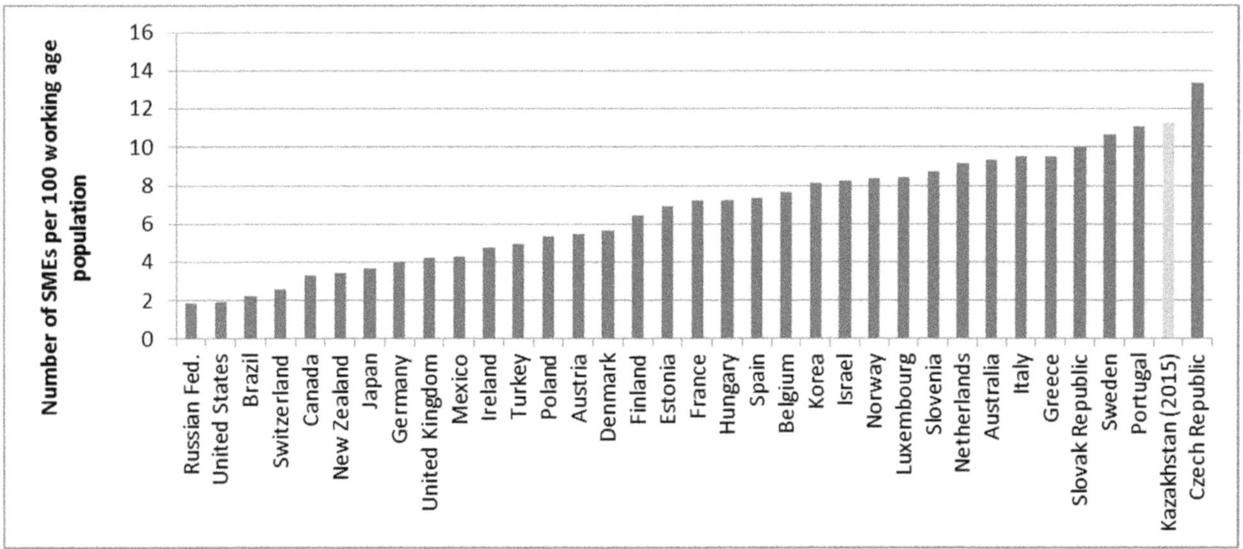

Note: Owing to changes in the definition of SMEs, 2015 is used for the purpose of comparability rather than more recent data.

Source: OECD (2016), Ministry of National Economy, Committee on Statistics. Figures for 2013 or latest available year. Figures for Kazakhstan for 2015.

StatLink http://dx.doi.org/10.1787/888933827669

Moreover, there has been steady growth of the SME sector in recent years in Kazakhstan in terms of numbers, employment and value added (Figure 2.2). Between 2002 and 2013, on average the number of SMEs increased by 12% per annum, employment by 10%, and GDP by 19%. While these are impressive figures, the average size of SMEs has decreased over the period.

Figure 2.2. Evolution of number, employment and GDP in the SME sector

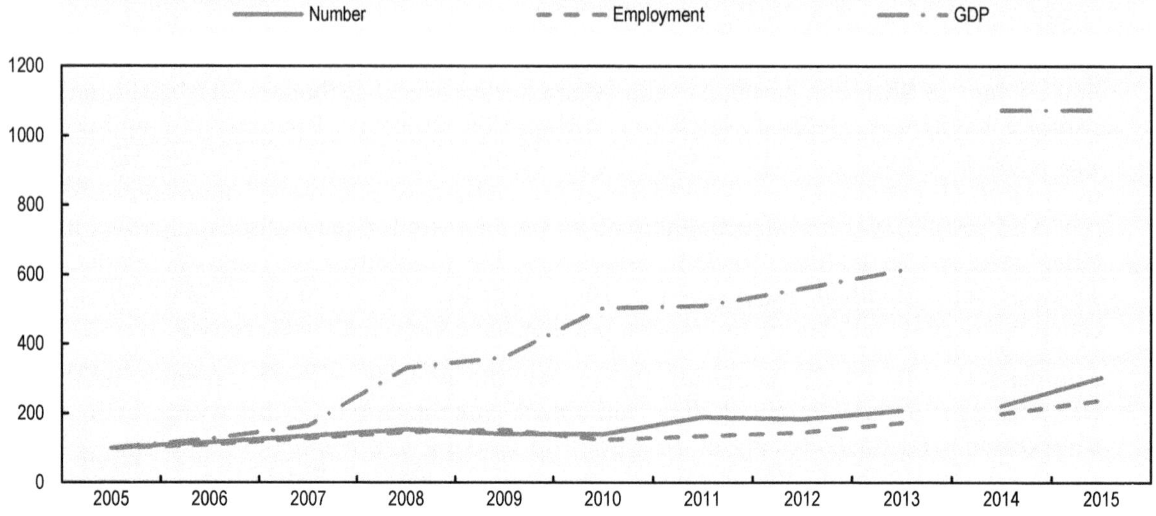

Source: Ministry of National Economy, Committee on Statistics, 2005 =100. Note that owing to changes in definition, figures for 2013 and 2014 are not directly comparable.

StatLink http://dx.doi.org/10.1787/888933827688

SMEs have a small share of employment and value added, and are concentrated in trade and services

Kazakhstan's SME population includes a large number of very small firms (particularly those run by independent entrepreneurs). Accordingly, the SME contribution to business economy employment and value added is small compared to a wide range of OECD and Commonwealth of Independent States (CIS) countries (Figure 2.3 and Figure 2.4).

Figure 2.3. SME share of business sector employment

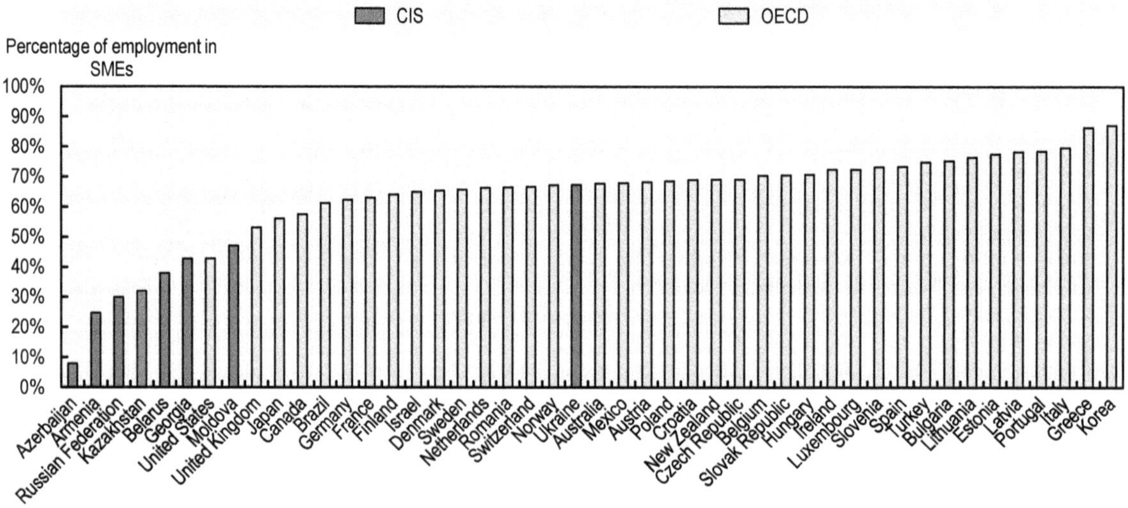

Source: OECD (2016), OECD/European Union/EBRD/ETF (2015), Ministry of National Economy, Committee on Statistics. *Note:* Figures for 2013 or latest available year. Figures for Kazakhstan for 2015.

StatLink http://dx.doi.org/10.1787/888933827707

Figure 2.4. SME share of total business economy gross value

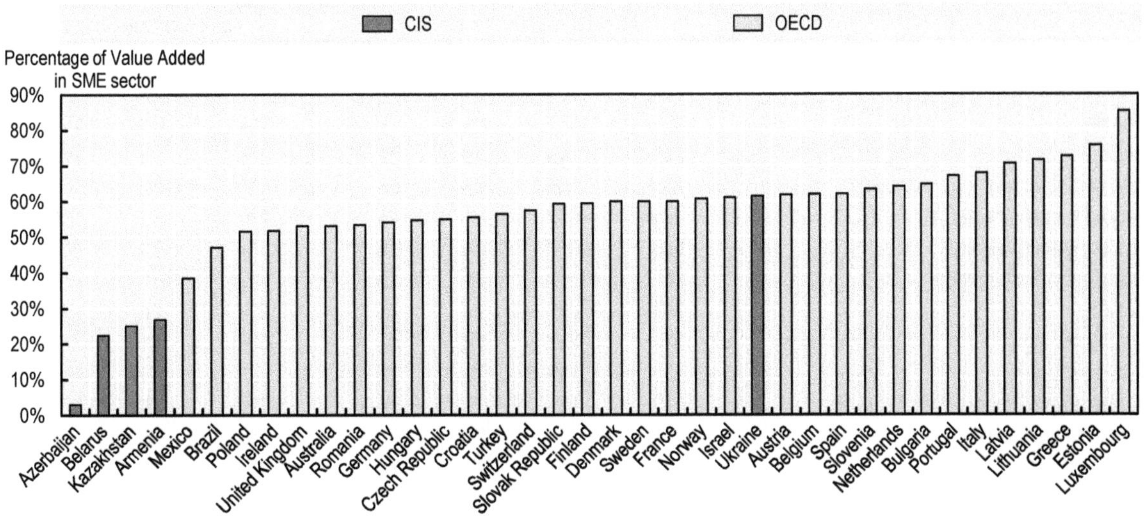

Source: OECD (2016), OECD/European Union/EBRD/ETF (2015), Ministry of National Economy, Committee on Statistics.

Note: Figures for 2013 or latest available year. Figures for Kazakhstan for 2015.

StatLink http://dx.doi.org/10.1787/888933827840

Kazakhstan's SMEs are strongly weighted towards the wholesale and retail trade. On the other hand, medium and large enterprises are particularly concentrated in manufacturing and construction. Independent entrepreneurs form the largest number of enterprises in all sectors, but are particularly concentrated in the wholesale and retail trade, service activities, and transportation and warehousing (Table 2.1).

Table 2.1. Number of enterprises by sector and size class

	As percentage of sector				As percentage of size class			
	Independent	Small	Medium	Large	Independent	Small	Medium	Large
Arts, entertainment and recreation	80%	20%	0%	0%	1%	1%	2%	1%
Construction	43%	56%	1%	0%	2%	16%	15%	14%
Education	55%	44%	1%	0%	1%	3%	4%	5%
Electricity, gas, steam and air conditioning	23%	66%	4%	7%	0%	0%	2%	6%
Financial and insurance activities	8%	91%	1%	1%	0%	3%	2%	5%
Health care and social services	62%	37%	1%	0%	1%	2%	4%	3%
Information and communication	65%	34%	0%	0%	1%	3%	2%	2%
Manufacturing	69%	29%	1%	1%	3%	7%	18%	20%
Mining and quarrying	4%	89%	4%	3%	0%	1%	4%	6%
Other service activities	89%	11%	0%	0%	17%	10%	3%	2%
Professional, scientific and technical activities	57%	43%	0%	0%	2%	8%	6%	4%
Public administration and defence	74%	26%	1%	0%	3%	5%	9%	9%
Real estate transactions	86%	13%	0%	0%	7%	6%	3%	1%
Services for accommodation and meals	91%	9%	0%	0%	3%	2%	3%	2%
Transportation and warehousing	92%	8%	0%	0%	10%	5%	8%	6%
Water supply; sewerage system, control over the collection and distribution of waste	41%	57%	2%	1%	0%	1%	1%	2%
Wholesale and retail trade; repair of motor vehicles and motorcycles	90%	10%	0%	0%	49%	28%	14%	11%

Source: Ministry of National Economy, Committee on Statistics. Figures for operating enterprises as of January 2017.

There is a still a large state-owned sector in Kazakhstan, accounting for approximately one-third of employees. However, figures from the Committee on Statistics show that average wages in the private sector were around 50% higher than in the state sector in 2013. The scale of state ownership is likely to hamper the ability of the private sector to enter the economy. The current round of large-scale privatisation, which began in 2016, should support private sector development.

Entrepreneurship

Attitudes to entrepreneurship are positive

Entrepreneurship is seen as a desirable career choice in Kazakhstan by almost 60% of the adult population and as high status by slightly more than 80%. Almost half of adults consider that there is high media attention for entrepreneurship. In addition, the share of the population giving high status to successful entrepreneurs is high by an international comparison (Singer et al, 2018).

Table 2.2. Entrepreneurial attitudes in the adult population, 2017

	Entrepreneurship as a good career choice	High status to successful entrepreneurs	Media attention for entrepreneurship
Kazakhstan	59.7	80.1	49.1
Bosnia and Herzegovina	62.7	65.6	26.4
Qatar	65.9	77.3	54.0
Taiwan	71.1	60.1	81.3
Thailand	74.7	74.5	84.3
Indonesia	70.0	81.0	83.8
Vietnam	62.1	74.8	81.1
China	66.4	74.6	71.0
United States	63.1	75.5	74.5
India	53.0	56.2	44.8
Canada	65.6	74.0	76.5
European Union	58.5	67.3	54.3
Australia	53.9	68.9	74.0
Iran	48.3	79.4	49.4
Malaysia	77.1	69.9	83.2
Switzerland	53.0	73.2	59.0
Japan	24.3	52.0	56.2

Note: Good career choice refers to the percentage of the adult population between the ages of 18 and 64 years who believe that entreprenurship is a good career choice.

High status refers to the percentage of the adult population between the ages of 18 ans 64 years who believe that high status is afforded to successful entrepreneurs.

Source: Singer, S., Herrington M.,Menipaz Ehud (2018), Global Entrepreneurship Monitor, Global Report 2017/18. Babson College, Universidad del Desarrollo, Universiti Tun Abdul Razak, Korea Entrepreneurship Foundation. Figures for 2017.

Furthermore, entrepreneurial attributes and intentions in the population are positive (Singer et al, 2018). Relatively high proportions of adults in Kazakhstan perceive themselves to have the capabilities necessary for successful entrepreneurship and relatively low proportions cite fear of failure as a reason not to pursue entrepreneurship. Fear of failure has reduced considerably since 2007, when more than 41.9% of the population noted this as a problem, compared to less than 25% in 2014. Slightly more than half of the adult population perceive opportunities for business creation in Kazakhstan, which is a high rate in an international context (Table 2.3). Similarly, the level of entrepreneurial intentions, at 46.2 in 2017, is also high.

Table 2.3. Attributes of potential entrepreneurs and entrepreneurial intentions in the adult population, 2017

	Perceived opportunities	Perceived capabilities	Fear of failure	Entrepreneurial intentions
Qatar	45.6	41.1	41.9	15.7
Canada	60.2	55.6	43.8	14.1
United States	63.6	54.3	33.4	14.5
Thailand	49.1	48.9	52.7	37.4
Australia	51.4	49.3	41.4	13.2
Indonesia	47.4	57.3	46.7	28.1
Switzerland	47.2	42.1	29.5	10.5
Malaysia	45.1	46.1	45.0	17.6
Vietnam	46.4	53.0	46.6	25.0
India	44.9	42.1	39.6	10.3
European Union	41.4	43.4	37.0	10.8
Taiwan	26.6	25.9	39.2	25.7
China	35.2	27.2	41.5	15.3
Iran	33.6	53.4	39.9	38.8
Kazakhstan	50.4	64.7	18.4	46.2
Bosnia and Herzegovina	13.4	35.5	27.2	4.6
Japan	7.4	10.8	41.2	3.7

Notes:

Perceived opportunities refers to the percentage of the population aged 18-64 who see good opportunities to start a firm in the area in which they live.

Perceived capabilities refers to the percentage of the population aged 18-64 who believe they have the required skills and knowledge to start a business.

Fear of failure refers to the percentage of the adult population aged 18-64, perceiving good opportunities to start a business but who indicate that fear of failure would prevent them from setting one up.

Entrepreneurial intentions refers to the percentage of the population aged 18-64 who are latent entrepreneurs and who intend to start a business within three years (individuals involved in any stage of entrepreneurial activity are excluded).

Source: Singer, S., Herrington M.,Menipaz Ehud (2018), Global Entrepreneurship Monitor, Global Report 2017/18. Babson College, Universidad del Desarrollo, Universiti Tun Abdul Razak, Korea Entrepreneurship Foundation. Figures for 2017.

There is a reasonable level of early-stage entrepreneurial activity

Total early-stage entrepreneurial activity in Kazakhstan is slightly below the average for efficiency-driven economies but substantially higher than in the Russian Federation and Georgia (Table 2.4). The rate of established business ownership is also less than the average for efficiency-driven economies, but higher than the Russian Federation and comparable with Georgia.

Table 2.4. Share of the adult population involved in entrepreneurship activities, 2017

	Nascent entrepreneurship rate	New business ownership rate	Early-stage entrepreneurial activity (TEA)	Established business ownership rate	Discontinuation of businesses
Thailand	10.6	12.1	21.6	15.2	9.2
Qatar	4.7	2.8	7.4	1.3	5.8
Iran	6.8	6.9	13.3	10.6	6.6
China	3.7	6.4	9.9	6.8	2.8
Vietnam	2.5	20.8	23.3	24.7	4.2
Indonesia	3.6	3.9	7.5	10.4	4.8
United States	9.4	4.6	13.6	7.8	4.0
Kazakhstan	8.0	3.8	11.3	2.4	7.5
Australia	6.4	5.9	12.2	9.0	3.8
Canada	11.3	8.1	18.8	6.2	6.9
Taiwan	3.6	5.0	8.6	12.1	4.0
European Union	5.1	3.1	8.1	7.0	2.9
Bosnia and Herzegovina	2.5	1.4	4.0	1.4	1.3
Switzerland	4.7	3.9	8.5	10.5	1.1
India	4.9	4.6	9.3	6.2	3.2
Malaysia	15.4	6.6	21.6	3.8	8.3
Japan	3.2	1.6	4.7	6.3	1.5

Note: Nascent Entrepreneurship Rate – Percentage of the adult population aged between 18 and 64 years that have started a business that is less than 4 months old and that has not paid salaries or wages

New Business Ownership Rate – Percentage of the adult population aged between 18 and 64 years that have started a business that is between 4 and 42 months old and is paying salaries or wages

Total Early-stage Entrepreneurial Activity – TEA - Percentage of the adult population between the ages of 18 and 64 years who are in the process of starting a b usiness or already started a business (a nascent entrepreneur or owner-manager of a new business) which is less than 42 months old.

Established Business Ownership Rate – EB –Percentage of the adult population aged between 18 and 64 years who are currently an owner manager of an established business, i.e. owning and managing a running business that has paid salaries, wages or any other payments to the owners for more than 42 months.

Discontinuation of Businesses – Percentage of the adult population aged between 18 and 64 years that have discontinued a business in the past 12 months, either by selling, shutting down or otherwise discontinuing an owner/management relationship with the business.

Source: Singer, S., Herrington M.,Menipaz Ehud (2018), Global Entrepreneurship Monitor, Global Report 2017/18. Babson College, Universidad del Desarrollo, Universiti Tun Abdul Razak, Korea Entrepreneurship Foundation. Figures for 2017.

Self-employment

There is a significant population of unproductively self-employed

In 2014, an estimated 2.6 million people were self-employed in Kazakhstan, 30.2% of the working population. Of these, 1.2 million were registered individual entrepreneurs, and only 166 000 were employers (6.4% of all self-employed and 2% of all employed). The two largest sectors for self-employment were agriculture and retailing. Although they make up nearly one-third of the employed population, the self-employed produce only approximately 10% of the gross value added in the country and their productivity is six times lower than that of those who are formally employed (Syrlybaeva, 2011).

Up to 44% of self-employment is informal, i.e. the income is not fully declared. Much of this informal self-employment activity is at the subsistence level. Overall, there is a high proportion of the "unproductively self-employed" (World Bank, 2015), including those in informal self-employment activity, those employed in private farms producing goods for their own consumption, unpaid family workers, members of cooperatives engaged on an individual basis and people employed in private farms with monthly income below the subsistence minimum.

One of the barriers to increasing returns from self-employment is that the self-employed tend to have lower education levels than wage earners. While 41% of the employed have higher education, only 19% of the self-employed have higher education (25% among the self-employed with higher earnings and only 11% among the "unproductive self-employed") (World Bank, 2015).

Women and youth entrepreneurship

Kazakhstan scores well on gender equality in entrepreneurship, but issues remain

A high proportion of the self-employed in Kazakhstan are women (48%) by international comparison (see Figure 2.5). Furthermore, the labour force survey shows that women constitute around 45% of "productive" self-employment in Kazakhstan (unproductive self-employment is defined as that which does not produce sufficient income on which to survive). This share is high compared to OECD countries.

Figure 2.5. Percentage of the self-employed who are women

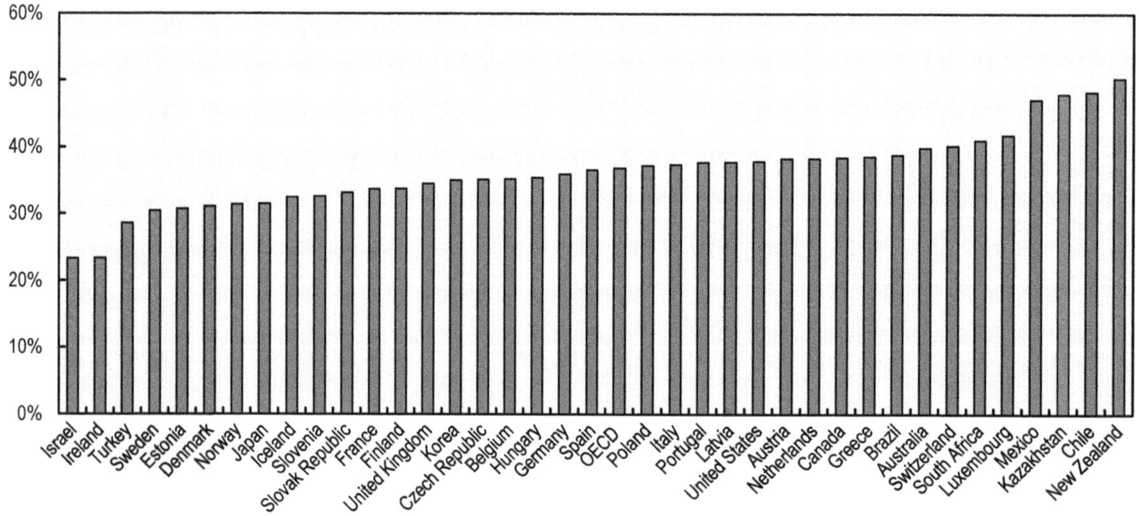

Source: OECD (2016), Ministry of National Economy, Committee on Statistics. Figures for 2015 or latest available year.

StatLink http://dx.doi.org/10.1787/888933827859

However, women entrepreneurs tend to operate smaller businesses than men in Kazakhstan. The labour force survey shows that only 28% of the managers of incorporated enterprises are women[1]. Only 3.8% of the female self-employed were employers compared to 8.3% of the male self-employed[3]. Female-owned enterprises also averaged only 2.32 employees compared with an average of 3.73 employees in male-owned enterprises. They were also significantly less likely to be of medium-size and tended to have more modest capital assets, working capital, and annual turnover (ADB, 2013; Sange Research Centre, 2013).

In the same vein, the Global Entrepreneurship Monitor shows that the rate of opportunity-oriented entrepreneurship by women in Kazakhstan was 7 percentage points behind the rate for men in 2016 (Khanin et al, 2017). This is a relatively small difference compared with many countries, but it is still a significant gap to close. This indicates a deficit in the numbers of women-owned businesses with scale and growth orientation in Kazakhstan.

There are also differences in the sectors of activities pursued by women and men entrepreneurs in Kazakhstan. Women entrepreneurs tend to be more concentrated in lower value added activities in the areas of hotels and catering, financial services, trade, and personal services, according to a survey by Damu in 2010, suggesting potential to facilitate the participation of women in growth sectors. This is confirmed by an ADB-funded survey, which shows that women-owned business tend to be more involved in trade and hospitality services and less in construction, farming and material production (Sange Research Centre, 2013).

Furthermore, although on average for Kazakhstan as a whole, the share of women in entrepreneurship is near to that of men, there is considerable variation in women's participation in entrepreneurship across the regions of Kazakhstan. For example, while women-headed SMEs accounted for 48% of all active SMEs in the Kostanay and Karaganda regions, this dropped to only one-third in the South Kazakhstan region (Damu, 2015, p. 19). There therefore appears to be scope to increase women entrepreneurship rates significantly in certain regions.

In terms of the barriers affecting the rate and nature of women entrepreneurship activity, evidence points to a relative lack of experience and expertise in starting and operating a business, lack of access to start-up capital and collateral, lack of access to and control over land and property, and lack of digestible information on business opportunities (Shakirova, 2014). These constraints are exacerbated by the greater difficulty for women in reconciling the requirements of growth-oriented entrepreneurship with family obligations (Sange Research Centre, 2013).

Figure 2.6 suggests that many of the barriers to entrepreneurship are gender neutral. However, businesses with female senior managers are twice as likely as other businesses to identify access to finance and business licensing as the most important obstacles to business.

Figure 2.6. Gender differences regarding major obstacles to business

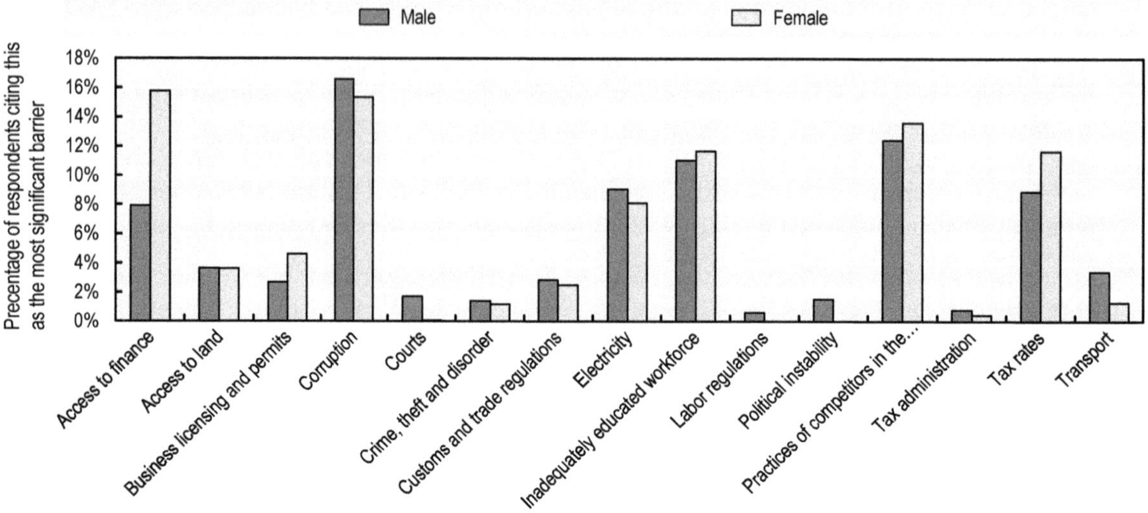

Source: OECD calculations from data from European Bank of Reconstruction and Development (EBRD) / World Bank Business Environment and Enterprise Performance Survey (BEEPS) V, 2014.

StatLink http://dx.doi.org/10.1787/888933827878

The quality of youth self-employment often needs to be upgraded

In 2012/13, an estimated 185 000 graduates from technical and vocational education and 172 000 from higher education entered the labour market (World Bank, 2015a). The private sector is not large enough and growing fast enough to absorb these new graduates. Although the official youth unemployment rate is low (6.6% in 2013), this masks a large number of young people who turn to informal work and necessity-driven self-employment activity. In fact, in 2013, the Agency of Statistics reported that 30.4% of working 15-29 year-olds were self-employed (Scientific-Research Centre "Youth", 2013, p. 207). A large number of these "self-employed" young people are in low productive activity in the informal sector.

Better alternatives for low productivity young self-employed people should be developed. A number of the young self-employed could be supported to develop higher value added enterprises and grow them to scale. Relevant measures for this group would include offering entrepreneurship education and entrepreneurship training programmes and support with access to finance. General vocational training could also support some of these young people to transition into more productive paid employment.

Informal economy

The size of the informal economy is an important obstacle to growth

Kazakhstan has a very large informal economy. The IMF estimates the size of the informal economy at around 33%, ranking it 62 of 67 countries researched (Figure 2.7). While other CIS countries perform even worse in this ranking, the informal economy is smaller than in Kazakhstan in most middle-income countries in other regions of the world (Medina and Schneider, 2018).

Figure 2.7. Comparison of size of the informal economy, 2015

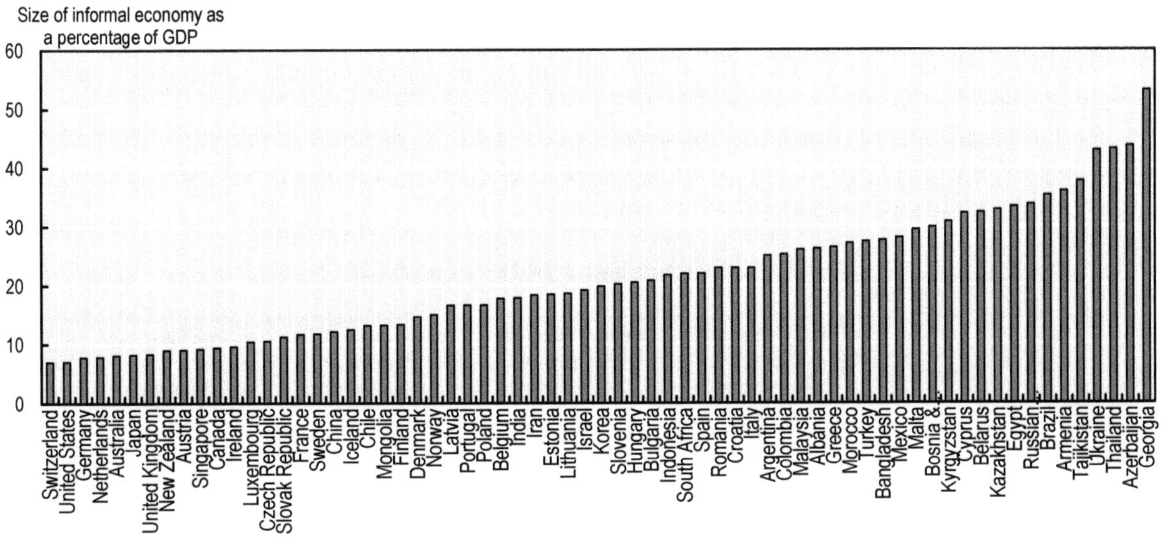

Source: Medina and Schneider (2018).

StatLink http://dx.doi.org/10.1787/888933827897

The size of the informal economy (i.e. businesses which are neither taxed nor monitored by the state) has an adverse impact on the development of SMEs and entrepreneurship. It is notable that competitors in the informal sector were identified as one of the most important obstacles in the business environment in Kazakhstan in the EBRD BEEPS V survey (Figure 2.8).

Figure 2.8. Major obstacles to business

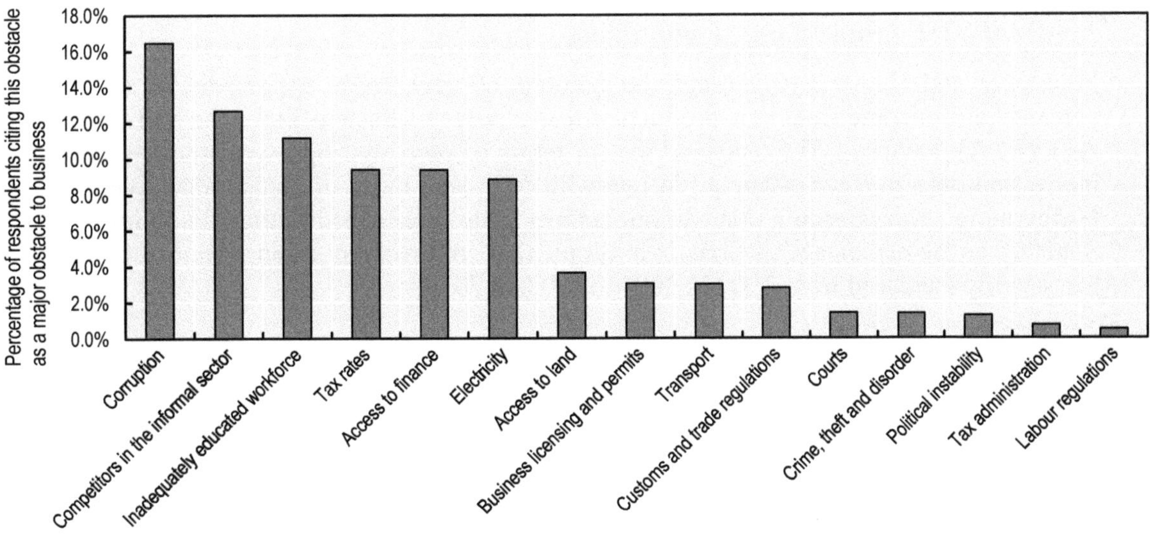

Source: OECD calculations from data from EBRD BEEPS V survey, 2014.

StatLink http://dx.doi.org/10.1787/888933827916

Trade

Few firms export, but many use imported goods

Only a small proportion of SMEs in Kazakhstan are exporters compared to other upper middle income countries or countries in Eastern Europe and Central Asia, even though a similar proportion of firms use imported goods. Part of the reason for this lies with problems in customs efficiency, with times taken to clear both imports and exports being very high relative to comparable countries (Table 2.5).

Table 2.5. Participation of SMEs in trade, 2013

	All firms – Kazakhstan	Small Firms (1-19 Employees) - Kazakhstan	Medium Firms (20-99 Employees) - Kazakhstan	Large Firms (100+ Employees) - Kazakhstan	All firms – Eastern Europe & Central Asia	All firms – Upper middle income
% of Exporter Firms	5.2	2.5	6.8	16.3	22.8	19.1
% of Firms that Use Material Inputs and/or Supplies of Foreign origin	64.0	59.9	65.3	73.7	64.8	67.5
Average Time to Clear Direct Exports Through Customs	7.2	N/A	10.9	3.3	4.4	7.2
Average Time to Clear Imports from Customs (days)	11.2	16.0	6.1	10.0	6.1	9.4

Source: World Bank (2013).

Innovation

Levels of SME innovation are improving

Figure 2.9 and Figure 2.10 present the number of new products introduced and the percentage of income from new products across a range of Eastern European and Central Asia (ECA) countries. They suggest that in terms of recently improved products, SME innovation rates in Kazakhstan are in line with or exceed those of comparable countries. Furthermore, Kazakhstan's innovation activity rate (defined by the Committee on Statistics as the percentage of firms in a sample that are involved in innovation activities) has steadily increased from 2.3% in 2004 to 8.1% in 2015.

Figure 2.9. Number of new products introduced, country comparison

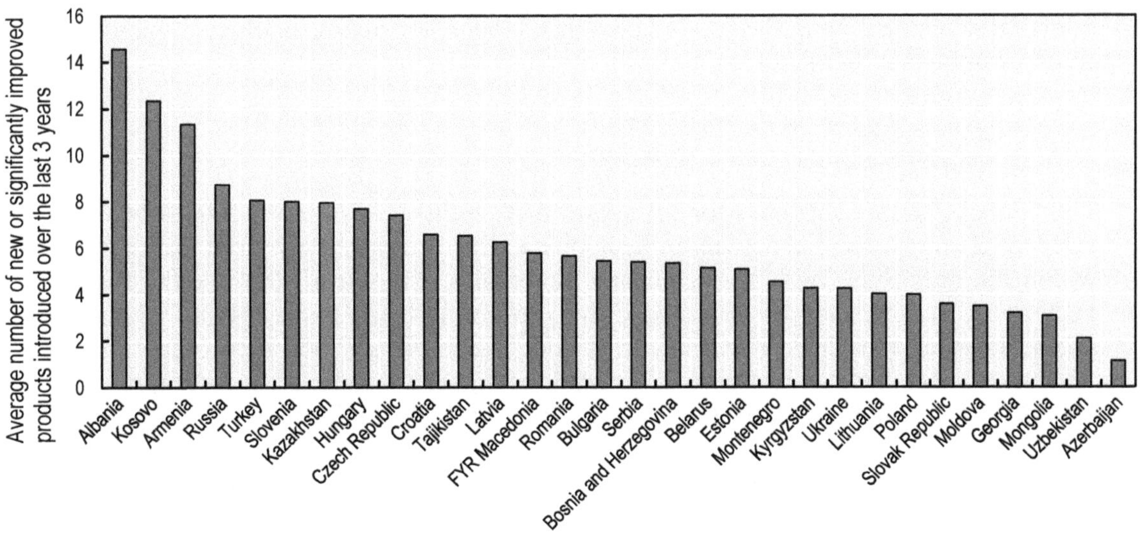

Source: OECD calculations from data from EBRD BEEPS V survey 2014.

StatLink http://dx.doi.org/10.1787/888933827935

Figure 2.10. Percentage of sales accounted for by new products, country comparison

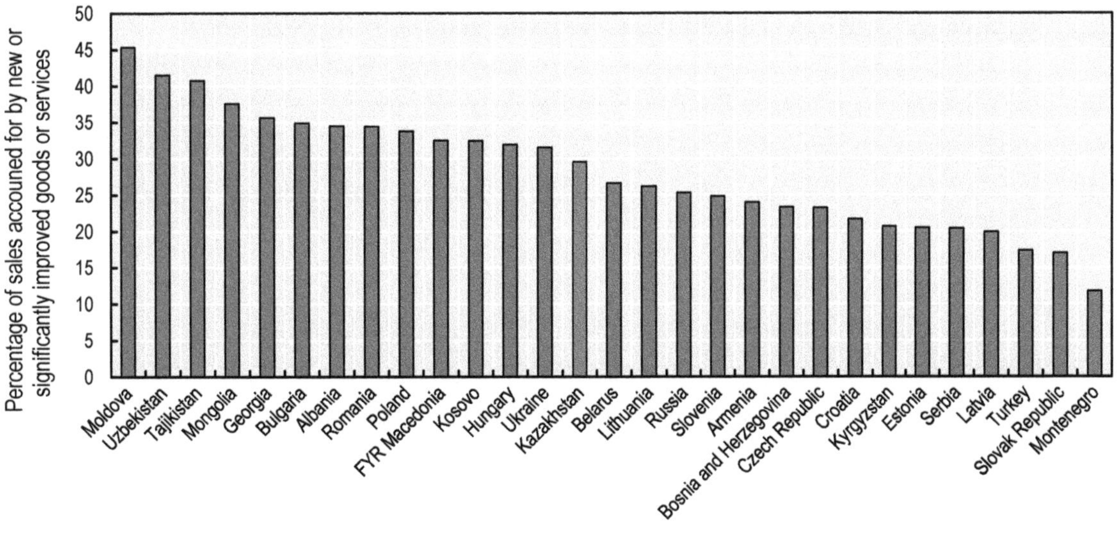

Source: OECD calculations from data from EBRD BEEPS V survey 2014.

StatLink http://dx.doi.org/10.1787/888933827726

Business use of the internet lags behind government usage

On the other hand, the World Economic Forum's Networked Readiness Index for 2015 shows that, although overall Kazakhstan scored well at 40th out of 143 countries (and performed better than the average for upper middle income group countries on all sub-indices), it performed badly on firm-level technology absorption (90th out of 143 countries), capacity for innovation (69th), business to business internet use (64th) and business to consumer internet use (59th). This suggests that there are obstacles to address in digital adoption among SMEs, and also that support for non-technological innovation could be important (WEF, 2015).

High-growth enterprises

The Global Entrepreneurship Monitor shows that, in 2016, 33.1% of adults involved in early-stage entrepreneurial activity in Kazakhstan expected to employ more than 5 people within the next five years. This compares favourably with Brazil (4.4%), the Russian Federation (18.7%), India (5.2%), and China (26.7%) (Khanin et al, 2017). It should be noted, however, that these entrepreneurs do not necessarily include high proportions of "gazelles", since the standard growth threshold is higher for these businesses (growth of 10%-20% per year for 3 years from a base of at least 10 employees) and since growth expectations may not translate into real achieved growth (OECD, 2016). There is a strong need for such high-growth enterprises in Kazakhstan given the government's objectives for growth of value added and employment in the SME sector.

Notes

1. It can be noted that the proportion of women-managed enterprises is considerably higher for state-owned enterprises (43%), suggesting that the gap does not relate to ability or to the general status of women.

2. Based on Kazakhstan labour force survey data reported by ILOStat.See: http://www.ilo.org/ilostat/faces/help_home/data_by_country/country-details/indicator-details?country=KAZ&subject=EMP&indicator=EMP_TEMP_SEX_STE_NB&datasetCode=YI&collectionCode=YI&_afrLoop=32212163743579#%40%3Findicator%3DEMP_TEMP_SEX_STE_NB%26subject%3DEMP%26_afrLoop%3D32212163743579%26datasetCode%3DYI%26collectionCode%3DYI%26country%3DKAZ%26_adf.ctrl-state%3D1cm2dt30da_158.

References

ADB (2013), *Kazakhstan Country Gender Assessment*, Asian Development Bank, Manila, Philippines.

Damu (2015), "Report on the Status of Development of Small and Medium Enterprises in Kazakhstan and its Regions 2014", Issue 7, Damu, Ministry of National Economy and Baiterek, Almaty.

Khanin, D., Subramanian, V., Uvaliyeva, A., Turganbayev, Y., Ospanova, B., Kulbatyrov, N., Tourez, C. (2017) National Report, Global Entrepreneurship Monitor: Kazakhstan 2016/17. Nazarbayez University, Economic Research Institute and National Chamber of Entrepreneurs, Astana.

Medina, L and Schneider, F. (2018), "Shadow Economies Around the World: What Did We Learn Over the Last 20 Years?," IMF Working Paper 18/17, https://www.imf.org/en/Publications/WP/Issues/2018/01/25/Shadow-Economies-Around-the-World-What-Did-We-Learn-Over-the-Last-20-Years-45583.

OECD (2016), Entrepreneurship at a Glance 2016, OECD Publishing, Paris. http://dx.doi.org/10.1787/entrepreneur_aag-2016-en.

OECD/European Union/EBRD/ETF (2015), SME Policy Index: Eastern Partner Countries 2016: Assessing the Implementation of the Small Business Act for Europe, OECD Publishing, Paris. http://dx.doi.org/10.1787/9789264246249-en.

Sange Research Centre (2013), "Kazakhstan: Improving Capacity to Support SME Development - SME Survey – A Needs Assessment", May, Asian Development Bank, Manila.

Shakirova, S. (2014), "The Development of Women's Entrepreneurship in Kazakhstan", *DIALOGUE*, Vol. 15(3), January—March: 163–170. (Accessible online at: http://www.astnaharati.org/Dia_Jan%20014.pdf/)

Singer, S., Herrington M., Menipaz E. (2018), Global Entrepreneurship Monitor, Global Report 2017/18. Babson College, Universidad del Desarrollo, Universiti Tun Abdul Razak, Korea Entrepreneurship Foundation.

Syrlybaeva (2011), "New Employment Strategy for Kazakhstan", Kazakhstan Institute for Strategic Studies, http://kisi.kz/en/categoroes/economy-and-energy/posts/new-employment-strategy-for -Kazakhstan384/.

World Bank (2013), *Kazakhstan Country Profile 2013: Enterprise Surveys*, Washington DC. http://www.enterprisesurveys.org/~/media/GIAWB/EnterpriseSurveys/Documents/Profiles/English/Kazakhstan-2013.pdf.

WEF (2015), The Global Information Technology Report 2015. World Economic Forum, Geneva.

World Bank (2015a), "Kazakhstan - Skills and Jobs Project", World Bank Group: Washington, DC, http://documents.worldbank.org/curated/en/2015/03/24162685/kazakhstan-skills-jobs-project/.

Chapter 3. The Business Environment for SMEs and Entrepreneurship in Kazakhstan

This chapter assesses business environment conditions for SMEs and entrepreneurship in Kazakhstan. It examines macroeconomic conditions, a summary of business perceptions of the main obstacles in the business environment, regulations, corruption and governance, human capital, the innovation system, access to finance, and foreign direct investment.

Key messages and policy recommendations

The Kazakhstan macro-economy has offered stability and steady growth since 2000, providing positive opportunities for entrepreneurship and the development of small and medium-sized enterprises (SMEs).

Kazakhstan has also made considerable progress in improving its regulatory environment for SMEs and entrepreneurship, including simplifying the administration process for starting a business. There are nevertheless some further challenges in strengthening the regulatory environment, notably concerning the regulation of international trade. Furthermore, corruption is identified by many enterprises as a serious constraint to business, despite ongoing efforts to increase transparency and improve public governance. The establishment of a business ombudsman is a welcome development, since it enables SMEs and entrepreneurs to signal unfair treatment by government and seek redress. However, the post needs to be independent of government. Furthermore, the requirement that non-governmental organisations (NGOs) must reapply for approval of their legal status every three years has a negative impact on their ability to represent small business to government and provide independent and critical views.

Access to a skilled workforce remains a barrier to small business development in Kazakhstan. Government and education spending levels are relatively low. More could be done at school level to strengthen literacy skills, including through better training of teachers and increased mother tongue based instruction, and achieving more equal education standards across the country. The government is making reforms to the vocational education system that should improve the supply of skilled workers to SMEs, including the development of a national qualifications framework and occupational standards, establishment of sector skills councils with participation of employer firms, and implementation of a dual training system involving partnerships between colleges and employers for work placements. Specific efforts are needed to involve SMEs, including actions to identify the skills needs of SME employers and respond to them in vocational training provision in colleges. At the tertiary level, the government has set the objective of seeing two Kazakhstan universities ranked among the top 500 in the world. This objective should be matched with efforts to achieve generalised improvements of standards in higher education institutions across the country as a whole. Priorities including renewing university resources and ensuring that university graduates leave with skills that align with SME needs.

The government recognises the potential of entrepreneurship education but policy initiatives to support it are currently fragmented and small scale. A more co-ordinated and strengthened approach would be merited in school education. In addition, higher education institutions and vocational education and training institutions could play important roles in stimulating innovative start-ups by their graduates, both through introducing an entrepreneurship curriculum across disciplines and providing support to students and graduates who are interested in developing their business ideas.

Kazakhstan has an early-stage innovation system, in which government expenditure on research and development (R&D) is still a major driver. There has been a very welcome recent increase in numbers of R&D employees in the country. However, the level of government R&D expenditure remains low, and expenditure has not increased in line with increases in numbers of R&D personnel. Increased R&D expenditure and increased targeting of R&D expenditure to activities with commercialisation potential would help stimulate further SME innovation and innovative entrepreneurship.

Access to finance remains a key constraint for SME and entrepreneurship development. Credit history information is not yet widespread and banks have relatively limited involvement in SME lending without public sector incentives.

There has been substantial inward foreign direct investment (FDI) to Kazakhstan, which could be a support to SME development. However, the concentration of existing FDI in resource extraction activities is a barrier to intense linkage development with domestic businesses. Efforts to diversify the sectors of inward FDI activity should therefore be continued.

The key recommendations of the report on strengthening the business environment for SMEs and entrepreneurship in Kazakhstan are set out below.

Key recommendations on the business environment for SMEs and entrepreneurship

- Continue to take actions in the framework of the government's anti-corruption policy to ensure a change of culture regarding corruption and to reduce the consequences of corruption for SME and entrepreneurship development.
- Increase enrolment rates in tertiary education, for example through increasing the alignment of university degrees with private sector needs and enhancing access to scholarships. Ensure the achievement of minimum tertiary education quality standards throughout the national territory, for example through strengthened faculty training and faster renewal of university resources.
- Strengthen the literacy skills of Kazakh youth at secondary education level, including through better training of teachers and provision of mother-tongue-based instruction, and reduce inequalities in the education system in order to build a broad base of young people with skills for more productive SMEs and entrepreneurship.
- As part of regular surveys of SMEs, identify SME skills needs in Business Road Map 2020 priority sectors. Ensure that these skills are incorporated in the National Qualifications Framework and that appropriate training is provided in vocational education and training programmes. This should include the generic skills as well as the technical skills needed for SME development, for example in business management, marketing and sales, and accounting/finance.
- Expand and strengthen entrepreneurship education in schools and universities, including support facilities for entrepreneurship teachers and encouragement of national and international exchanges of good practice.
- Encourage higher education and vocational education institutions to complement entrepreneurship teaching with extracurricular programmes to support graduate start-ups, such as student business incubators and student entrepreneurship clubs.
- Augment government R&D spending in line with the increase in the size of the R&D workforce in the economy. Increase the emphasis on SMEs in the targeting and management of public R&D spending.
- Ensure access of a wide range of financial institutions to financial information gathered by the State Credit Bureau.
- Continue to reform the banking sector so that in the longer term banks lend to SMEs under normal banking terms without public intervention.

Macroeconomic conditions

GDP has been growing steadily

There was continuous economic growth between 2000 and 2017, providing a positive context for SME and entrepreneurship development with respect to demand and investment. The economy generated 2.3 million jobs between 1999 and 2013, and the unemployment rate fell from 13.5% to 4.9% between 1999 and 2017 (Figure 3.1).

Figure 3.1. Employment and GDP Growth, 1991-2017

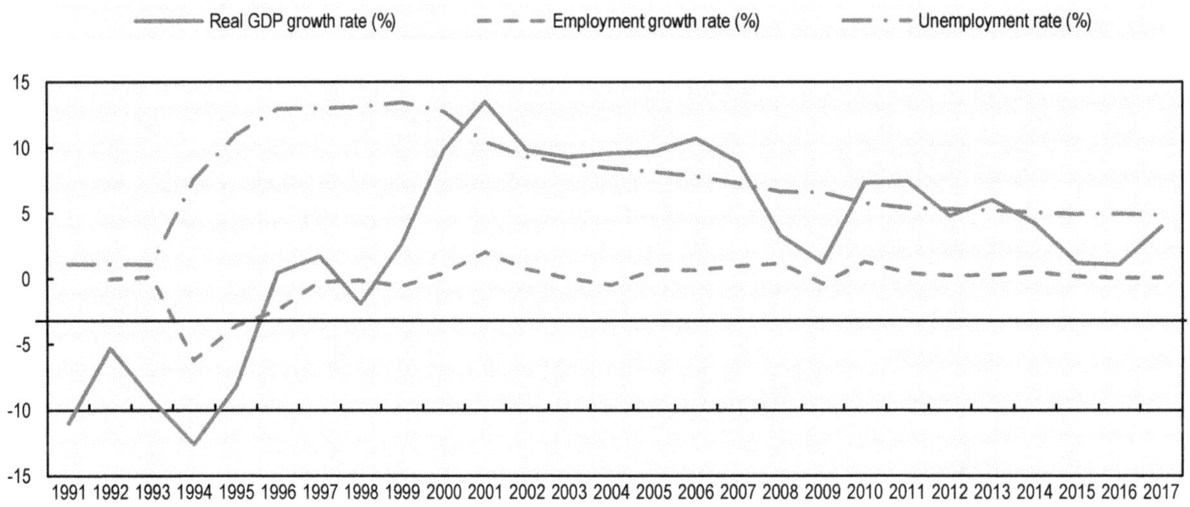

Source: World Bank Open Data, https://data.worldbank.org/country/kazakhstan.

StatLink http://dx.doi.org/10.1787/888933827954

The labour force participation rate is high. Some 71.6% of adults of at least 15 years of age participated in the labour market in Kazakhstan in 2017, compared with an average of 58.4% in Eastern Europe and Central Asia, according to the International Labour Organisation labour market indicators. Similarly, Kazakhstan's employment-to-population ratio was 67.5% in 2017, higher than most OECD countries and significantly higher than the Eastern Europe and Central Asia average, although this participation level is likely to reduce as the ageing of the population accelerates in the coming decade. Youth unemployment is also low. In 2013, it stood at 5.5% for 15-28 year olds compared to an average for the population as a whole of 5.2% according to Ministry of Labour and Social Statistics data.

Kazakhstan has a relatively narrow economic base, as extractive industries generate a large share of value added (Figure 3.2). After the Russian Federation, Kazakhstan has the largest oil reserves and oil production of the former Soviet republics. Activities related to resource extraction also account for a substantial share of manufacturing, transport, trade and services. By some estimates, the oil and gas sector generates around 30% of gross domestic product (GDP), almost one-third of budget revenues and close to two-thirds of exports. Because of Kazakhstan's dependence on the oil and gas sector, global declines in commodity prices have large repercussions on the current account, budget revenues and growth. This has also led to a strong political commitment to economic diversification, including through the development of SMEs and entrepreneurship.

Figure 3.2. Sectoral Share of GDP, average 2015-2017

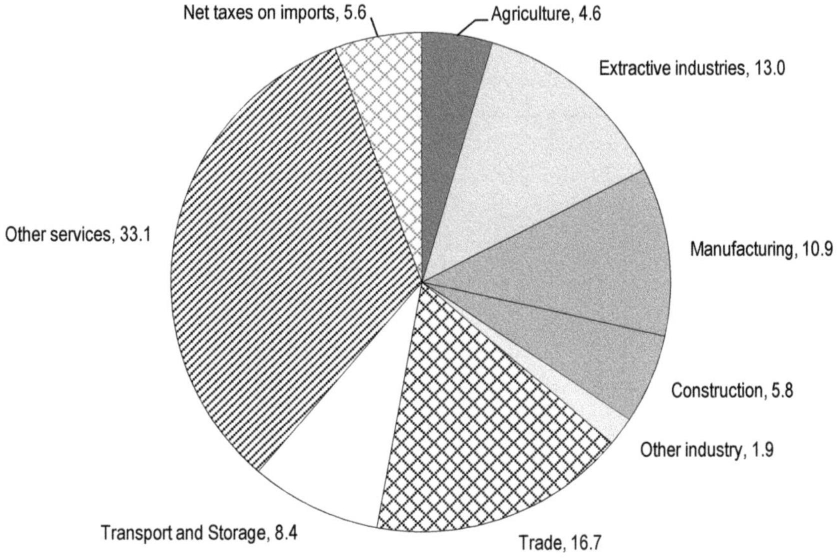

Source: Committee on Statistics, www.stat.gov.kz.

StatLink http://dx.doi.org/10.1787/888933827973

Overview of business perceptions of obstacles in the business environment

Key obstacles cited by SMEs include corruption, informal sector practices, electricity connection, and tax rates

The top five main obstacles in the business environment identified by Kazakh entrepreneurs in the 2013 World Bank Enterprise Survey 2013 were: corruption; informal sector practices; inadequately educated workforce; tax rates; and access to finance (Figure 3.3). These were also the top five obstacles identified in the 2009 survey. On the other hand, regulations (e.g. trade regulations, business licensing and permits, tax administration and labour regulations) have consistently been reported as minor issues.

Figure 3.3. Main obstacles in the business environment of Kazakhstan, 2013 and 2009

Percentage of firms that identify the problem as the main obstacle

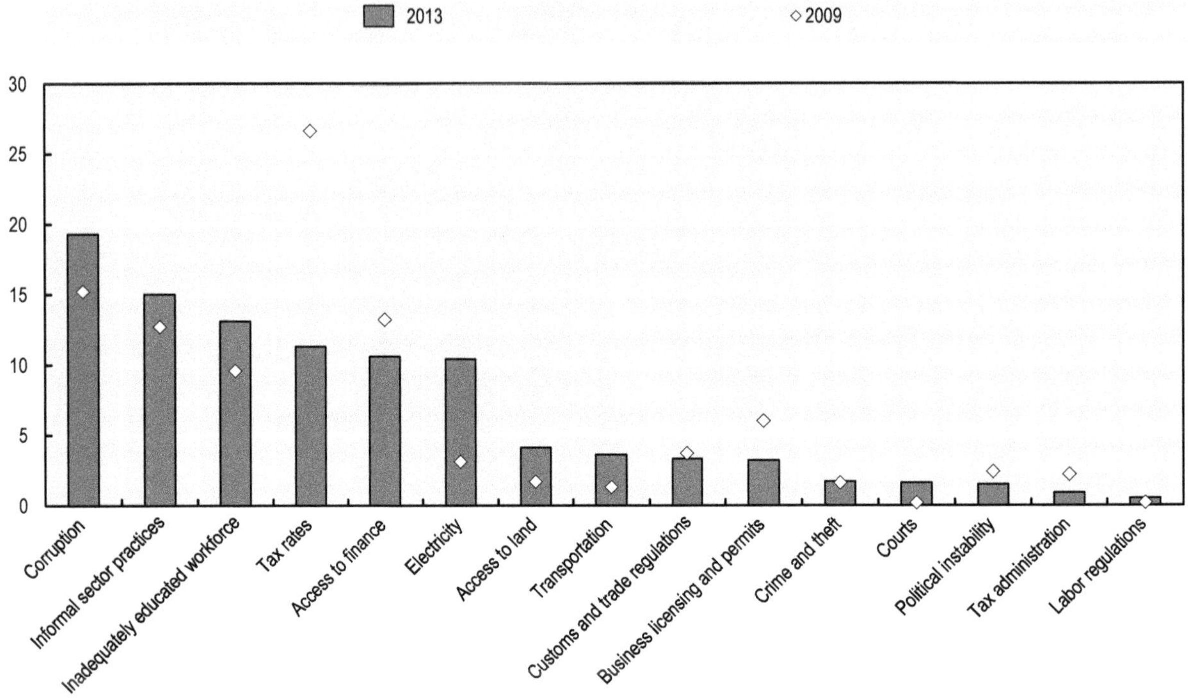

Source: World Bank Enterprise Survey Database.

StatLink http://dx.doi.org/10.1787/888933827992

A disaggregated analysis of the perceived barriers by firm size shows that for small firms (1-19 employees), the top three problems were corruption, informal sector practices and electricity connection. Informal businesses may be a source of unfair competition particularly for similarly small-sized enterprises. For medium-sized firms (20-99 employees) the top three obstacles were tax rates, corruption and inadequately educated workforce (World Bank, 2013).

In comparison with other Eastern Europe and Central Asian (ECA) countries, business perceptions of the regulatory burden are low in Kazakhstan, but issues related to corruption, an inadequately educated workforce, and electricity supply are relatively high (Figure 3.4).

Figure 3.4. Major obstacles to business, 2013

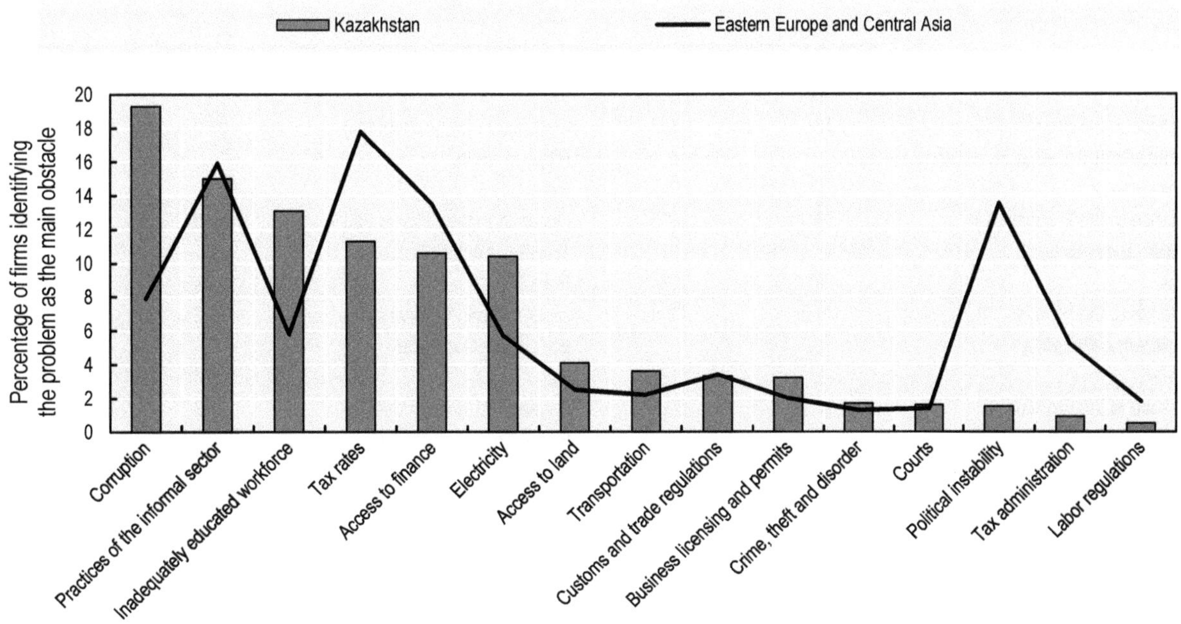

Source: World Bank (2013).

StatLink http://dx.doi.org/10.1787/888933827745

Regulations

Kazakhstan has greatly improved its regulatory environment

The government of Kazakhstan explicitly uses the results of the World Bank Doing Business Survey to benchmark its progress on regulatory simplification and has a stated aim of reaching a ranking among the top 30 countries in the survey on ease of doing business. Kazakhstan has made rapid inroads on this measure, moving from the 74th ranking in 2010 to the 36th ranking in 2018.

Table 3.1. Doing Business in Kazakhstan, 2015-2018 provides a breakdown of Kazakhstan's regulatory performance in the survey. Progress has been especially notable in several areas with strong relevance to SME and entrepreneurship development, notably the ease of starting a new business, an effective insolvency regime and protecting minority investors.

Table 3.1. Doing Business in Kazakhstan, 2015-2018

Rank and Distance to the Frontier (% values)

	2018	2015		2018	2015
Starting a Business			**Protecting Minority Investors**		
Rank	41	53	Rank	1	64
Distance to the Frontier (%)	92.0	90.2	Distance to the Frontier (%)	85.0	56.7
Dealing with Construction Permits			**Paying Taxes**		
Rank	52	100	Rank	80	17
Distance to the Frontier (%)	73.3	67.3	Distance to the Frontier (%)	79.5	89.9
Getting Electricity			**Trading Across Borders**		
Rank	70	68	Rank	123	121
Distance to the Frontier (%)	76.8	73.5	Distance to the Frontier (%)	63.2	60.4
Registering Property			**Enforcing Contracts**		
Rank	17	25	Rank	6	14
Distance to the Frontier (%)	84.6	80.3	Distance to the Frontier (%)	77.6	73.9
Getting Credit			**Resolving Insolvency**		
Rank	77	71	Rank	39	63
Distance to the Frontier (%)	55	50	Distance to the Frontier (%)	67.5	51.5
Doing Business (Overall)					
Rank	36	53			
Distance to the Frontier (%)	75.4	69.6			

Source: World Bank Doing Business Database.

In terms of starting a business, it now takes only 9 days and 5 procedures on average to open a new company in Kazakhstan, in line with the OECD average. Registration costs for individual businesses are 0.3% of per capita income, much lower than the OECD average (3.2%). There are capital requirements for limited liability companies (i.e. Kazakhstan Tenge (KZT) 200 000, i.e. USD 600), but SMEs are exempted, thus effectively benefiting from a preferential treatment.

The improvements in the regulatory environment have been the result of major reforms undertaken by the Kazakhstan Government over recent years, including eliminating registration fees for SMEs, shortening registration time at the public registration centre, and eliminating the obligation to register at the local tax office. Entrepreneur Service Centres have also been set up, offering free information and consultations on regulatory requirements. Further regulatory simplification is on top of the future policy agenda. For example, the government has set the objective of cutting by half the number of permits and licenses, which amounted to around 700 at the end of 2015.

Despite these major improvements, the Doing Business survey shows that further work is needed to improve regulatory design in the areas of getting credit, trading across borders and getting electricity. In addition, it is important that good legislation is followed by good implementation to ensure that regulatory reforms are enacted and achieve the expected outcomes. Kazakhstan has put in place many elements of a full regulatory policy, but this still needs to be strengthened through an improved consultation process and full elaboration of the regulatory impact analysis system (OECD, 2014a).

A system of industry-level self-regulatory organisations has been introduced

In May 2016, the government introduced a system of sector-based self-regulatory organisations (SROs) to govern licenses and permits as well as controls and sanctions at the industry level. SROs are responsible for overseeing the activity of industry members, in compliance with national laws, while the government limits itself to overseeing the activity of SROs. Membership of SROs is expected to be compulsory. The aim of this reform is to enable entrepreneurs to take ownership of the development of their industry by giving them an incentive to improve the quality of administrative services.

Resolving insolvency has become easier but challenges remain

"Resolving insolvency" is another area where Kazakhstan has made major recent progress in the World Bank Doing Business Survey, moving from 63rd rank in 2015 to 39th rank in 2018. Government reforms to the national insolvency regime in the last five years include: allowing creditors to initiate re-organisation proceedings; authorising post-commencement finance (i.e. finance provided to the debtor after the commencement of the insolvency process) and granting it priority over existing unsecured claims; introducing an accelerated rehabilitation proceeding and extending the period for rehabilitation; authorising payment in kind to secured creditors; and encouraging the sales of assets of a liquidated business as a going concern[1].

However, the gap with the best-performing countries is still wide. The average duration of insolvency proceedings is 1.5 years in Kazakhstan, less than in OECD countries (2.3 years). However, the recovery rate (i.e. the percentage of credit that secured creditors recover from an insolvent firm at the end of insolvency proceedings) is 41% in Kazakhstan, much lower than in OECD countries (72%), and the average cost of insolvency (as a percentage of the estate's value) is 15%, higher than in OECD countries (9%).

Effective insolvency regimes are important to SME and entrepreneurship development for a number of reasons: i) in their absence, businesses which are viable but experience short-term liquidity problems cannot seek protection from creditors and, therefore, may become unable to rehabilitate their business; ii) lenders will be hesitant to provide credit if they feel creditor rights are not protected should the borrower business become unviable; iii) at a broader scale, messy insolvency proceedings will imply greater losses for both creditors and debtors and thus a less efficient reallocation of resources in the economy than if both rights were adequately protected.

The credit market legal framework and accessibility to credit information require improvement

Access to finance is an important barrier in the business environment of Kazakhstan, with the credit market legal framework being one of the main causes. The main reasons for Kazakhstan's low scores in this area relate to the poor coverage of private credit registries and the comparative weakness of the legal rights index. According to the World Bank Doing Business Survey, Kazakhstan's index score on the legal rights index was only 4/12 in 2018 (although it had strengthened from 2/12 in 2010), whereas the OECD's index was 6/12. This index measures the protection of the rights of borrowers and lenders through collateral laws and the protection of secured creditors' rights through bankruptcy laws. Kazakhstan's public credit bureau was estimated to cover only 54% of the adult population in 2018. On the other hand, the available credit information is relatively deep, with Kazakhstan scoring 7/8 on the Doing Business depth of credit information index.

This has been achieved partly by integrating information from utility companies and recording loans regardless of their size in the public credit bureau system.

In order to take advantage of the good quality credit information held by the public credit bureau system for much of the population, it is important to ensure the access of a wide range of private financial institutions to the information systems of the State Credit Bureau and the First Credit Bureau. Access to this information would enhance the capabilities of financial institutions in predicting corporate risks and processing loan applications of SMEs and entrepreneurs.

Corruption and governance

Corruption is seen as a major problem by business

Nineteen percent of respondents to the World Bank Enterprise Survey identified "corruption" as the main obstacle in the national business environment. Similarly, 14% of business leaders surveyed for the World Economic Forum (WEF) Global Competitiveness Report cited "corruption" as among the five most problematic factors, and "inefficient government bureaucracy" featured third in the ranking of problematic factors (WEF, 2017).

One of the most widely referred to measures of perceptions of corruption in the population is the Corruption Perception Index (CPI) of the NGO Transparency International, which classifies countries on a scale from 0 (highly corrupt) to 100 (very clean) based on the computation of 13 different sources of information. Kazakhstan's ranking in the 2016 index was 131st (out of the 176 covered countries and territories), totalling a score of 29. This was close to that of other Eurasian Customs Union (EACU) members but lower than BRICS countries, barring the Russian Federation, and less than half the value of the OECD average (Figure 3.5). The performance has not improved significantly over the last three years.

Figure 3.5. Corruption Perception Index, 2016

From 0 (highly corrupt) to 100 (very clean)

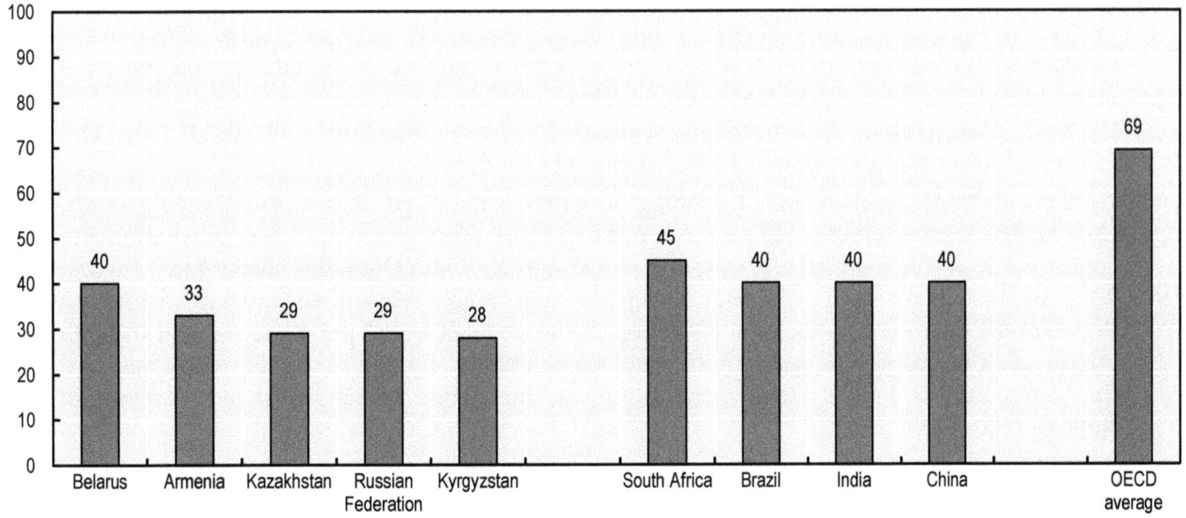

Note: The Corruption Perception Index relies on 13 different sources of information: African Development Bank Governance Ratings 2015; Bertelsmann Foundation Sustainable Governance Indicators 2016; Bertelsmann Foundation Transformation Index 2016; Economist Intelligence Unit Country Risk Ratings 2016; Freedom House Nations in Transit 2016; Global Insight Country Risk Ratings 2015; IMD World Competitiveness Yearbook 2016; Political and Economic Risk Consultancy Asian Intelligence 2016; Political Risk Services International Country Risk Guide 2016; World Bank - Country Policy and Institutional Assessment 2015; World Economic Forum Executive Opinion Survey (EOS) 2016; World Justice Project Rule of Law Index 2016; Varieties of Democracy Project 2016.
Source: OECD based on Transparency International (http://www.transparency.org/cpi2014/results).
StatLink http://dx.doi.org/10.1787/888933828011

Combating corruption requires a coordinated approach. An example of good practice in this respect is given by the Independent Commission against Corruption (ICAC) in Hong Kong, which has produced dramatic changes in a comparatively short period of time (Box 3.1). Kazakhstan has recently put in place a comprehensive framework for combating corruption including the Law on Anti-Corruption, which gives legal protection and financial rewards for whistle-blowers, the Anti-Corruption Strategy for 2015-2025 and within this an Action Plan for 2015-2017. These measures include actions to support a culture against corruption. The results of these actions need to be carefully monitored.

Box 3.1. Independent Commission Against Corruption, Hong Kong

Description of the approach

In the 1950s and 1960s, Hong Kong was noted for its high level of corruption, particularly in the public sector but also in private business. Despite the existence of a Police Anti-Corruption Office, corruption was seen as widespread and deep rooted, and people were resigned to it as a way of life. However, a number of high-profile scandals during 1973 made the authorities realise that there was a need for decisive action, and the Independent Commission Against Corruption (ICAC) was established in 1974.

As well as being independent of existing authorities, the ICAC has a wide-ranging remit. Despite being enforcement-led, it takes a three-pronged approach: deterrence, prevention and education. It consists of three corresponding departments: the Operation Department (taking 70% of resources) to investigate corruption and prosecute offenders; the Corruption Prevention Department to examine systems and procedures in the public sector and through this to identify corruption opportunities and make recommendations to plug loopholes; and the Community Relations Department to educate the public and to enlist their support in fighting corruption.

ICAC has had notable success, changing the practices and perceptions concerning corruption in less than a decade. Hong Kong is now rated as one of the cleanest places regarding corruption. It is still seen as an important institution and is allocated almost 0.4% of the economy's public budget.

Factors for success

As well as an enforcement-led approach within a wider remit (the three-pronged approach), key success factors relate to the following:

- Employment of professional staff, including specialist knowledge of a wide range of disciplines;
- Clear and public strategies in the three areas: for deterrence, commitments to fast responses, confidentiality and zero tolerance; for prevention, investigation of all public sector systems; for education, a wide range of activities from school onwards;
- An effective legal framework and law. ICAC cases are prosecuted by a selected group of public prosecutors to ensure quality and integrity. Conviction rates are very high, around 80%; and
- Equal emphasis on public and private sector corruption. Private sector corruption is seen as key, not only because of public safety (dangerous structures through corruption in construction, unstable markets through corruption in finance) but also because effective enforcement against private sector corruption is seen as a safeguard for foreign investment.

Obstacles and responses

ICAC has maintained its key strategy but has had to adapt its detailed approach to changing circumstances and the reactions of criminals. Current challenges include the internationalisation of corruption and, coupled with this, the rise in cyber-crime. These require more clear and structured relationships with anti-corruption agencies in other countries, including exchange of information.

Relevance for Kazakhstan

This example shows that it is possible to move relatively quickly from a position where a country has endemic corruption to one where it is seen as relatively clean. Corruption is seen as a serious problem in Kazakhstan by both local businesses and by foreign investors and priority needs to be given to decisive action in this sphere.

Source: http://www.icac.org.hk/en/home/index.html, Kwok Man-wai (2011).

A more detailed analysis is available through the World Bank Worldwide Governance Indicators (WGI), which measure governance strength by six aggregate indicators on a -2.5/+2.5 scale in which positive indicators represent better conditions[2]. Of these six aggregate indicators, three are most relevant to the effectiveness of the state and its public administration, i.e. "control of corruption", "government effectiveness", and "rule of law". The first of the three indicators (control of corruption) confirms that perceived corruption is high in Kazakhstan, especially if compared to OECD countries. Kazakhstan scores are closer to those of BRICS countries on this measure. Kazakhstan does better in the "rule of law" (for example, the quality of contract enforcement, the policy and the courts) and "government effectiveness" (for example, the quality of public services and the degree of its independence from political pressures), ranking second and first respectively within the Eurasian Customs Union (EACU). In the case of government effectiveness, Kazakhstan is also ahead of three of the BRICS countries (Brazil, India and the Russian Federation).

Figure 3.6. Governance in Kazakhstan compared to EACU, BRICS and OECD, 2015

Scale from -2.5 to 2.5

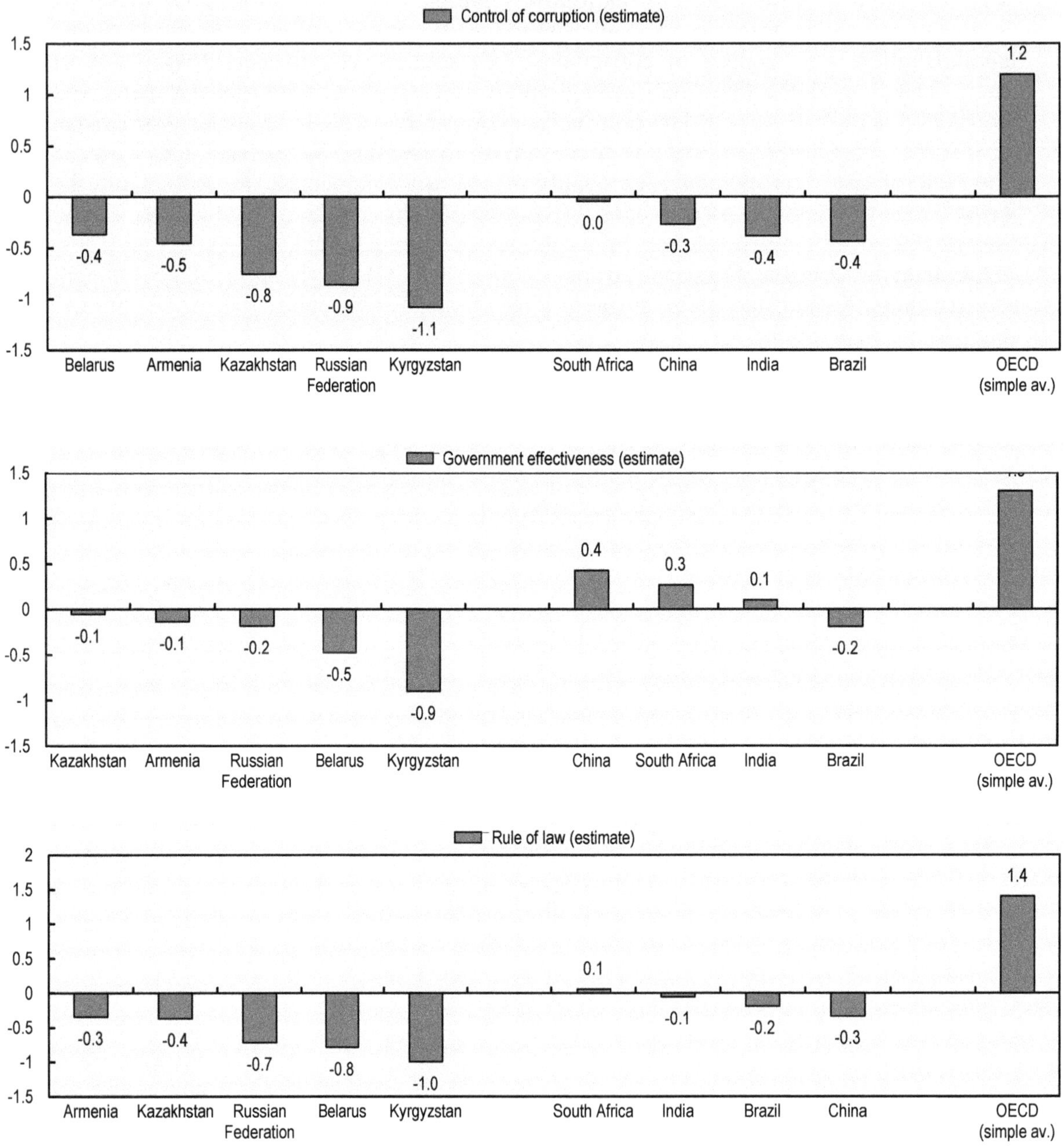

Note: Based on the World Bank's definitions: A) "Control of Corruption" captures perceptions of the extent to which public power is exercised for private gain, including both petty and grand forms of corruption, as well as "capture" of the state by elites and private interests. B) "Rule of Law" captures perceptions of the extent to which agents have confidence in and abide by the rules of society, and in particular the quality of contract enforcement, property rights, the police, and the courts, as well as the likelihood of crime and violence. C) "Government Effectiveness" captures perceptions of the quality of public services, the quality of the civil service and the degree of its independence from political pressures, the quality of policy formulation and implementation, and the credibility of the government's commitment to such policies.

Source: World Bank Worldwide Governance Indicators, http://info.worldbank.org/governance/wgi/index.aspx#home.

StatLink http://dx.doi.org/10.1787/888933828030

Increasing transparency of governance can assist in the fight against corruption. In this respect, the growth of e-government can be important, since it allows for consistency and neutrality of procedures as well as greater openness of data. Kazakhstan rates quite well in international comparisons, being ranked 33rd out of 193 countries in the United Nations E-Government Survey 2016. This base of relatively strong e-government can help in the wider fight against corruption.

The new business ombudsman is a positive development

An important policy development in Kazakhstan is the creation in 2016 of a Commissioner for Protection of the Rights of Entrepreneurs of Kazakhstan. This is a type of "business ombudsman" function in line with good practice in many countries (OECD, 2015). The Commissioner is housed in the National Chamber of Entrepreneurs (NCE). The office will ensure the judicial protection of the rights of businesses, elaborate the consultation procedures to be followed in conducting regulatory impact assessments (RIAs) on new legislative acts, design more precise rules for carrying out government inspections of business activities, and make provisions for the self-regulation of private business and professional associations.

The Commissioner is a senior figure who reports directly to the President, and is included in the NCE Presidium. In particular, the Commissioner can receive complaints from business owners about perceived unfair treatment in government relations, including those regarding instances of maladministration and unfair law enforcement such as repetitive audits or inspections, unreasonable fines and penalties, or threats and acts of retaliation by government officers. Businesses can deliver messages confidentially to an email hotline or postal address of the Commissioner about cases of corruption, fraud or other illegal actions. The Commissioner may make recommendations to state bodies on actions that should be taken to restore the rights of entrepreneurs, call for prosecuting authorities to intervene and signal systematic violations of entrepreneurs' rights to the President for top-level state intervention. This new office offers businesses an alternative to going to the court system for the resolution of conflicts between the state and business.

Public consultations on regulatory design also support the development of regulations that are conducive to SME and entrepreneurship activity in Kazakhstan, helping reduce the scope for corruption. Advisory councils based in each ministry commonly include NGOs representing small businesses, giving an opportunity to hear the concerns of SMEs and entrepreneurs about regulatory issues that they see as detrimental to business development. However, the requirement for NGOs to re-apply every three years for their legal status is likely to have a negative impact on their ability to provide overly independent and critical views, including through the advisory councils (OECD, 2014a).

Furthermore, there is scope to develop a stronger advocacy for the needs of SMEs and entrepreneurs within government with an independent office established for this purpose. An example of an effective approach is shown by the SBA Office of Advocacy in the USA (Box 3.2).

Box 3.2. SBA Office of Advocacy, USA

Description of the approach

The U.S. Small Business Administration's (SBA) Office of Advocacy was first established in 1976 with a mission to "serve as an independent voice for small business within the federal government".

The Office of Advocacy operates as an independent office serving as a voice for small business, a unique position within the federal government. The Regulatory Flexibility Act (RFA) is the primary legal tool that gives small businesses a voice in the rulemaking process. The Office of Advocacy oversees federal agencies' compliance with the RFA, which establishes in law the principle that government agencies must analyse the effects of their regulatory actions on small entities – small businesses, small non-profit organisations, and small governments – and consider alternatives that would minimise the economic burden on small entities while still achieving their regulatory objectives.

Specifically, the mission of the Office of Advocacy is to encourage policies that support the development and growth of American small businesses by:

- Early intervention in the regulatory development process of federal agencies concerning proposals that affect small businesses, and providing RFA compliance training to federal agency policymakers and regulatory development officials;
- Producing research to inform policymakers and other stakeholders on the impact of federal regulatory burdens on small businesses, to document the vital role of small businesses in the economy, and to explore and explain the wide variety of issues of concern to the small business community; and
- Fostering two-way communication between federal agencies and the small business community. Advocacy reaches out to its many stakeholders to solicit their views on issues of concern to small firms. In addition to seeking feedback through meetings and roundtables, Advocacy also communicates with small business owners through various platforms including Regulatory Alerts and comment letters.

The Office of Advocacy employs around 50 staff with 10 regional advocates located in SBA regional offices. In 2014, its budget was USD 8.75 million.

Factors for success

The key factors of success relate to:

- The clear and guaranteed independence of the Office. Although it is associated with the SBA, it remains independent of it, with a Chief Counsel for Advocacy directly appointed by the president and confirmed by the Senate; and
- A remit that includes not only outreach and advocacy, but also rights related to regulatory review, and appropriate resources for background economic research.

Obstacles and responses

During its operation, the independence of the Office has been seen as a key attribute and has been successively strengthened. The improvements have included separating its funding from that of the SBA as a whole, by using a separate budget line, and reforming the way in which it reports.

Relevance for Kazakhstan

The establishment of a business ombudsman in Kazakhstan is a welcome step in dealing with specific complaints about unfair government treatment of SMEs. In addition, advisory councils in ministries provide a voice to small business on specific issues. However, there is an additional need for a broad and independent advocacy office to signal the needs of SMEs and entrepreneurs to government ministries and bodies.

Source: OECD (2015).

Human capital

Kazakhstan suffers from a low-skilled workforce

A low-skilled labour force is frequently reported as a weakness in the business environment of Kazakhstan. This is likely to have adverse impacts on productivity and innovation in SMEs and on the growth prospects of many business start-ups. Approximately 12% of firms surveyed by the World Bank Enterprise Survey point to "inadequately educated workforce" as the main obstacle in the business environment of Kazakhstan, making this the third most cited major problem after corruption and unfair competition from the informal sector. Among SMEs, the problem is felt most strongly by medium-sized (20-99 employees) and large firms (100+ employees), rather than the smallest enterprises (1-19 employees). The latter are more concentrated in lower value-added sectors where worker skills are often less of a competitive factor. The World Economic Forum's (WEF) Executive Opinion Survey also highlights the problem. Some 6.8% of the survey's respondents reported "inadequately educated workforce" as one of the top five problems in 2014, a slight progress compared to 8.1% in 2009.

A factor likely to be contributing to the poor performance on skills levels is relatively low public spending on education (Figure 3.7).

Figure 3.7. Government expenditure on education, 2013 or latest available year

Percentage of GDP

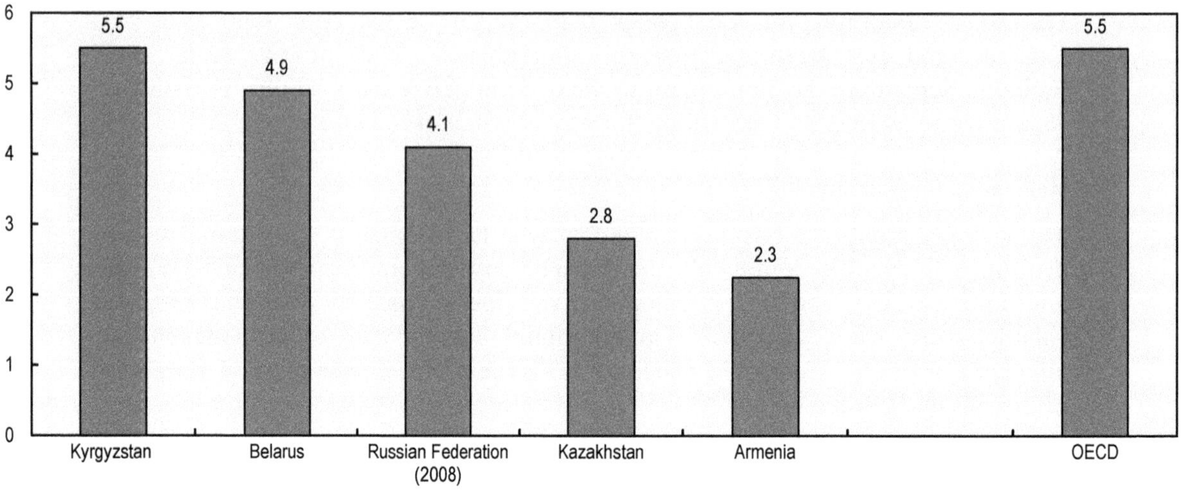

Source: World Bank World Development Indicators Databank.

StatLink http://dx.doi.org/10.1787/888933828049

Secondary education exhibits large inequalities and significant shares of low achievers

Kazakhstan's gross enrolment rate in secondary education is high, estimated at 109% of the relevant age group in 2015[3]. However, the performance of Kazakh 15-year old students in maths, science and literacy was relatively weak in 2012 compared with OECD countries and the Russian Federation (Figure 3.8). Student performance was better in maths and science than literacy. Nonetheless, Kazakhstan's share of low achievers in maths (i.e. proficiency level of 2 or less) was 45% in 2012, nearly twice as high as in the OECD area (24%) and the Russian Federation (24%). Furthermore, the education system is associated with strong inequalities in outcomes (e.g. urban versus rural, Russian language schools vs. Kazakh language schools), in which many students run the risk of being at a disadvantage in the labour market (Inoue and Gortazar, 2014).

Figure 3.8. Kazakhstan's performance in the OECD Programme for International Student Assessment (PISA)

Mean scores

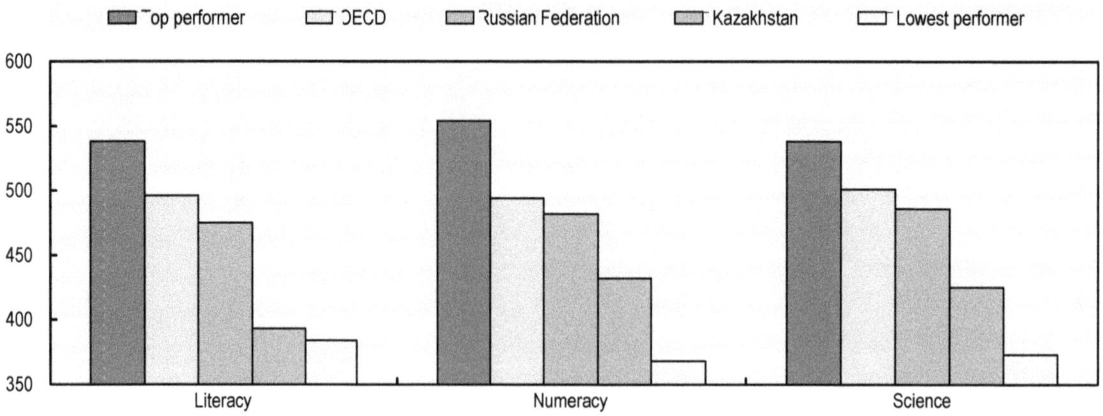

Source: OECD (2014b), *PISA 2012 Results: What Students Know and Can Do*, OECD Publishing, Paris.

StatLink http://dx.doi.org/10.1787/888933828068

Key priorities at secondary level are, therefore, strengthening literacy skills, for example through better training of teachers and provision of mother-tongue-based instruction (Inoue and Gortazar, 2014), and reducing inequalities in the education system to build a broad base of young people with adequate skills for the labour market.

There are gaps in skills in the vocational education system offer

The vocational education and training system in Kazakhstan has a number of weaknesses in providing appropriately skilled workers to businesses. This is manifested, for example, in a shortage of scientific, technical and engineering workers, lack of harmonisation of professional and educational standards, and poor knowledge of the English language among engineering and technical staff (see Burnston et al, 2011; Álvarez-Galván, 2014; OECD, 2014c).

However, the government has made considerable progress in reforming the vocational education and training system in the last decade, with support from the World Bank Technical and Vocational Education Modernisation Project, which ran from 2010 to 2013, and the World Bank Skills and Job Project, running from 2015 to 2020 (World Bank, 2015a). Significant reforms include the establishment of a national qualifications framework setting out occupational standards and training programmes for 147 occupations, creation of sector skills councils to support partnerships between colleges and employers in the development, delivery and assessment of the curriculum, and modernisation of training capacity (World Bank, 2015b).

Another highly important reform involves the recent introduction of a dual training system based on the German model. This involves a substantial component of training through employer work placements mixed with periods spent in vocational training colleges. In 2012, 500 vocational training institutions had workplace-based learning agreements with employers, involving over 170 000 students. In 2014, the NCE and the Ministry of Education and Science introduced measures to expand this coverage by launching a roadmap for the implementation of dual training covering 11 priority industries – mechanical engineering, metallurgy, agriculture, tourism services, transportation, telecommunications, maintenance, construction trades, clothing and fashion design, etc. The implementation support applied to some 170 colleges, 10 000 trainees and 400 enterprises in 2014-16, with students spending 70% to 80% of their time working in an enterprise environment. The system received a further boost in 2017 through an amendment to the Education Law that made the dual training system a mandatory requirement for vocational education and training colleges.

The relevance of public vocational education and training for SMEs could be increased by introducing more formal consultation of SMEs in the development of vocational training programmes to be used in colleges, including by ensuring specific SME representation on national and regional sector skills councils and conducting a survey to identify the skills needs of SMEs in priority sectors. The identified SME skill requirements can then be incorporated in the national qualifications framework and reflected in core- and competency-based curriculum programmes. Alongside demands for specific technical or sector-based skills, an assessment should be made of the need for qualified workers in transversal business competences such as small business management, marketing and sales, accounting and finance, and information technology.

Enrolment in higher education is decreasing

According to World Bank and National Committee on Statistics figures, Kazakhstan's gross enrolment rate in higher education dropped from a peak of 57% in 2005 to 46% in 2015, a figure very similar to that of 2002. Higher education enrolment trends in Kazakhstan have been symmetrical to wider economic growth trends, with a reduced appetite for higher education among young people during phases of economic expansion. The risk in the long term is a low-skill equilibrium, where the economy becomes locked in to non-knowledge-intensive industries and stages of production.

From a comparative perspective, Kazakhstan's gross enrolment rate in tertiary education lags behind the OECD average and the Russian Federation, although it is more in line with ECA countries and other EACU members such as the Kyrgyz Republic and Armenia (Figure 3.9). In seeking to boost higher education participation, particular attention is required to securing greater equity of access to affordable higher education, including support for students from rural areas, students with disabilities and students of lower socio-economic status (OECD, 2017a).

Figure 3.9. Gross enrolment ratio in tertiary education, 2015

Total number of people enrolled in tertiary education as a share of population in the relevant age

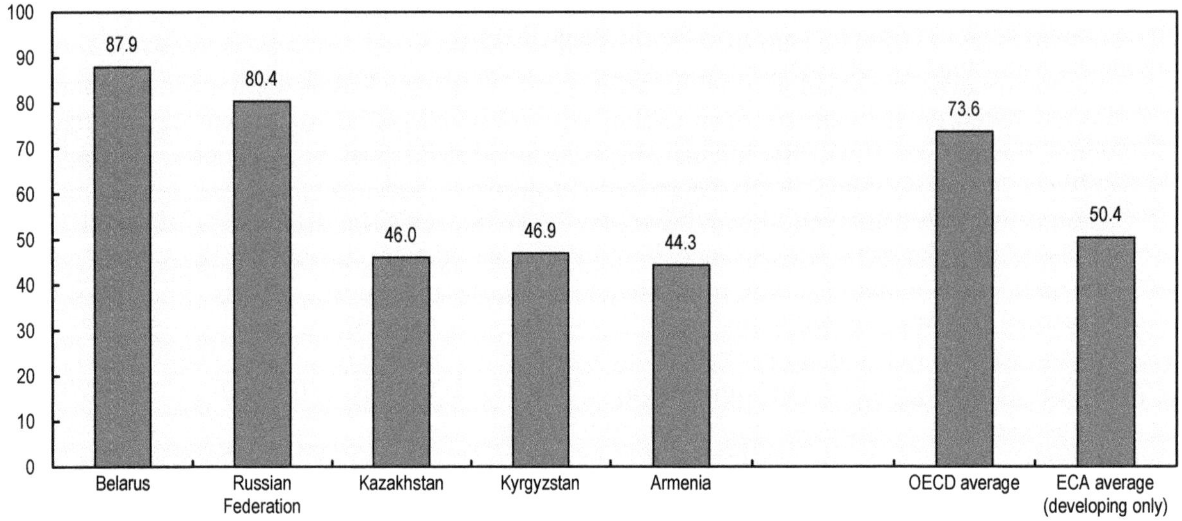

Note: World Bank's Europe and Central Asia (ECA) countries group (developing only) comprises: Albania, Armenia, Azerbaijan, Belarus, Bosnia and Herzegovina, Bulgaria, Georgia, Kazakhstan, Kosovo, Kyrgyz Republic, Macedonia FYR, Moldova, Montenegro, Romania, Serbia, Tajikistan, Turkey, Turkmenistan, Ukraine and Uzbekistan.
Source: World Bank World Development Indicators.

StatLink http://dx.doi.org/10.1787/888933828087

In 2010, Kazakhstan entered the European "Bologna Process" on comparability in the standards and quality of higher education qualifications in Europe and neighbouring regions. In this context, Kazakhstan has prioritised the international accreditation of national universities, the improvement of existing institutions and greater access to tertiary education to overcome regional inequalities (UNECE, 2012). The government has also set the objective of having at least two national universities ranked among the top-500 of the Shanghai University's Academic Ranking of World Universities. Achieving this objective would certainly bring prestige to the country. However, it should be matched by other objectives that ensure minimum quality standards across all tertiary education institutions. For example, it would be important to guarantee faculty training and faster renewal of university resources (Government of Kazakhstan, 2010), and strive for increased enrolment in tertiary education, e.g. through university degrees more in line with private sector needs and enhanced access to scholarships.

Entrepreneurship education is still not fully established in primary and secondary schools

Entrepreneurship education can play an important role in instilling an entrepreneurship culture and promoting business start-up in younger generations. The more exposure students have to entrepreneurship courses and activities while in the formal education system, the more likely they are to become entrepreneurs in the future and to develop higher quality and more innovative entrepreneurial activity (WEF, 2009; Levie and Autio, 2008; EC, 2012).

The vocational education system in Kazakhstan has included entrepreneurship education as a mandatory activity in economic disciplines since 2012, such as through the "Fundamentals of the Market Economy" and "Fundamentals of Tax Law" modules. Since 2016, the "Fundamentals of Business" course has been introduced into all vocational education disciplines, with the number of hours devoted to tax culture and entrepreneurship ranging from 16 to 20 hours. This has gone a long way to strengthening entrepreneurship education provision in vocational education and training institutions.

However, entrepreneurship education is less widespread at primary and secondary school levels. The "basics of business and financial management" course in the current curriculum offers basic business knowledge but does not go as far as offering entrepreneurship learning experiences focused on developing entrepreneurship mind-sets and competencies. One of the key actors is the worldwide Junior Achievement (JA) programme, which has been active in Kazakhstan for more than two decades[4]. One of its most successful initiatives is the Company Programme, in which students in teams gain the experience of starting and running their own (mini) enterprise for at least one school year, are mentored by business leaders for the duration of the programme, and compete in competitions for the best JA Company at the end of the experience (JA Worldwide, 2014). As early as 1996, the Minister of Education instructed regional departments of education to evolve from optional to obligatory inclusion of two hours of JA business and entrepreneurship classes per week, but take-up was very slow due to limited resources of JA, the resistance of state schools, and lack of corporate sponsorship to cover the costs of the programme and provide volunteer instructors and mentors. As a result, JA programmes do not reach all schools in Kazakhstan. In many other countries, JA programmes have been encouraged and supported by government stakeholders and authority granted by ministers of education for the introduction of JA programmes into classroom activity, including on a credit basis.

In Kazakhstan, integrating entrepreneurship in the education system is not identified as a priority in government strategies for business or education. However, it is increasingly viewed as an important component of SME and entrepreneurship internationally (Potter, 2008; WEF, 2009). A number of OECD countries, European Union Member States, and transition and developing economies are implementing national strategies on entrepreneurship education to integrate entrepreneurship into the curriculum at all levels of the education system from Kindergarten through to university. Australia, Finland,

Norway, the Netherlands and the United Kingdom are examples where the national government has made entrepreneurship education a priority of their SME development and entrepreneurship policy efforts. Furthermore, the "Small Business Act" for Europe encourages European Union member states to introduce entrepreneurship as a key competence in school curricula, particularly in general secondary education, and to ensure that it is correctly reflected in teacher training. The Kazakhstan Ministry of National Economy could support such a process by developing a policy for entrepreneurship education in co-operation with the Ministry of Education and Science, including a strategy, action plan and resourcing for implementation.

More could be done to promote entrepreneurship education in universities

Further efforts are also needed to offer entrepreneurship education at higher education institutions (HEIs), where the entrepreneurial activity rates of student leavers tend to be higher and where their business start-ups tend to be more innovative and have higher growth aspirations (Singer al., 2015; Gries and Naudé, 2008). Basic courses are offered across the higher education system on "Fundamentals of Law" and "Fundamentals of Economic Theory", which have some relevance to entrepreneurship. However, at present, only a few of the more than 100 universities in Kazakhstan have adopted a strong focus on entrepreneurship education, including Nazarbayev University, Al-Farabi Kazakh National University, South Kazakhstan State University, and the International Academy of Business (Almaty School of Management).

To reinforce the entrepreneurship education offer, various HEIs in Kazakhstan are working on developing content for new elective courses on entrepreneurship, including courses on the "risks of entrepreneurship" and "taxation of business entities" within undergraduate degrees in economics and finance. Student incubators have also been established at Miras University and Kazakh National University.

In general, HEIs in Kazakhstan should be encouraged and supported to experiment and innovate in the provision of entrepreneurship teaching and start-up support. Rolling out of relevant initiatives across the higher education system would be supported by the creation of an inventory of the entrepreneurship teaching and start-up support activities of each HEI. In addition, the government could create a shared learning platform for university teachers, managers and others involved in supporting entrepreneurship in higher education, which could provide access to a national observatory of pedagogical practices in entrepreneurship (including international examples), a repository of useable teaching materials and methods, and training for entrepreneurship teachers in universities.

Information and experience exchange in entrepreneurship education can also be important. It can be supported in Kazakhstan by encouraging the formation of a national professional association, such as on the lines of the Russian Association for Entrepreneurship Education (Box 3.3). HEIs could also be supported to participate in an international exchange of good practices, such as through the use of the OECD/European Commission HEInnovate assessment and guidance tool (see: http://www.heinnovate.eu/).

Box 3.3. Russian Association for Entrepreneurship Education (RUAEE)

The Russian Association for Entrepreneurship Education (RUAEE) was founded in 2008. It results from a decision of the Russia Centre for Entrepreneurship, representatives of leading Russian universities and business schools, and a number of entrepreneurs to address an insufficient focus on entrepreneurial skills in the Russian education system. Members of the association are entrepreneurship educators, researchers, and mentors from universities, vocational education colleges, and secondary schools in Russia and Commonwealth of Independent States (CIS) countries.

The association develops and disseminates new quality standards in entrepreneurship education, best practice teaching methodologies, guidance in developing educational programmes, educational materials on entrepreneurship, and offers opportunities for teacher qualification and professional development in the field of entrepreneurship and upgrading opportunities for entrepreneurship faculty and mentors. One of its educational programmes is the "Dynamic Entrepreneurship Classroom" course, which helps teachers to develop entrepreneurship programmes by providing knowledge of teaching methods focused on the practice and development of business skills. It also expands opportunities for members to influence educational policy.

The Kazakhstan government could encourage formation of a similar national network to support the exchange of experience in introducing and integrating entrepreneurship at various levels of the educational system.

Source: http://www.ruaee.ru/.

The innovation system

The innovation system in Kazakhstan is at an early stage of development

The quality of national innovation systems has an important impact on the stimulation of innovative start-ups and high-growth SMEs and on innovation in SMEs more generally. Kazakhstan's innovation system is still at an early development stage. A relevant measure is provided by the World Bank's Knowledge Economy Index (KEI) for 2012, which compares 154 countries on four sub-indexes: the education index (i.e. average years of schooling and enrolment in secondary and tertiary education), the innovation index (royalty payments, patent count, and journal articles), the ICT index (telephones, computer, and internet users), and the broader institution-regime index (tariff and non-tariff barriers, regulatory quality, and rule of law). Kazakhstan ranked in the 72nd position on the overall index, an improvement of five positions since 2000, but still worse than most other EACU partners. Kazakhstan's performance was relatively weak on the innovation sub-index, while it was relatively better positioned on the institution-regime sub-index (UNECE, 2012).

R&D activity is a crucial element in innovation systems, particularly for high-technology industries. However, although the number of R&D researchers increased rapidly from 2011 to 2014 (OECD, 2017b), both the share of R&D researchers in the population and the share of R&D expenditures in GDP are relatively low in Kazakhstan compared with the OECD and ECA averages (Figure 3.10). Furthermore, R&D expenditure is very concentrated geographically, almost half of R&D expenditures occurring in the city of

Almaty, and extramural (to the country) R&D expenditure is substantial, accounting for 38% of the total in 2010 (UNECE, 2012). The relatively weak domestic R&D performance in Kazakhstan is partly the result of the economy's industry composition, in which non-R&D-intensive resource-based activities (mainly oil and gas) play a prime role.

Figure 3.10. R&D intensity in selected economies and in Kazakhstan, 2005-15

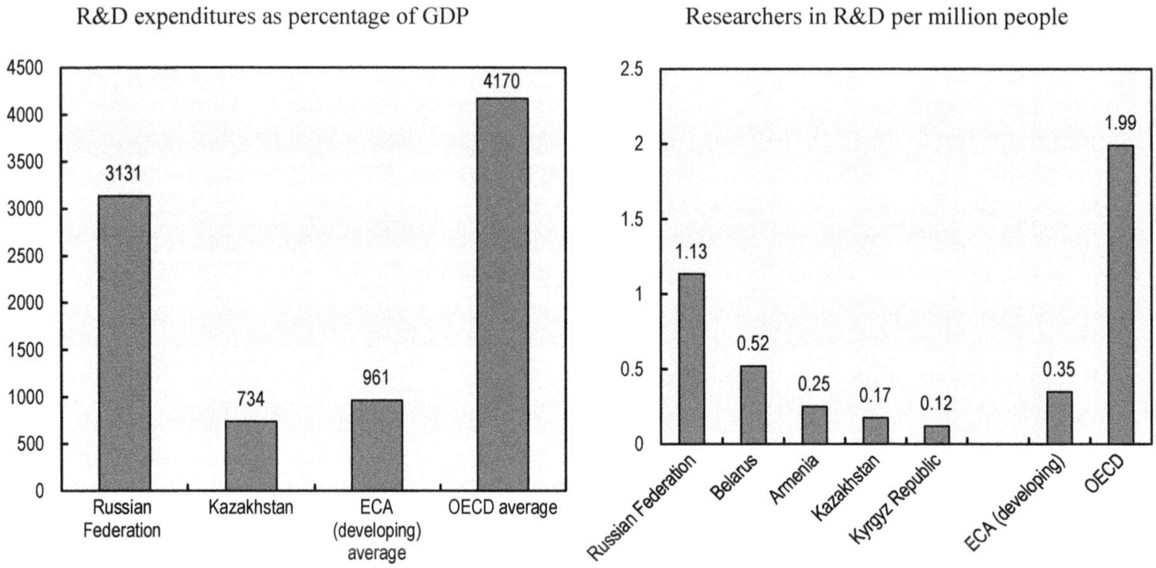

Note: World Bank's Europe and Central Asia (ECA) countries group (developing only) comprises: Albania, Armenia, Azerbaijan, Belarus, Bosnia and Herzegovina, Bulgaria, Georgia, Kazakhstan, Kosovo, Kyrgyz Republic, Macedonia FYR, Moldova, Montenegro, Romania, Serbia, Tajikistan, Turkey, Turkmenistan, Ukraine and Uzbekistan.
Source: World Bank World Development Indicators.

StatLink http://dx.doi.org/10.1787/888933828106

Government expenditure on R&D makes up a larger share of the total than in other EACU members (e.g. the Russian Federation and Belarus). This primarily involves universities and research institutes under the responsibility of the Ministry of Education and Science.

Kazakhstan's R&D is strongly weighted to applied research. This accounts for 56% of total R&D expenditures, while 30% are accounted for by development activities and 14% by basic research. The high proportion of applied research is linked to the strong role of state-owned enterprises (SOEs) as contractors of R&D projects, especially in sectors such as oil, metallurgy and electrical equipment, a situation which is openly encouraged by the government's current policy agenda (UNECE, 2012). This applied research could be a significant catalyst for technology commercialisation in start-ups and SMEs on condition that good policies are in place to promote commercialisation.

In this respect, Kazakhstan could benefit from a strategic approach to government R&D expenditure that seeks to develop commercialisation opportunities particularly among technology-intensive start-ups and SMEs. The Israel Innovation Authority illustrates how such an approach can be implemented successfully (Box 3.4).

Box 3.4. R&D Support by the Israel Innovation Authority

Description of the approach

The Israel Innovation Authority (formerly the Office of the Chief Scientist), based in the Ministry of Economy, leads government innovation policy in Israel. It is empowered under the 1984 Law for the Encouragement of Industrial Research & Development (the "R&D Law").

One of the Authority's major instruments is the R&D Competition Fund. This is a Fund of approximately NIS 1 billion (USD 300 million), which can back anything related to R&D, from pre-seed-stage conceptual projects to industrial R&D and research commercialisation. Supported projects are funded annually, with funding confirmed if the projects meet agreed milestones. Approximately 80% of the R&D Competition Fund goes to SMEs for industrial projects, mainly in the fields of ICT and biotechnologies.

The Authority is also responsible for: twenty-seven technology incubators, which provide finance and advice to early-stage technology entrepreneurs; the TNUFA programme, which helps entrepreneurs to prepare patent applications and to assess the technological and financial viability of their pre-seed stage projects (budget: USD 40 million); the MAGNET programme, which encourages collaborative research in the form of research consortia where industry and university staff members work together on precompetitive research projects (budget: USD 57 million); and NOFAR, which focuses on finding industry applications from R&D in biotechnology and nanotechnology.

Factors for success

The Israel Innovation Authority and the R&D Law represent a long-term commitment to innovation that has paid off over many years. The concentration of all funding in one agency helps to co-ordinate R&D policy while the emphasis on involving SMEs and start-ups in applied R&D projects has helped Israel to be a leading country in the commercialisation of research.

Obstacles and responses

This R&D-based approach to innovation support has some disadvantages in that it has tended to favour high-technology industry development rather than broader-based innovation across the economy. Nonetheless, dedicated support to non-technological innovation is provided by the Traditional Industries Programme of the Israel Innovation Authority and by the general SME support offered through the Small and Medium Business Agency.

Relevance for Kazakhstan

This example shows a way of exploiting government R&D support for SME and entrepreneurship development.

Source: OECD (2016b), http://economy.gov.il/English/RnD/Pages/RnD.aspx.

Access to finance

Domestic credit collapsed following the global financial crisis but has recovered

Figure 3.11 illustrates the severe impact the 2008 global financial crisis had on the Kazakhstan banking system, which led to a credit crunch that has particularly affected SMEs. Domestic credit to the private sector in relation to GDP in Kazakhstan, a proxy for the size of the domestic credit market, constantly outgrew the average for the Europe and Central Asia (ECA) developing countries until 2008, only to collapse to well below the ECA developing countries average and all other EUCA members except Belarus in the aftermath of the crisis.

Figure 3.11. Domestic credit to the private sector, 2001-2014

Percentage of GDP

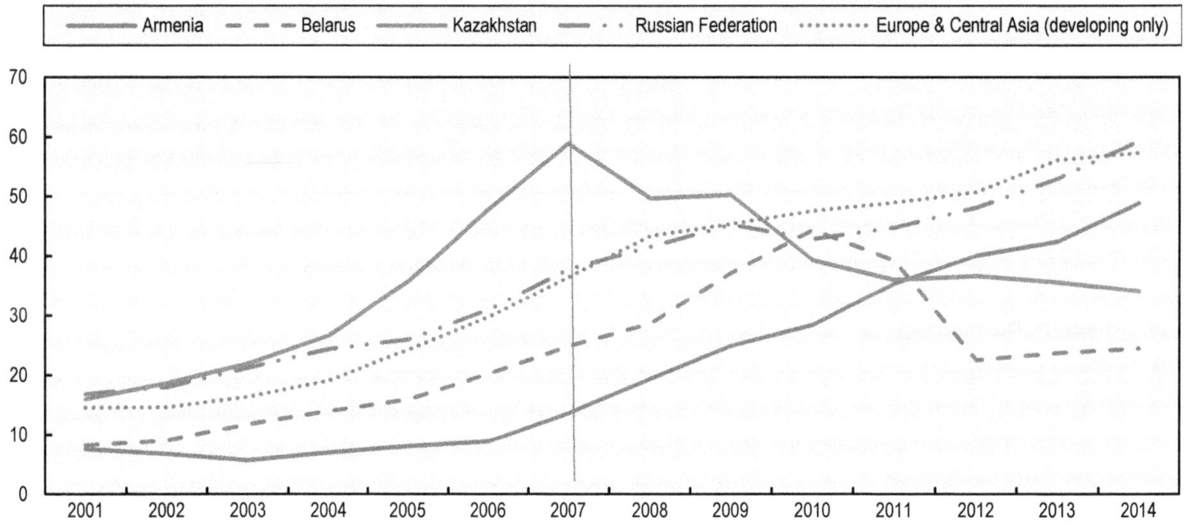

Note: World Bank's Europe and Central Asia (ECA) countries group (developing only) comprises: Albania, Armenia, Azerbaijan, Belarus, Bosnia and Herzegovina, Bulgaria, Georgia, Kazakhstan, Kosovo, Kyrgyz Republic, Macedonia FYR, Moldova, Montenegro, Romania, Serbia, Tajikistan, Turkey, Turkmenistan, Ukraine and Uzbekistan.
Source: World Bank Indicators.

StatLink http://dx.doi.org/10.1787/888933828125

Between 2005 and 2007, Kazakhstan-owned banks borrowed massively from foreign sources, primarily European banks, and loaned a substantial part of these funds to non-tradable sectors, primarily construction. With the global financial crisis in 2008, Kazakhstan banks found themselves deprived of access to foreign capital and were forced to deleverage aggressively, resulting in a significant drop in the number of new loans. This drop is perhaps best reflected by trends in the SME sector. Between 2007 and 2010 annual volumes of new SME lending contracted by 63.1%. These declines were probably tied to the devaluation of the tenge, which reduced banks' net worth and led to massive intervention by the Kazakhstan Government, which acquired majority and minority stakes in major banks. In 2011, however, following intervention, lending volumes began recovering. In 2016, new lending volumes had completely recovered, reaching levels 2.5 times those of 2011 and 6% higher than those of 2007.

An important contribution to the recovery was made by the government's KZT 500 billion effort to rekindle the economy, with half of this funding going to banks at a subsidised rate to incentivise lending to SMEs at below market-level interest rates (OECD, 2018). The government also worked actively with International Financial Institutions to improve conditions for SME lending. For example, IFC provided nearly USD 900 million in investments to Kazakhstan's financial sector between 2010 and 2014, via equity participation, subordinated loans, senior debt, and trade finance products[5].

The issue of non-performing loans needs to be addressed

Although lending has returned to normal levels following the financial crisis, the volume of non-performing loans (NPLs) remains relatively high in Kazakhstan. To reduce the level of NPLs, the government of Kazakhstan created a Problem Loan Fund (PLF) (i.e. a state asset management company) in 2012 to which NPLs could be sold. Banks were allowed to place NPLs in organisations for managing stressful and uncollectible assets, acting as sorts of decentralised asset management companies. In 2017, the only stakeholder of the PLF became the Ministry of Finance. Previously, the National Bank of Kazakhstan was the only stakeholder of the Fund.

The National Bank of Kazakhstan also gradually reduced its maximum appropriate NPL levels for banks to 15% in 2015 and 10% in 2016. The standards required banks to take actions to address NPLs, including the write-off/forgiveness of bad loans, restructuring of loan portfolios, recovery in judicial and extrajudicial procedures, broader acceptance of collateral, and transfer of loans to subsidiaries of banks (that acquired problem assets) or collection agencies. Finally, several, reforms were made to the tax code and regulatory acts of the National Bank to complement these two interventions.

The interventions were successful in reducing the share of loans with arrears of more than 90 days in banks' portfolios. In 2016, non-performing business loans dropped from 8.0% to 6.7% and non-performing SME loans fell from 12.7% to 8.8% (OECD, 2018). Despite the progress, however, these NPL levels remain relatively high by international standards, with top performing countries in this category often having NPL volumes of less than 5%. It is likely that further action will be needed to reduce NPLs and stabilize NPL levels to a desirable threshold.

SMEs confirm the problems in accessing bank loans

Bank loans constitute the primary source of external finance for SMEs in Kazakhstan. However, they are difficult for SMEs to access. Of 1.5 million registered SMEs only 60 000 had bank loans, and SME loans represented no more than 20% of the loan portfolio in mid-2016 according to the National Bank of Kazakhstan (NBK).

The importance of the constraints in SME lending is confirmed by the 2013 World Bank Enterprise Survey results. Nearly one in ten entrepreneurs surveyed in Kazakhstan considered access to finance as a major obstacle. While this is lower than other EUCA countries, it nevertheless represents an important obstacle. Moreover, some of the detailed findings on specific financing conditions suggest that the situation is worse in certain respects in Kazakhstan than in other EUCA members (Table 3.2).

Table 3.2. Access to finance conditions in Kazakhstan and other EUCA members, 2013

	Per cent of firms identifying access to finance as a major constraint	Percent of firms with a checking or savings account	Percent of firms with a bank loan/line of credit	Percent of firms whose recent loan application was rejected	Percent of firms with an annual financial statement reviewed by external auditors	Value of collateral needed for a loan (% of the loan amount)	Percent of firms using banks to finance working capital	Percent of firms using banks to finance investments	Proportion of working capital financed by banks	Proportion of investment financed internally
Armenia	26	91	46	3	20	264	39	17	16	73
Belarus	16	92	30	5	43	154	32	27	12	78
Kazakhstan	9	92	19	31	13	196	13	16	6	83
Kyrgyzstan	26	95	29	4	31	188	23	18	9	80
Russian Federation (2012)	28	100	22	26	23	154	21	11	8	84

Source: World Bank Enterprise Survey.

High interest rates are one of the constraints to SME lending, reflecting risk averse attitudes of banks. The interest rates on commercial loans were about 15% as of September 2015. Another issue is very stringent collateral requirements. Close to 9 out of 10 loans require collateral of some kind and, on average, borrowers have to pledge collateral worth twice as much as the loan value to have their credit application approved. These numbers are relatively high compared with other mid-income countries (Figure 3.12). Low levels of financial literacy as well as the problems associated with transparency, informality and lack of documented credit history of SMEs are the main reasons for high collateral requirements.

Figure 3.12. Collateral requirements

In per cent, 2013 or most recent

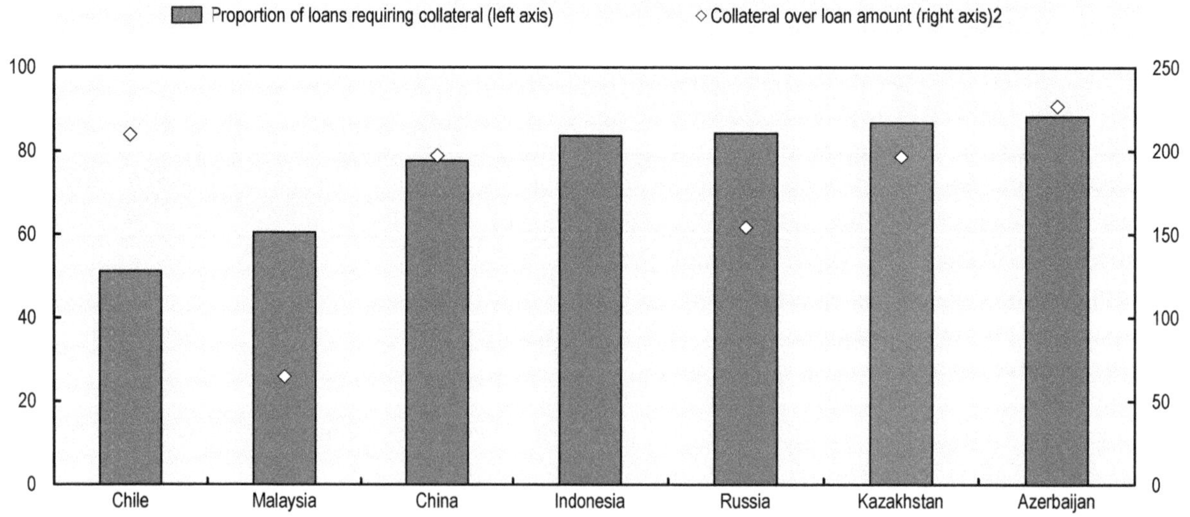

Note: No comparable data on collateral values available for Indonesia. Latest data for Chile (2012), China (2012), Indonesia (2009) and Malaysia (2007).

Source: Authors' calculations based on World Bank (2015a), Enterprise Surveys (database), http://www.enterprisesurveys.org.

StatLink http://dx.doi.org/10.1787/888933827764

The Kazakhstan banking industry is highly concentrated and there is limited banking presence for SMEs, particularly in rural areas. The 35 second-tier banks had only 353 branches in 2015, and the largest five banks (Bank Centercredit, Halyk Bank, Kazkom Bank, Sberbank, and Tsesnabank) held 61% of the total bank loan portfolio (NBK, 2016). Measures to increase banking competition could encourage banks to cover better the potential market.

Alternative financing mechanisms for SMEs are assuming more prominence in the financing market in Kazakhstan, including microfinance, leasing and factoring, and can also help to address the problem of limited SME lending. In 2016, total leasing and hire purchases stood at KZT 167.0 billion, 2.8 times their value in 2010 and micro-finance organisations provided KZT 74 396 million in total microcredit for business purposes. The factoring market is also developing dynamically having attracted the interest of commercial banks after having originated primarily with independent factoring companies.

Foreign direct investment

Kazakhstan has relatively few restrictions on inward foreign direct investment (FDI), as shown in Figure 3.13. As a proportion of GDP, Kazakhstan attracts large volumes of inward FDI. Among Central Asian countries, Kazakhstan received 85% of all investment in 2012; among the Commonwealth of Independent states the share was 42% (International Trade Center, 2015). The substantial scale of inward FDI offers a potential lever for supporting SME development via FDI-SME linkage creation.

Figure 3.13. FDI restrictiveness index, 2013

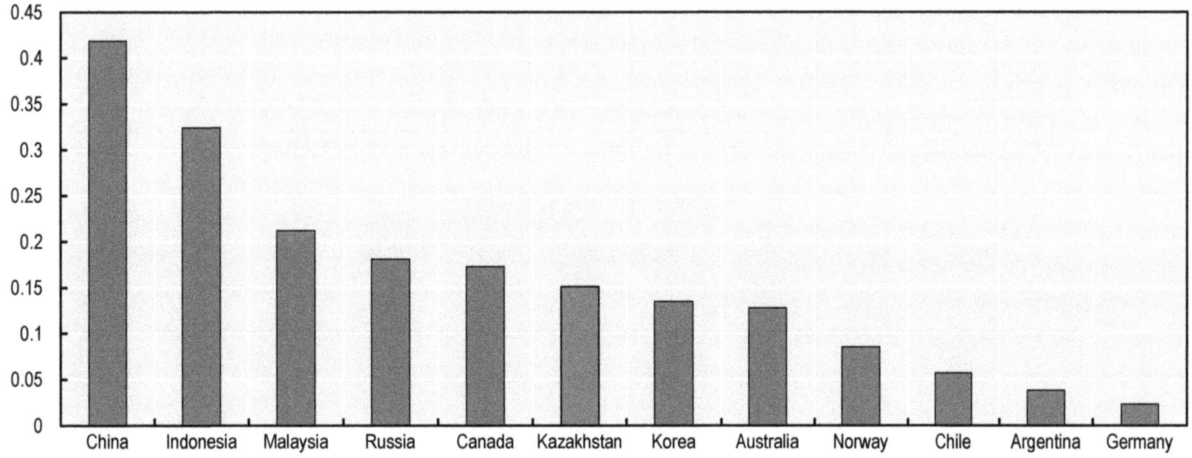

Source: OECD (2016b).

StatLink http://dx.doi.org/10.1787/888933828144

Nevertheless, inward FDI flows have recently been failing to keep up with economic growth in Kazakhstan (Figure 3.14) as important oil-related projects reach completion and the risk appetite of foreign investors remains subdued in the aftermath of the financial crisis. Although in nominal terms net investment was close to its 2007 level in 2013, net inflows relative to the size of the economy were only about half their pre-crisis level.

Furthermore, inward FDI tends to be concentrated in resource extraction and related activities (Figure 3.15). The share of inflows of FDI into activities related to natural resources stood at around 50-60% in Kazakhstan over 2010-14, while 55% of the total FDI stock is in exploration and prospecting activities and another 15% in mining. The share of foreign investment in manufacturing remained at around a modest 15% in 2014. Although FDI-SME linkages can be developed around resource-seeking FDI, extractive industries typically have very short and specialist supply chains and the opportunities for driving SME development through FDI-SME linkages are often greater from manufacturing FDI. This suggests a need both to continue to attract inward FDI and to diversify its sectors.

Figure 3.14. Inward FDI flows and stocks

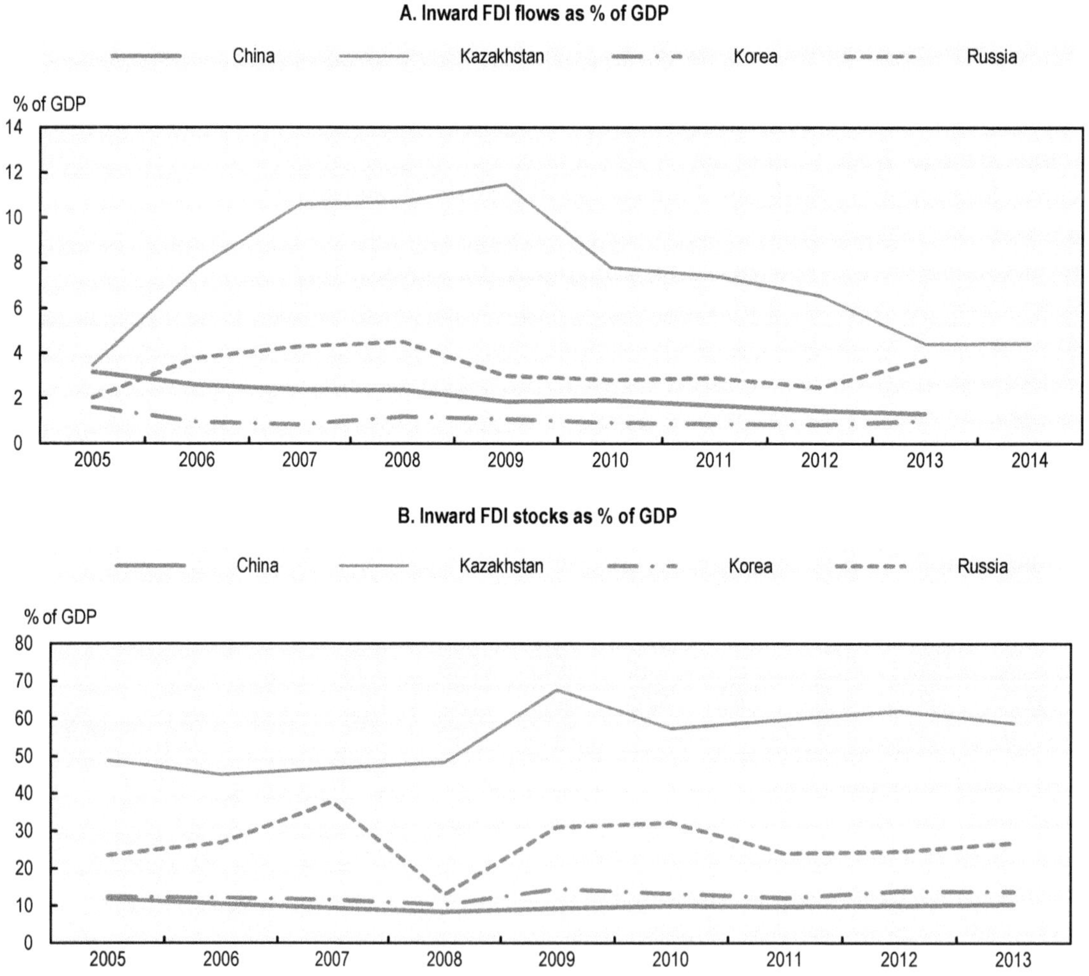

Source: OECD (2016a).

StatLink http://dx.doi.org/10.1787/888933828163

Figure 3.15. Share of FDI inflows by sector

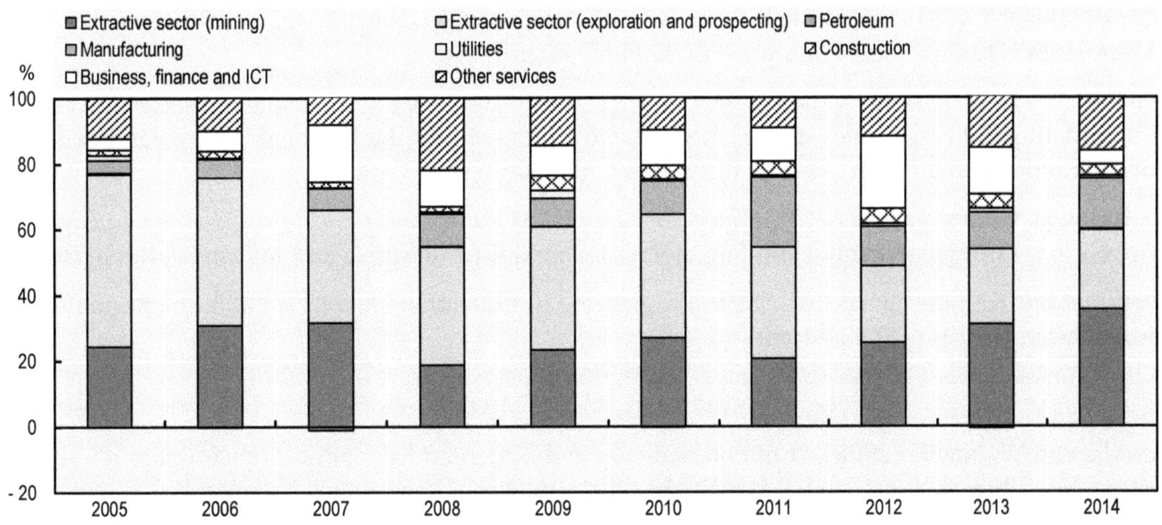

Source: OECD (2016a).

StatLink http://dx.doi.org/10.1787/888933828182

Notes

1. Information retrieved from: http://www.doingbusiness.org/reforms/overview/topic/resolving-insolvency#kazakhstan.
2. These are Voice and Accountability; Political Stability and Absence of Violence; Government Effectiveness; Regulatory Quality; Rule of Law; Control of Corruption. These indicators combine the views of a large number of enterprise, citizen and expert survey respondents and are based on over 30 individual data sources produced by a variety of survey institutes, think tanks, non-governmental organizations, international organizations, and private sector firms.
3. The gross enrolment rate in secondary education is given by the number of students, irrespective of age, enrolled in the first step of the main secondary and general secondary education (ISCED 2,3) and in the technical and professional education (ISCED 3) to the total number of population of secondary school age (11-17 years). Information retrieved from the Kazakh National Committee on Statistics, http://www.stat.gov.kz.
4. http://www.junior.kz/about/.
5. http://ifcext.ifc.org/IFCExt/pressroom/IFCPressRoom.nsf/0/1D8879069160E8F985257D7B00273751?OpenDocument.

References

Álvarez-Galván, J. (2014), A Skills Beyond School Review of Kazakhstan, OECD Reviews of Vocational Education and Training, OECD Publishing, Paris.

Burnston, J., T. Chadotsang, X. Dong, M. Ghosh, K. Grinstein, I. Vasileiou, and T. Wirkes (2011), "Stimulating industrial innovation in Kazakhstan", prepared for the National Innovation Fund, School of International and Public Affairs, Columbia University, New York, NY.

EC (European Commission) (2012), *Effects and Impact of Entrepreneurship Programmes in Higher Education*, Entrepreneurship Unit, Directorate-General for Enterprise and Industry, March, Brussels.

Government of Kazakhstan (2010), "State Programme of Education Development in the Republic of Kazakhstan for 2011-2020, Astana. http://planipolis.iiep.unesco.org/upload/Kazakhstan/Kazakhstan_State_Program-of-Education-Development-in-the-Republic-of-Kazakhstan_2011-2020.pdf.

Gries, T., and W. Naudé (2008), "Entrepreneurship and Structural Economic Transformation", Research Paper No. 2008/62, June, UNI-WIDER, World Institute for Development Economics Research, United Nations University, Helsinki.

Inoue, K. and L. Gortazar (2014), *Strengthening Kazakhstan's Education Systems: An Analysis of PISA 2009 and 2012*, World Bank Group, Washington DC.

International Trade Center (2015), FDI database, www.intracen.org/itc/market-info-tools/statistics-inwardcountry-industry/.

JA Worldwide (2014), Impact: Making a Measurable Difference - Statistics and Stories from the Field, Junior Achievement Worldwide, Boston.

Kwok Man-wai, Tony (2011), Successful anti-corruption strategy, effective investigation and the role of government agencies in combating corruption. 15th UNAFEI UNCAC training programme visiting experts' papers: resource material series 89.

Levie, J. and E. Autio (2008), "A Theoretical Grounding and Test of the GEM Model", *Small Business Economics*, 31(3), 235–263.

OECD (2018) *Financing SMEs and Entrepreneurs 2018: An OECD Scoreboard*. OECD Publishing Paris. https://doi.org/10.1787/fin_sme_ent-2018-en.

OECD (2017a) *Higher Education in Kazakhstan 2017, Reviews of National Policies for Education*, OECD Publishing, Paris. http://dx.doi.org/10.1787/9789264268531-en.

OECD (2017b), *OECD Reviews of Innovation Policy: Kazakhstan 2017*, OECD Publishing, Paris, http://dx.doi.org/10.1787/9789264270008-en.

OECD (2016a), *Multi-dimensional Review of Kazakhstan: Volume 1. Initial Assessment, OECD Development Pathways*, OECD Publishing, Paris. http://dx.doi.org/10.1787/9789264246768-en.

OECD (2016b), *Review of SME and Entrepreneurship Issues and Policies in Israel*, OECD Publishing, Paris. http://dx.doi.org/10.1787/9789264262324-en.

OECD (2015), SME Ombudsman: International Profiles and a Policy Proposal for Mexico, unpublished report.

OECD (2014a), *Regulatory Policy in Kazakhstan*, OECD Publishing, Paris. http://dx.doi.org/10.1787/9789264214255-en.

OECD (2014b), *PISA 2012 Results: What Students Know and Can Do, Student Performance in Mathematics, Reading and Science (Volume I, Revised Edition, February 2014)*, OECD Publishing, Paris. http://dx.doi.org/10.1787/9789264208780-en.

OECD (2014c), Reviews of National Policies for Education: Secondary Education in Kazakhstan, OECD Publishing, Paris. http://dx.doi.org/10.1787/9789264205208-en.

Potter, J. (Ed) (2008) Entrepreneurship and Higher Education, OECD Publishing, Paris.

Singer, S., Herrington M., Menipaz E. (2018), Global Entrepreneurship Monitor, Global Report 2017/18. Babson College, Universidad del Desarrollo, Universiti Tun Abdul Razak, Korea Entrepreneurship Foundation.

UNECE (2012), *Innovation Performance Review: Kazakhstan*, Geneva

WEF (2009), *Educating the Next Wave of Entrepreneurs: Unlocking entrepreneurial capabilities to meet the global challenges of the 21st Century*, Geneva: World Economic Forum.

WEF (2017) *The Global Competitiveness Report 2017-18*, World Economic Forum, Geneva.

World Bank (2018) *Doing Business 2018: Reforming to Create Jobs*, World Bank, Washington DC.

World Bank (2018). Kazakhstan Open Data. https://data.worldbank.org/country/kazakhstan. World Bank,Washington D.C.

World Bank (2015a), "Kazakhstan - Skills and Jobs Project", World Bank Group: Washington, DC. Online at: http://documents.worldbank.org/curated/en/2015/03/24162685/kazakhstan-skills-jobs-project/.

World Bank (2015b), "Kazakhstan - Technical & Vocational Education Modernization (TVEM): P102177 — Implementation Status Results Report: Sequence 10", World Bank Group, Washington, DC, http://documents.worldbank.org/curated/en/2015/01/23921525/kazakhstan-technical-vocational-education-modernization-tvem-p102177-implementation-status-results-report-sequence-10/.

World Bank (2013), *Kazakhstan Country Profile 2013: Enterprise Surveys*, Washington DC, http://www.enterprisesurveys.org/~/media/GIAWB/EnterpriseSurveys/Documents/Profiles/English/Kazakhstan-2013.pdf.

Chapter 4. Strategic Framework and Delivery System for SME and Entrepreneurship Policy in Kazakhstan

This chapter examines arrangements for the formulation, co-ordination and delivery of SME and entrepreneurship policy in Kazakhstan. It reviews the legal basis of policy in the Entrepreneurial Code, assesses the vision and objectives set out for SME and entrepreneurship policy, and examines the arrangements for leadership and co-ordination of the policy within government. The distribution of SME and entrepreneurship policy expenditures in the Business Road Map 2020 is also examined. The chapter then turns to an assessment of the main agencies and structures for the delivery of business support services to SMEs and entrepreneurs including the National Chamber of Entrepreneurs and the Damu Entrepreneurship Development Fund. Finally, arrangements for monitoring and evaluation of SME and entrepreneurship policies and programmes are reviewed.

Key messages and policy recommendations

Following the Soviet period, Kazakhstan's government has invested consistently in encouraging the emergence of SMEs and entrepreneurship. These efforts were given a major boost with the 2006 Law on Private Entrepreneurship, which introduced a range of new policy measures and programmes, backed up with support from international organisations. The government has taken this further in the current decade, and set out new and ambitious targets to increase the role of SMEs and entrepreneurship in the economy, including a doubling of the share of SMEs in GDP between 2011 and 2030.

The five-year Business Road Map 2020 (BRM 2020) programme is the government's main tool for meeting its SME and entrepreneurship policy objectives. It includes investments in a broad set of business support measures including financing, investment, consultancy and innovation. The support is targeted to 14 economic priority sectors in manufacturing and certain services. Alongside BRM 2020, various other programmes include some SME and entrepreneurship support actions, for example Employment Road Map 2020 and Agribusiness 2020. These plans set out a clear strategic vision for policy, although there are some gaps in detailed objectives and targets for individual programme interventions.

Effective mechanisms exist for leading and co-ordinating SME and entrepreneurship policies across government. The focal government department is the Entrepreneurship Development Department (EDD) in the Ministry of National Economy (MNE), which is mandated to co-ordinate with other ministries and agencies in this field. The EDD co-ordinates policy to improve the business environment, including on regulatory impact assessment and state control over private enterprises and advocates for taking account of the impacts on SMEs and entrepreneurs in the policies of other ministries. It is also active in leading SME and entrepreneurship programme development. It is supported by an inter-ministerial committee and clear mechanisms for consultation with business representative organisations.

The major programme for business support to SMEs and entrepreneurs is BRM 2020. Its expenditure mix across different types of intervention is currently strongly focused on financial support, including interest rate subsidies, capital equipment grants, support for business loans and microfinance. Greater attention to non-financial supports is warranted, such as consultancy and mentoring, in order to help improve management and productivity in existing SMEs. BRM 2020 also includes little dedicated support for high-growth potential enterprises or for increasing the numbers of medium-sized enterprises and their productivity and these should be a priority for further development. A full assessment of BRM 2020 expenditures broken down by type of programme intervention and the types of SME and entrepreneur principally targeted by each intervention would help to assess how far the current mix of policy expenditures matches with policy objectives and needs.

Arrangements for delivering business support to SMEs and entrepreneurs are relatively streamlined in Kazakhstan. The Damu Entrepreneurship Development Fund delivers financial support. In parallel, the National Chamber of Entrepreneurs (NCE) provides non-financial support. Other key agencies with responsibilities in the area of business support are the National Agency for Technological Development and the Autonomous Cluster Fund. The NCE was set up in 2013 and took over the main responsibility for delivering business development services from the Damu Entrepreneurship Development Fund in 2015. It has introduced a network of Entrepreneurship Support Centres (ESCs), which functions as a single-window service to SMEs and entrepreneurs. However, the network is relatively new and the ESC advisors and consultants have received only a limited length of training in delivering services. Ongoing professional development support is needed to help ensure high quality. Although the Damu Entrepreneurship Development Fund now concentrates largely on providing support for access to finance to SMEs and entrepreneurs, it has not updated its strategic vision to that of a specialist public financial institution focused on this role.

SME and entrepreneurship programme interventions have traditionally been provided measure by measure in Kazakhstan, with SMEs and entrepreneurs needing to go through different application procedures for different types of support. More cross-referencing across different types of support or packaging of support would help increase the accessibility of support to businesses and to ensure that related constraints in enterprises are addressed. The recent re-organisation of several public business support agencies under the umbrella of the Baiterek Holding Company is an example of a reform that is helping to deliver more integrated packages of support.

A key challenge for strengthening business support in Kazakhstan is to increase the density of business incubators and the scope of their services. This infrastructure would be very beneficial in offering follow on support to promising new and early-stage innovative entrepreneurs that participate in entrepreneurship training programmes. The incubators could also offer a locus of advice and support for potential entrepreneurs who have not participated in public entrepreneurship training.

There is a systematic approach to the monitoring of SME and entrepreneurship measures in the BRM 2020. This includes mandatory procedures for regular and timely monitoring of expenditures, numbers of SMEs and entrepreneurs that benefit from programmes, their satisfaction with the support, and feedback from certain beneficiary firms on the perceived impact of the programmes. However, there is much less emphasis on the evaluation of the impacts of programmes on targeted SMEs and entrepreneurs using robust methodologies such as control groups and using independent evaluators. Such evaluation would be an important aid to policy making in this area, and should be used systematically across different SME and entrepreneurship programme areas to identify their contributions to meeting explicit policy impact targets.

The key recommendations of the report on strengthening the strategic framework and delivery arrangements for SME and entrepreneurship policy in Kazakhstan are set out below.

Key recommendations on strategic framework and policy delivery system

The policy framework and strategic directions

- Present and review the distribution of expenditures on SME and entrepreneurship support across different types of programme and target enterprise in order to guide decisions on the most appropriate policy mix.
- Review the balance between financial support and non-financial support measures in the Business Road Map 2020 in relation to evidence on policy needs and impacts, noting that although the demand expressed by businesses tends to be for financial subsidies, the greatest needs are often for management development and workforce training.
- Place greater policy emphasis on stimulating high-growth potential enterprises and productivity growth in existing SMEs.

Policy delivery structure

- Fully implement the proposal to deliver the SME and entrepreneurship support tools of the Damu Entrepreneurship Development Fund, the National Agency for Technological Development, the Autonomous Cluster Fund and related state organisations in the form of "packages" that offer SMEs and entrepreneurs access to combinations of financing and competency-building actions that meet their needs in a more holistic manner.
- Continue to invest in the ongoing professional development of the business development advisors and consultants in the network of Entrepreneurship Support Centres and incubators.
- Assess the need for further business incubators and for different types of incubators (e.g. full-service versus partial-service incubators; technological versus non-technological incubators) and offer public support for the development of additional business incubators in function of this analysis.
- Review the strategic plan of the Damu Entrepreneurship Development Fund, noting that it no longer has main responsibilities for non-financial support programmes and that therefore the benchmarks in the current strategy are not appropriate. Create a long-term vision for the future of the Fund based on comparison with the activities of public SME financial institutions in other countries.

Monitoring and evaluation

- Increase the use of robust policy impact evaluations, using independent evaluators and techniques such as control groups, and seek comparability of measures of policy performance across evaluations.

The legal framework

The Entrepreneurial Code specifies the definitions and support tools of policy

In 1991, Kazakhstan transformed from a Soviet Republic to an independent state with the ambition of growing private sector economic activity. It started from a base of very little private sector activity; for example only 4.2% of the Kazakhstan population was self-employed. In 1992, a law "On protection and support of private enterprise № 1543" laid the general foundations for the promotion of private enterprises, such as in the areas of regulation, tax policy, and access to financing, production facilities, raw materials and information. However, it was 1994 before the legal freedom of individuals to engage in private entrepreneurial activities was guaranteed in the Civil Code of the Republic of Kazakhstan. Kazakhstan's history with SME and entrepreneurship development is thus relatively recent.

Since then, there have been several further milestones in the development of the strategic framework for SME and entrepreneurship policy. In 1997, the Law "On state support of small enterprise № 131" and the Law "On individual enterprise" gave high policy priority to the support of small enterprises as a vehicle for generating employment and increasing competition. Further measures were taken in the period 1996 to 2001 to reduce regulatory barriers, ease the tax burden, create a business support infrastructure, make financing more accessible, provide knowledge and information support, support women's entrepreneurship, and modernise private and small enterprises. All these separate actions were brought together in a wide-ranging "Law on Private Entrepreneurship № 124", which was introduced in 2006 and amended in 2013 and 2015.

Since the beginning of 2016, Kazakhstan's SME and entrepreneurship policy has been governed by the Entrepreneurial Code of 29 October 2015, which aimed to systematise the vast array of regulatory acts and business laws in the Republic as well as to address gaps in the legal regulation of business. The Entrepreneurial Code repealed the 2006 Law on Private Entrepreneurship and a large number of other previous laws, including the 1998 Law on Peasant Farming, the 2003 Law on Investments, the 2008 Competition Law, the 2011 Law on State Control and Supervision, and the 2012 Law on State Support for Industrial and Innovative Activities. Much of the Entrepreneurial Code applies to regulation and state support for private enterprises of all sizes. This includes actions for SMEs and start-ups, but they are not the sole concern of the Code.

Among the important contributions of the Entrepreneurial Code are the:

- Revision of the size-band definitions for small, medium and large enterprises originally established in the 2006 Law and addition of a new category of "microenterprise";
- Definition of legal safeguards to the freedom of entrepreneurship and the interaction of businesses and the State;
- Identification of the main lines of State business development support. These include: 1) financial and property support; 2) infrastructure support (*e.g.* creation of a network of business support centres, business incubators, technology parks, and industrial zones in each region); 3) institutional support (*i.e.* creation and development of financial institutions and state research institutions to study the problems of private enterprises and prepare business development proposals); and 4) information support (including advice and training to assist enterprises in their

business operation methods, marketing, engineering, management and legal issues, and commercialisation of technology);

- Specification of the roles of different government bodies in supporting business, including the competences of the National Chamber of Entrepreneurs, the Damu Entrepreneurship Development Fund, local executive bodies, and financial institutions; and
- Introduction of a Commissioner for Protection of the Rights of Entrepreneurs of Kazakhstan (a "business ombudsman").

Several chapters and articles of the Code make explicit reference to SMEs. For example, the Code outlines the role of accredited SME associations (and the rules of such accreditation) in the examination of draft laws and regulations affecting businesses as part of the Regulatory Impact Assessment (RIA) regime; prohibits random inspections of micro and small enterprises within three years of state registration; and sets limits on the number of working days required to undertake scheduled inspections of microenterprises and SMEs.

The Entrepreneurial Code includes a chapter on state support for SMEs. This covers regulatory and procedural simplifications, establishing financing mechanisms, establishing support centres and other facilities to assist the development of new and existing SMEs, providing training, consulting and technical/material support to SMEs, providing access to public procurement opportunities, and defining conditions for transfer of State property to SMEs (Box 4.1).

Box 4.1. Directions for SME policy in the Entrepreneurial Code of the Republic of Kazakhstan

- Simplifying procedures for the State registration of SMEs and their reorganisation or voluntary liquidation, and simplified requirements for record keeping and accounting.
- Establishing an optimal tax regime.
- Introducing SME loan programmes.
- Using foreign direct investment (FDI) attraction and embedding to develop SMEs.
- Promoting the foreign trade activities of SMEs.
- Guaranteeing an allocation of not less than 15% of the total public procurement of goods, works and services to SMEs and providing advice for SMEs on participation in procurement processes.
- Organising training, retraining and advanced training to SMEs through existing and newly-created educational and research centres, consulting organisations, and information support systems.
- Implementing international programmes and projects for the exchange of experience in the development of SMEs.
- Establishing business incubators to offer educational, marketing, consulting, and other organisational and administrative services to new and small businesses.
- Transferring free of charge the ownership of state-owned property to SMEs in non-trading and intermediary activities one year after conclusion of a leasing or asset management contract.
- Supporting peasant farms with exemption from utilities connection charges, simplification of accounting records and taxation calculations, investment incentives for agricultural production, and information and marketing support.

Source: Republic of Kazakhstan (2015b), "Entrepreneurial Code of the Republic of Kazakhstan", No. 375-V, 29 October, Chapter 22.

The strategic vision for SME and entrepreneurship policy

The policy vision is clear

In addition to the provisions of the Entrepreneurial Code, the Government of Kazakhstan has developed two long-term vision statements that recognise the importance of SMEs and entrepreneurship to national development. The Kazakhstan 2030 and Kazakhstan 2050 documents set out strong ambitions for the economy, including becoming one of the top 30 developed countries in the world by 2050. The development of SMEs and entrepreneurship is identified as a cornerstone of the vision, and the ambition is set out to double the share of SMEs in GDP from 17.5% in 2011 to 36% in GDP and to progress to 50% of GDP by 2050, which would bring the structure of the Kazakhstan economy closer into line with other economies. In 2017, the government also approved a medium-term national 2025 Strategic Development Plan focused on seven major reform areas, including business competitiveness. This places strong importance on productivity growth in existing industries, expanding export-oriented production, and developing new industries, including through building supply chains and promoting knowledge exchange.

The plans emphasise how the medium- and long-term objectives should be achieved through actions to create the infrastructure for a knowledge-based economy, improve the institutional environment for business, raise the level of human capital, establish a national innovation system, modernise infrastructure and improve energy efficiency, and promote stronger integration of Kazakhstan in international relations and markets. The following are among the key actions to be taken, as identified in the Kazakhstan 2050 Strategy:

- Creating a system to encourage, stimulate and support SME and entrepreneurship activity, including in the areas of research and innovation;
- Minimising the amount of regulation in the internal market, such as by reducing the need for permits and licensing;
- Establishing a more rigorous system of accountability for government officials in order to remove any artificial barriers to businesses;
- Improving support mechanisms for the protection and promotion of the interests of domestic producers, especially in light of Kazakhstan's participation in the Eurasian Economic Space;
- Creating the necessary conditions to enable individual entrepreneurs and small businesses to grow into medium-sized enterprises; and
- Strengthening domestic entrepreneurship through large-scale privatisation of non-strategic enterprises and services.

Five-year plans translate the vision into policy directions

An overarching framework – the State Programme of Accelerated Industrial-Innovative Development

The overarching five-year plan relevant to SME and entrepreneurship policy is the State Programme of Accelerated Industrial-Innovative Development of Kazakhstan (SPAIID), which currently covers the period 2015–2019 (Republic of Kazakhstan, 2014b). The goal of the plan is to stimulate diversification of the economy and improve manufacturing competitiveness. One of its six objectives is to promote entrepreneurship and develop SMEs in the manufacturing sector.

The SPAIID seeks to address three major barriers with respect to SME and entrepreneurship development: (1) a high concentration of quasi-state ownership of business activity, which limits market access for new entries and SME growth; (2) a complex business licensing and regulatory system; and (3) lack of access of SMEs to financial resources and other business supports. However, the programme has set no specific targets for SME and entrepreneurship development.

The major business development policy directions set out in the SPAIID include:

- Regulatory improvements, with particular reference to simplifying all procedures for opening and running a business and for issuing permits and licences;
- Reducing the negative impact of monopolistic practices on SME and entrepreneurship development through competition policy;
- Increasing availability of financial resources for business development with an emphasis on priority sectors (using the instruments of public institutions and in partnership with second-tier banks and other financial institutions);
- Providing specialised non-financial services to enhance the competitiveness of enterprises by aiding the introduction of modern technologies and quality standards and increasing productivity and efficiency;
- Improving the quality of human capital, both of entrepreneurs and SME managers (enhancement of technological and managerial competencies), and of workers (technical skills in areas required of priority sectors);
- Developing exports; and
- Improving SME access to supplier markets, including through the procurement policies of state-owned enterprises, supplier linkages between SMEs and large enterprises, and participation of SMEs in regional cluster initiatives.

The SPAIID also sets out the framework for innovation policies focusing on creation of knowledge-intensive industries and development of new economy sectors. These priorities are also relevant to SME and entrepreneurship development, particularly with respect to encouraging innovative start-ups and stimulating innovation in SMEs. The main innovation related policy objectives in the SPAIID with relevance to SME and entrepreneurship development are to:

- Promote technology transfer and high technology production in priority sectors (through use of innovation grants for prototyping, purchase of technology, and industrial research, optimisation of technological parks and industrial design offices, and creation of innovation clusters);
- Stimulate demand for innovations among enterprises (*e.g.* through regulatory measures, a "support for innovative companies" package, and financial measures to stimulate innovation activities, including among SMEs); and
- Increase the innovation capabilities of the top management of enterprises (technological and managerial competencies) by co-financing consultants to perform technical diagnostics and help enterprises to implement improvements.

The key innovation targets in the SPAIID 2015–2019 are to increase the share of innovation-active enterprises to 20% of the total number of enterprises (from 8.1% in 2014) and the share of innovative products in GDP to 2.5%.

Detailed sector programmes

Achievement of the goals and objectives of the SPAIID depend entirely on the implementation of a range of five-year socio-economic programmes, including 27 sector programmes and master plans. The key five-year sector programmes relevant to SMEs and entrepreneurship are the Business Road Map (BRM) 2020, Agribusiness 2020, the Productivity 2020 Programme (primarily targeting large industrial enterprises), the Export 2020 Programme, and the Employment Road Map (ERM) 2020. Of these, the

Business Road Map (BRM) 2020 programme is the most important tool for implementing policy measures to support the development of SMEs and entrepreneurship.

These programmes are implemented through approved one-year operational plans, which fit within three-year budget plans providing the basis for public spending and determining the priorities for each government agency.

The detailed SME and entrepreneurship objectives are mainly set out in Business Road Map 2020

The main state programme for SMEs and entrepreneurship is the Business Road Map 2020 (BRM 2020). There have been two editions of the BRM 2020. The current edition covers the period 2015–2019, updating the previous 2010-2014 plan. The BRM 2020 identifies 10 objectives for policy action (Republic of Kazakhstan, 2015a):

- Increase access to financing for entrepreneurs in rural settlements, mono-industry towns and small towns;
- Increase production capacities of entrepreneurs and SMEs in rural settlements, mono-industry towns and small towns;
- Increase new business initiatives of entrepreneurs and SMEs in rural settlements, mono-industry towns and small towns;
- Prevent transformation of currency risks to credit risks;
- Increase the amount of local output from SMEs in priority economy sectors and manufacturing;
- Create new competitive enterprises in priority economic sectors and manufacturing;
- Provide information and analytical support to entrepreneurship.
- Improve entrepreneurial competencies (train entrepreneurs and SME managers; management support to existing SMEs);
- Enhance the productivity of entrepreneurs (use of external experts; technology upgrading/development; quality certification); and
- Promote business connections of Kazakh SMEs with foreign partners; promote local manufactured goods.

It also sets the higher-level objective of increasing employment in SMEs with a target of achieving a 50% increase by 2019 compared with 2014.

Employment Road Map 2020, Agribusiness 2020 and other programmes also include SME and entrepreneurship objectives

Other state programmes also contribute to SME and entrepreneurship development. For example, the Employment Road Map 2020 includes an objective of stimulating entrepreneurial initiative in rural communities and middle and high development potential villages in order to increase economic activity through the establishment or expansion of businesses (mainly self-employment). Associated measures provide free training in the basics of entrepreneurship for unemployed individuals and marginally self-employed persons, access to microcredit for business start-up, and advisory services in support of start-up business projects for up to one year. In addition, Agribusiness 2020 includes the objective of developing SMEs in agricultural processing and trade in order to support the diversification of the economy. Measures include provision of microcredit for small agri-food producers and other small village enterprises.

The strategic direction of policy is well developed

In order to obtain a complete picture of SME and entrepreneurship policy directions in Kazakhstan, it is necessary to consider together the various key policy documents, including Kazakhstan 2050, the 2015 Entrepreneurial Code, the SPAIID and the BRM 2020. These imply ten policy priorities:

- Improving the business environment for SMEs and entrepreneurs through simplification of business licensing and permit requirements, taxation and accounting records and financial reporting, and rigorous assessment of the impact of new legislative and regulatory proposals and drafts on private enterprises;
- Supporting the start-up of new business by offering advice, counselling and training in the basics of entrepreneurship to potential entrepreneurs, including young people, women, people with disabilities and people over the age of 50;
- Enhancing the management capability and growth capacity of existing SMEs through the provision of training to SME owners and their senior and middle managers;
- Strengthening the productivity of existing SMEs, particularly in the manufacturing sector, through access to subsidised domestic and foreign experts and consultants to transfer technologies and best management practices in the areas of production efficiency, quality standards, and certification of products and management systems to international standards, including the training of SME workers to execute these practices;
- Expanding markets for SMEs by supporting SMEs in developing connections and networks with foreign firms and enabling the formation of joint ventures, supporting exporters and potential exporters, making room for SMEs to become suppliers of quasi-public bodies and large multinationals, and ensuring that SMEs are integrated into cluster initiatives and supply chains;
- Improving access to financing for SMEs and entrepreneurs. Policy tools include: Conditional Placement of Funds with second tier banks for relending to SMEs[1]; partial credit guarantees to compensate lenders (second tier banks, leasing companies and microcredit organisations) for the lack of collateral of SMEs and start-up entrepreneurs; interest rate subsidies to reduce the cost of borrowing for targeted enterprises; and start-up grants to new entrepreneurs in priority economy sectors. Further stipulation of eligibility criteria for these policy instruments seeks to steer financial support in particular to priority sectors and manufacturing and mono-industry towns, small towns and rural settlements;
- Improving the skills of SME workers through access to subsidised training and retraining meeting the needs of SME employers;
- Improving access to business development services through the establishment and operation of a unified system of one-stop-shop Entrepreneurship Support Centres (ESCs) in all regions of Kazakhstan. These centres are to provide information and advice to potential and new entrepreneurs and existing SMEs on a broad range of

business-related topics, and including access to entrepreneurship and management training and linkages to all State financial and non-financial support measures and programmes;

- Provision of the physical infrastructure needed by new and existing SMEs through financing of production facilities (business and technology incubators, technology parks, sewer and water connections, waste systems, etc.); and allocation of State-owned property and land to operating SMEs; and
- Support for innovative start-ups and the innovative activity of SMEs through the provision of innovation grants, technological incubators, and commercialisation support.

These policy priorities appear to appropriate to creating conditions more conducive to the development of SMEs and entrepreneurship, although certain potential gaps in policy support are identified elsewhere in this chapter.

Policy lacks operational outcome targets and the highest-level outcome targets may be hard to achieve

Although conveying strong ambition for SME and entrepreneurship activity in Kazakhstan, it may be difficult to achieve the highest level policy target of increasing the share of SMEs in GDP from 17.5% in 2011 to 36% in 2030 and 50% in 2050. If the growth is to be achieved by contributing new GDP rather than by privatising or competing away existing large firm activity, a very high growth rate in SME GDP would be required. Even assuming a national GDP growth rate of only 2% per annum suggests a required annual average growth rate of approximately 9.1% in the SME share of GDP from 2011–2030, or 7.5% from 2011–2050. It is therefore appropriate to monitor progress in achieving the objectives and to revise targets if necessary.

The BRM 2020 sets some further high-level SME and entrepreneurship targets for the period 2015-2019:

- Increase SME output by 1.5 times compared to 2014;
- Increase the number of active SMEs by 50% compared to 2014; and
- Increase employment in SMEs by 50% compared to 2014.

The initial target is not far out of line with past performance. Indeed SME output increased by 1.6 times over the 2010–2014 period, which was a little above the new target. However, reaching the targets for SME numbers and employment may be more difficult. Achieving a 50% increase in the number of active SMEs by 2020 would require a net increase of some 475 000 SMEs over the five-year period, which is much greater than the net increase in SMEs during the 2010–2014 period of 263 400. Achieving a 50% increase in SME employment would mean a net increase of 1.38 million jobs in SMEs. However, over the 2010–2014 period, Kazakhstan experienced a net increase of only 473 338 SME jobs.

An additional target should also be considered, namely to increase the average employment size of SMEs. With the targeted increases in SME numbers being equal to the targeted increase in SME jobs, the average size of an SME would stay at around 3 workers. However, productivity generally tends to be higher in larger SMEs, and this would help achieve government objectives for the share of SMEs in value added. The growth in average SME size could be achieved by facilitating stronger start-ups with higher employment potential, and more transitions of microenterprises to small businesses, and small businesses to medium-sized businesses.

Beyond these high-level targets, there is little detail in BRM 2020 on targeted achievements and outcomes from policy objectives and actions. The high-level targets are the only policy objectives with quantifiable outcome targets. For more detailed policy objectives, the only targets are 'activity' targets in terms of the number of assisted SMEs and entrepreneurs or numbers of supported projects. More visible detailed targets would be useful to help steer and adjust policy over time and to encourage strong and consistent policy action by government ministries and agencies to achieve the high level national objectives.

Strategic directions for SME innovation and high-potential entrepreneurship are not specified

Strengthening innovation in SMEs should be a major strategic target

Despite low current innovation levels in SMEs in Kazakhstan and major government priorities for strengthening innovation and developing SMEs, the SPAIID 2015–2019 does not set any specific targets for increasing the level of innovative activity in SMEs. Achieving the government's goal of becoming an innovative, knowledge-based economy will require major policy initiatives to address the widespread constraints to innovative activities faced by SMEs, such as limited skills of staff, low levels of financial investment in innovation, and limited risk capital for innovative projects.

Similarly, BRM 2020 does not place a great stress on innovation. BRM 2020 certainly includes some SME innovation supports, in particular through the business incubators, certain training programmes, and targeting of SMEs involved in industrial innovative activities in some programme components. However, there are significant gaps in BRM 2020 with respect to innovation. In particular, there is no major programme that would assess the innovation potential and readiness of SMEs in manufacturing and priority sectors, encourage SMEs to examine opportunities to innovate, develop linkages between SMEs and research institutes, and support traditional, non-technological SMEs to pursue innovative activity.

There is also a need for further diagnostics of SMEs to determine their technological level and technological development opportunities, covering existing productivity, profitability and competitiveness, the potential availability of advanced technologies, possible equipment modernisation projects and training projects, and readiness for R&D. To date, technological foresight exercises have focused mainly on identifying the needs of medium and large firms and have not adequately taken into consideration the needs of smaller businesses.

High growth potential entrepreneurship and SMEs should also a key strategic area of policy

While the strategic directions of policy place strong attention on increasing the numbers of start-ups, there is less attention to the key concern for the Kazakhstan economy of nurturing a group of high growth potential start-ups and SMEs. The development of high-growth enterprises has become a strong focus of policy in many other countries, reflecting the disproportionate benefits they bring to economic development (OECD, 2013). While high growth potential enterprises are clearly eligible to participate in standard entrepreneurship and management training and financial support measures, more specific and targeted support is merited for this group. For example, an entrepreneurship training programme for high growth potential entrepreneurs would seek to attract and support starters with high entrepreneurial ability (measured for example in terms of their education, technical knowledge, experience, and social capital) and offer them more intensive training. Similarly, a high growth entrepreneurship policy would identify a small number of existing high growth potential SMEs and offer them business diagnosis, mentoring and consultancy support alongside the standard subsidies available to all SMEs. The total value of support offered per high growth potential entrepreneur or SME would generally be higher than for standard entrepreneurs and enterprises, but with many fewer companies supported than the standard policy schemes.

The policy approach of the Dutch government, having for some time recognised the importance of high growth firms to its employment and economic dynamism, provides an illustrative example of such targeting (Box 4.2).

Box 4.2. Policy approaches to stimulating high growth potential enterprises in the Netherlands

Description of the approach

The decision of the Dutch government to design and implement policies to encourage more high growth enterprises was based on evidence that the share of high growth SMEs in the Dutch SME population lagged behind key comparator OECD countries. In addition, the average annual turnover growth of its high growth enterprises was relatively low compared to other countries.

An analysis of the additional constraints faced by high growth SMEs compared to the typical Dutch SME revealed:

- Difficulties in finding enough new employees with the right qualifications and to accommodate phases of growth;
- Unique problems in accessing the financing needed to support rapid growth;
- Lack of growth management know-how and a clear management strategy to deal with the rapid changes required of fast growth; and
- Inadequate systems and processes to deal with new circumstances.

To deal with these obstacles, the government developed policy measures specifically designed for high growth potential enterprises. The resulting policy included a mix of targeted policy measures covering access to growth financing, supporting growth management capabilities, streamlined services to provide information, creation of new delivery mechanisms to improve the offer of public services specifically to high growth potential firms, and formation of networks and exchange platforms for high growth potential enterprises.

These were complemented and reinforced by more recent policy actions under the Agenda for Ambitious Entrepreneurship, the objective of which is to stimulate successful start-ups and growth (Ministry of Economic Affairs, 2014). The aim is to move the Netherlands to one of the top five countries within the OECD by 2020 regarding high growth enterprises and entrepreneurs with high growth ambition, from a ranking of 22nd in 2014 (Ministry of Economic Affairs, 2015).

The Agenda focuses on improving the following areas:

1. Access to capital: access to (risk and growth) funding;
2. Access to innovation and knowledge: use of schemes and developed knowledge;
3. Access to global markets: attracting international expertise and entrepreneurs and gaining access to international markets and customers;
4. Access to tax facilities: attractive tax conditions for growth;
5. Access to peer networks: strengthening the entrepreneur's social capital, the entrepreneur's own skills and how he/she deploys the human capital of the business; and
6. The conditions in which the entrepreneur operates, such as laws and regulations.

Some of these policy initiatives explicitly target existing high growth enterprises, while others target enterprises with high growth potential, such as innovative SMEs and techno-starters, and others seek to develop an eco-system to stimulate rapid growth of up-scalable start-ups led by "ambitious" growth-oriented entrepreneurs. Most of the initiatives were supported by the Ministry of Economic Affairs and led by a government agency such as the Netherlands Enterprise Agency (an agency of the Ministry of Economic Affairs responsible for supporting entrepreneurs in sustainable, agrarian, innovative and international business through help with grants, finding business partners, know-how and compliance with laws and regulations) or Syntens (the innovation network for SMEs in the Netherlands). The initiatives frequently involved collaboration of other ministries, universities and local government authorities, with some collaboration with private sector partners.

Examples of policy instruments include:

Policy pillar	Example of policy initiatives
Awareness	Initiatives to reinforce a growth culture, stimulate a "growth" mind-set among entrepreneurs, and present fast growers in a positive light, e.g. Annual High-Growth Forum; Gazelles Award.
Supporting managerial capabilities	Mastering Growth Programme implemented by Syntens with focus on addressing the pre-conditions for successful growth with masterclasses tailored to companies in various stages of their development. Linking entrepreneurs to mentors and coaches. Embedding entrepreneurship education in the performance commitments between the Ministry of Economic Affairs and the Ministry of Education, Culture and Science and higher educational institutions.
Improving public services through enterprise zones	Establishment of enterprise zones for start-ups and high-growth companies spearheaded by the Minister of Economic Affairs through agreements with three Dutch universities of technology and their associated local government authorities to offer special assistance to start-ups and high-growth companies. Growth Accelerator Programme to support and facilitate the growth of selected SMEs from a turnover of approximately EUR 2 million to a turnover of EUR 20 million over five years through mentoring, peer group learning sessions and leadership master-classes (one or two intakes of 15-20 companies a year).
Developing an ecosystem for ambitious entrepreneurs	Creation of NLevator, an ecosystem of stakeholders to facilitate growing businesses, respond to latent demand among existing businesses for more and better entrepreneurship education and mentoring/coaching and networking opportunities, and strengthen linkages among stakeholders. DutchBaseCamp, an initiative to organise and connect networks between the Netherlands and high-potential entrepreneurs in other countries for the purpose of attracting start-ups and fast growers to the Netherlands.
Improving access to growth financing	Growth Facility offering a government guarantee to investors in SMEs that covers 50% of newly invested risk capital (through an extension of the SME Credit Guarantee Scheme to non-bank

	investors).
	Dutch Venture Initiative to make more venture capital for ambitious entrepreneurs seeking to grow quickly.
	New facility for early-stage finance and business angels – implemented by the Netherlands Enterprise Agency in collaboration with regional players in the ecosystem.
	Creation of financing desk as part of the digital Business Link to provide better digital information and first-line advice and referral to the Netherlands Enterprise Agency, banks and private organisations.
	Stronger promotion of alternative finance opportunities for businesses, including government schemes, crowdfunding and credit unions, through meetings, events and other channels of communication.

Factors for success

Over a number of years, the Dutch government has gained knowledge on the needs of high growth enterprise and the factors determining the growth potential of new and existing firms. The results of research and analysis have been used to inform its policy formulation, which addresses the major barriers to high-growth SMEs in a comprehensive and integrated manner. Policy initiatives have evolved over time, largely as the result of policy learning from past approaches and initiatives. The policy has also benefited from consultation inputs from stakeholders on policy priorities and initiatives and partnership arrangements with various delivery agencies and institutions. Based on assessments of high growth enterprise policy in other countries, the interventions tend to actively solicit private sector participation given that private sector partners can bring experience-based knowledge, key industry contacts, and ability to identify and mobilise key external resources and can therefore help in screening deals, providing credibility to policy measures, mentoring, or in offering professional services for young firms (MTI, 2007; Lilischkis, 2011).

The higher level policy target of dramatically improving the Dutch ranking among OECD countries on benchmark indicators of high growth enterprises and the growth ambitions of entrepreneurs also provides a common vision for stakeholders delivering policy initiatives.

One of the strengths of the policy approach is the targeting of high growth potential firms at various stages of development (the life-cycle approach), starting with stimulating "ambitious entrepreneurship" and a growth mind-set among nascent entrepreneurs, and tailoring specific policy initiatives to high growth potential start-ups (including "born global enterprises"), traditional SMEs with under-utilised or hidden growth potential, and innovative enterprises in identified priority ("top") sectors for the Netherlands.

Obstacles and responses

The Dutch policy for stimulating high growth enterprises has evolved over a number of years, involving an expanding number of growth support initiatives both from public and private partners. A challenge is to maximise opportunities for co-operation and knowledge sharing among these initiatives. One of the ways in which the Ministry of Economic Affairs is seeking to enhance this is through support for stakeholder networks and networking, such as the NLevator platform.

Although not specific to the Netherlands, two other obstacles are routinely noted in studies of high growth enterprise policies. The first is the issue of selectiveness – establishing the selection criteria for which firms to support. In general, policy advice disfavours trying to "pick winners", especially on a sector basis, however, programmes should require an explicit orientation towards growth driven by demonstrable commitment of the firms' owner(s). The other issue relates to the level of proactivity of the policy delivery agents in identifying growth potential firms and encouraging them to engage in the policy support. The Finnish Growth Service for example, the "one-touch shop" for public services relevant to growth firms, makes use of its consultants to proactively identify promising growth firms and then to offer a growth analysis session to assess the specific needs for achieving growth and refer the firm to the appropriate support service. Other programmes may use competitive calls for programme support and select applicants based on a set of growth criteria and firm/leadership characteristics. In any event, the challenge is to direct the policy to firms with the greatest potential for rapid growth.

Another potential obstacle to success is that many high growth enterprise policies over-emphasise firms in technology sectors based on a perception that high growth is most likely in technology-push situations. However, rapid growth can also be found in business services, suggesting that an over-emphasis on technological innovation may be inefficient, and that policies should apply to growth potential firms and opportunities regardless of sector. In the Netherlands, the high growth enterprise policies are not restricted to technology firms although certain policy measures are directed to these firms specifically.

Relevance to Kazakhstan

Although the Committee on Statistics does not collect metrics on high growth enterprises, the large proportion of very small firms in the enterprise population and the relatively small contribution of SMEs to total employment and value-added suggests that there may be few high-growth start-ups and SMEs and obstacles to the rapid growth of firms. The Dutch example suggests that it would be useful for the Ministry of National Economy to conduct a study to determine factors hindering high growth entrepreneurship in Kazakhstan and then to design targeted policies to address the identified growth barriers.

Source: EIM and Ministry of Economic Affairs (2006); Suddle and Hessels (2007); Ministry of Economic Affairs (2015).

Policy leadership and co-ordination

SME and entrepreneurship development is influenced by policies pursued by a range of different government ministries and agencies, for example in trade policy, investment policy, labour and employment policy, regulatory policy, regional development policy, agricultural policy, technology policy, and gender policy. Table 4.1 shows the key ministries and agencies with a role in implementing SME and entrepreneurship policies in Kazakhstan. Advocacy and leadership of SME and entrepreneurship policy is therefore important to ensure that the objective of SME and entrepreneurship development is pursued widely across government and co-ordination is needed to minimise duplications and policy gaps across government policy areas.

The 2006 Law on Private Entrepreneurship indicated which institutional structures the Government of Kazakhstan should established. They include an authorised body on entrepreneurship to conduct the state policy and co-ordinate state support measures; an inter-ministerial entrepreneurship council; local executive bodies and expert councils to administer state support in the regions (Regional Co-ordinating Councils); advisory and consultative agencies on the issues of private enterprise; vehicles for providing information support and materials and reporting annually on the state of entrepreneurial development in the country; and defined roles for business associations. These structures have all been put in place.

Table 4.1. The SME and entrepreneurship policy activities of key national ministries and agencies

Ministry/ agency	Key areas of responsibility with relevance to SME and entrepreneurship policy
The Ministry of Economy, Entrepreneurship Development Department	Major responsibility for developing SME and entrepreneurship policy proposals and co-ordinating support for SMEs and entrepreneurship. Also co-ordinating the SME and entrepreneurship actions of five government institutions and advocating for a unified approach: National Bank of Kazakhstan (NBK), Ministry of Finance, Ministry of Justice, Ministry of National Economy directorates (department of international trade, department of construction, etc.), and the Ministry of Energy. The main co-ordination emphasis is ensuring that the views of SMEs and entrepreneurs are kept in view for the simplification of *Doing Business* reforms. Ultimate responsibility for policy measures under the BRM 2020. Assisted in its analytical work by the Economic Research Institute (ERI), including extensive enterprise surveys, investment climate assessments across different regions of the country; and research on the impact of impact of State programmes on SME and entrepreneurship performance.
Ministry for Investments and Development (MID)	Lead ministry on the industrial innovative development agenda with the aim of diversifying the economy away from its natural resource dependence through measures to develop new industries and stimulate technology transfer and growth of innovative firms. Responsible for the SPAIID programme and co-ordination of its implementation. The SPAIID Includes several references to policy objectives to strengthen SMEs in the priority and manufacturing sectors. Also responsible for the Productivity 2020 Programme (although the prime recipients of this programme are large enterprises).
Ministry of Healthcare and Social Development	Delivers micro-credit programmes, basic entrepreneurship training for the unemployed and fledgling self-employed (including youth, women, and people with disabilities, and in mono-industry towns and rural areas), advisory services to registered unemployed persons interested in starting a business, and job retraining for the unemployed and unproductively self-employed to improve their opportunities for paid jobs, and of existing workers to meet the skills demands of the employer firms.
Ministry of Agriculture	Delivers the AgriBusiness 2020 Programme; one objective is to support development of agribusinesses and encourage new start-ups in the sector.
National Agency for Development of Local Content	Involved in delivering aspects of the Productivity 2020 programme; ensuring that SMEs benefit from foreign direct investment activities.
The Kazakhstan Industry Development Institute (KIDI)	Mandated to develop and oversee the implementation of the clusters programme under the SPAIID and aspects of the Productivity 2020 programme.
Development Bank of Kazakhstan (DBK)	Strategic goals to support SMEs, the export activity of Kazakh companies, support the modern economy through industrial and innovation advances, and make investments in the non-oil sectors of the economy.
Autonomous Cluster Fund, Park of Innovation Technologies	The implementation of Start Up Kazakhstan, collaboration with multinational companies to open joint centres for technological development to localise production and finance R&D in the framework of sub-soil users' obligations (expenditure of 1% of their aggregate income from sub-soil operations), the opening of joint venture capital funds, and the acceleration and incubation of world class export-oriented companies.

A focal department is in place for policy leadership and co-ordination

Policy leadership and co-ordination can be facilitated by the establishment of a special department or dedicated focal point for ministries and departments involved in SME and entrepreneurship policy. Some countries have appointed Ministers for Small Business (or Entrepreneurship). However, the most common vehicle for leadership and co-ordination is a specific SME development department or agency. This may be housed within a government ministry or set up as a separate government department, a semi-autonomous agency, or an autonomous special government agency. Its role is to coordinate closely with other central and regional government bodies and with private sector and non-governmental organisations providing services to SMEs and entrepreneurs.

In Kazakhstan, the role is performed by the Entrepreneurship Development Department (EDD). This was created in 2008 in the Ministry of National Economy (MNE) with a clear mandate for co-ordinating SME and entrepreneurship policies across government. It has wide responsibilities, including the business environment and regulatory reforms (*e.g.* developing public policies to improve the state licensing system and state control over the activities of private entrepreneurs; co-ordinating and implementing state policy to improve the legal regulation of business activity; co-ordination of the state regulatory agencies on the implementation of regulatory impact analysis); formulating programme intervention proposals in favour of SME and entrepreneurship development (financial and non-financial support); creating the conditions for participation of SMEs in programmes related to innovation, investment and industrial development; contributing to the development of infrastructure for SMEs and entrepreneurship in the regions; and organising and co-ordinating the implementation of government measures to develop and support SMEs. By virtue of a ministerial order, the EDD also has wide powers of authority with respect to requesting and receiving information from other ministries, department and agencies of the government to enable it to carry out its tasks and effectively fulfil its co-ordination role.

A Co-ordinating Council supports inter-ministerial co-ordination

An inter-ministerial co-ordinating mechanism is also very important. In Kazakhstan, this takes the form of the Prime Ministry Co-ordinating Council on Development of Entrepreneurship, involving senior representatives of government and non-government bodies concerned by the policy area. It is a permanent advisory body directed by a Board represented by executive and legislative authorities, public associations, and business groups and unions and reporting to the President of the Republic[2]. This mechanism can define and agree the role of different departments, the mechanisms by which policies and programmes will be co-ordinated, and how interaction between the State and entrepreneurs will be organised. The main objectives of the Council are to: develop proposals to create the conditions to encourage the development of a market economy and support the development of entrepreneurship; develop recommendations for solutions to important problems of the State; consult with government agencies and officials to request and receive information on matters relating to the development of entrepreneurship; and participate in the discussion of issues of concern to entrepreneurs, professionals, academics, and independent experts. The meetings of the Council, to be held at least once a year, are organised by the MNE, which is also responsible for monitoring implementation of the Council's recommendations.

The BRM 2020 programme groups many SME and entrepreneurship actions

The BRM 2020, 2015-2019 issue, is additional evidence of the efforts to co- ordinate SME and entrepreneurship policy measures across the government. Under the heading of "Unified business support and development programme" the intent of this issue of the BRM was to consolidate sectoral programmes of support for the development of SMEs and entrepreneurship.

Input is gathered from SMEs and entrepreneurs to feed into policy formulation.

The design of SME and entrepreneurship policy in Kazakhstan benefits from several formal mechanisms for gathering and managing input from SMEs and entrepreneurs on their policy needs, primarily through representative business associations. The main organisation feeding into policy design is the National Chamber of Entrepreneurs (NCE). This was jointly established in late 2013 by the Government of Kazakhstan and the National Economic Chamber Atameken Union (essentially a replacement of the previous Chamber of Commerce and Industry) to address the government's problem of lack of feedback from the business community. Although businesses were (and are) free to set up their own associations, very few such associations wielded much influence. By contrast, membership in the NCE is mandatory for registered businesses[3], so it represents all active SMEs.

The main role of the NCE is to create an institutional framework for the growth and development of entrepreneurship by ensuring favourable legal and economic conditions, developing effective interactions between the business community and public authorities, and promoting and supporting the activities of associations of individual entrepreneurs and legal entities. The NCE works with the government in drafting legislation affecting business, and plays a direct role in providing expert opinions on the impact on SMEs of draft laws and legal acts affecting private enterprises as part of the government's regulatory impact assessment process. It also develops policy proposals for consideration. For example, it presented a proposal to the Ministry of Education and Science to include "Fundamentals of Entrepreneurship" in secondary schools. To support its work, the NCE regularly surveys its members on their needs and concerns.

The Damu Entrepreneurship Development Fund publishes an annual report on the state of development of SMEs and entrepreneurship in Kazakhstan and its regions and on the take-up of entrepreneurship support programmes, and the level of satisfaction of SMEs and entrepreneurs with the quality and usefulness of the support or service. This provides a good base of monitoring evidence to support the formulation of public policy.

In addition, other business associations survey their members on policy issues and provide this input to the government. Further, the public Economic Research Institute (ERI) conducts surveys and interviews with entrepreneurs and SMEs regarding their experiences with State support programmes as an input to assessing the impact of policy measures and making modifications to programmes.

The Government disseminates information on SME and entrepreneurship development issues

The Government of Kazakhstan is also active in disseminating information to the media, SMEs and entrepreneurs, other key stakeholders and the public at large on SME and entrepreneurship development issues and opportunities and the available state support. Through the BRM 2020 programme, provision is made for special television programmes, video films, media tours of state-supported entrepreneurship projects, and dissemination of leaflets and other programme materials. In addition, a unified business portal for entrepreneurs, www.business.gov.kz , provides, in an easily accessible format, information on all financial and business support measures and organisations, draft laws and regulations aimed at providing support for the development of entrepreneurship, news and analytical articles, "how-to" guides and case studies, market research and surveys, and procurement notices of public organisations and national companies, etc.

The policy mix and portfolio

Business Road Map 2020 offers a range of support and targets key sectors and geographies

BRM 2020 is structured in four policy action lines, and has a relatively strong focus on certain key sectors and geographies:

- Financial support for start-up entrepreneurs and for the modernisation or expansion of SMEs in rural settlements, mono-industry towns and small towns:
  - Interest rate subsidies, start-up grants, loan guarantees, microloans, construction grants for production infrastructure.
- Financial support to entrepreneurs in priority economy sectors[4] and manufacturing industries:
  - Interest rate subsidies, start-up grants, loan guarantees, construction grants for production infrastructure.
- Financial support to reduce currency risks:
  - Interest rate subsidies for loans to SMEs doing business in foreign currencies or markets.
- Non-financial support measures for developing entrepreneur and SME capabilities:
  - Information and advice for businesses; entrepreneurship and business management training; support making business connections and linkages; training of SME staff in productivity enhancement or product promotion management; consultancy on introduction of new management methods/technologies, quality systems, and international certification; consultancy for diagnosis of technological processes or a production organisation efficiency plan; reimbursement of costs incurred in promoting products in domestic and foreign markets.

Two of the four action lines target priority sectors and manufacturing or rural settlements, mono-industry towns and small towns. Some special emphasis on these targets is warranted given the need to diversify the economy, and recognising both the low share of SMEs in manufacturing (2.8% in 2014) and the objective of providing economic opportunities outside of the major cities of Astana and Almaty.

BRM 2020 expenditures have grown but are weighted to financial support measures

The scale of expenditure allocated to BRM 2020, the government's central programme for SME and entrepreneurship development, increased substantially for the period 2015-2019 as compared to 2010-2014, from Kazakhstan Tenge (KZT) 154.3 billion to a projected KZT 310.41 billion. This reflects the strong priority the government is now placing on SME and entrepreneurship development. Figure 4.1 shows the evolution of the annual budget.

Figure 4.1. Annual budget for implementation of the Business Road Map 2020

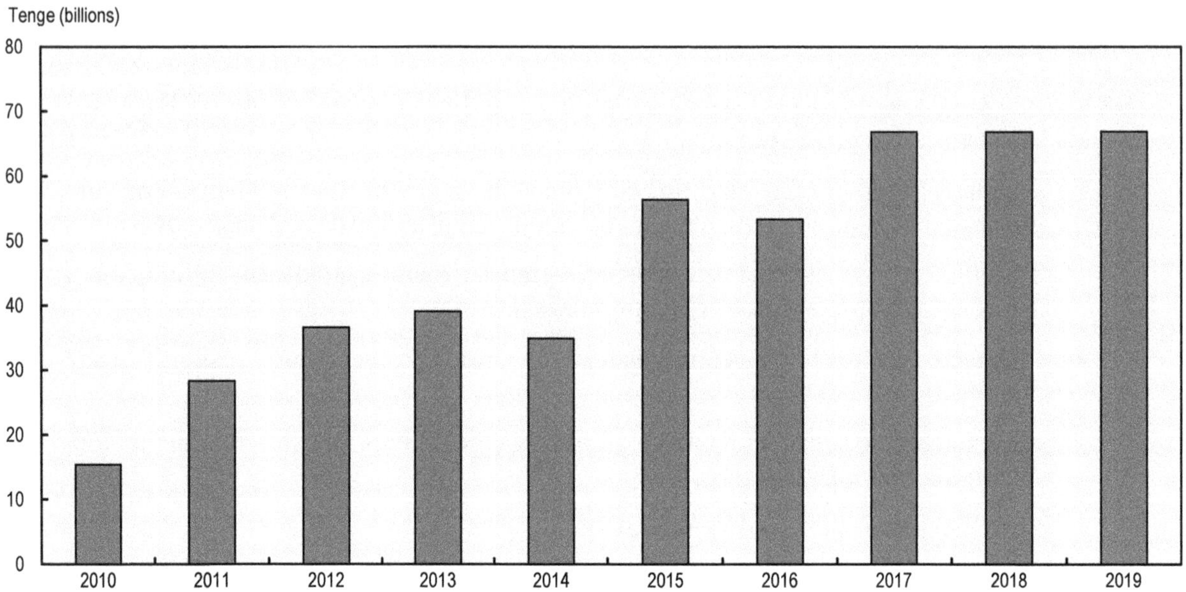

Source: Actual figures for 2010–2014 from the Ministry of National Economy; projected figures for 2015–2019 from Republic of Kazakhstan (2015a), "Resolution No. 168 of the Republic of Kazakhstan dated the 31st of March, 2015 on Approval of a Unified Business Support and Development Program 'Business Road Map 2020'", p. 2.

StatLink http://dx.doi.org/10.1787/888933828201

Figure 4.2 shows how the expenditures for 2015-2019 are distributed across the four BRM 2020 policy action lines. The vast majority of expenditures are allocated to policy action lines 2 and 3, namely financial support for SME and entrepreneurship development in priority economy sectors and manufacturing industries and financial support against currency risks, which is also accessed primarily by firms in these sectors (i.e. the sectoral dimension). Approximately 10% of expenditures are allocated to policy action line 1, namely financial support for start-up enterprises and SMEs in mono-industry towns, small towns and rural settlements (i.e. the regional dimension). Relatively little expenditure is allocated to policy action line 4 on building entrepreneur and SME capabilities, such as through consultancy and training.

Figure 4.2. Allocation of total projected spending by policy action area, Business Road Map 2020 (2015-2019)

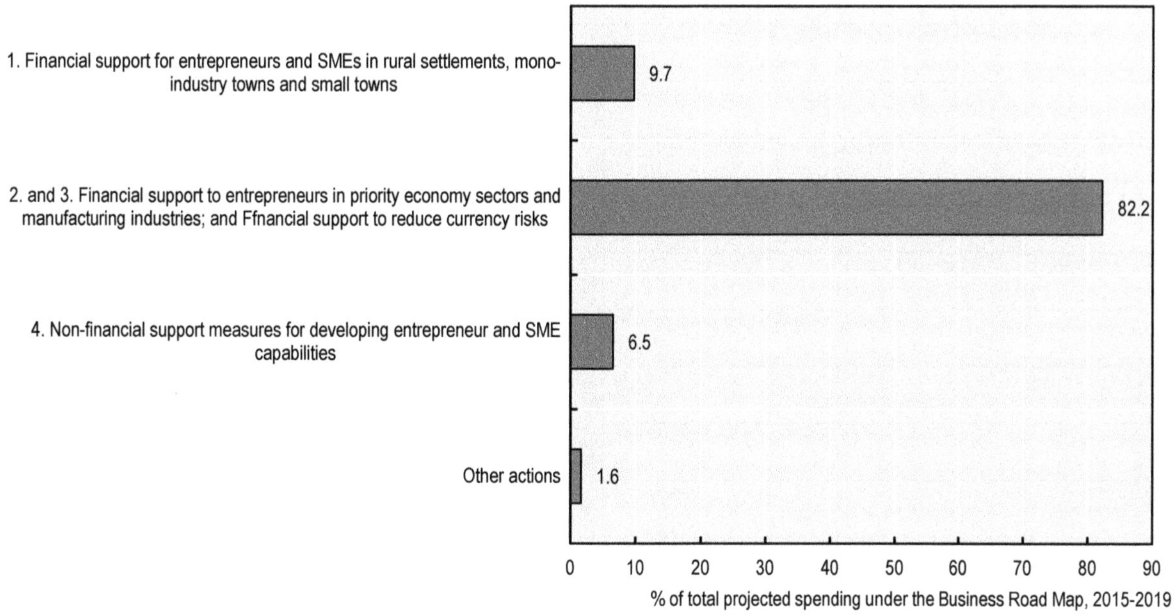

Source: Based on budget data in: Republic of Kazakhstan (2015), "Resolution No. 168 of the Republic of Kazakhstan dated the 31st of March, 2015 on Approval of a Unified Business Support and Development Program Business Road Map 2020", pp. 53–60.

StatLink http://dx.doi.org/10.1787/888933828220

Overall, 93.5% of expenditures are allocated in the form of financial supports (interest rate subsidies, loan guarantees, grants for new entrepreneur initiatives, microloans) compared with only 6.5% for non-financial business support (Figure 4.3). Interest rate subsidies take the largest share of the policy mix (57%), followed by the financing of infrastructure (28%), which covers costs of construction, reconstruction or modernisation of physical infrastructure for businesses (*e.g.* water supply, gasification, water conduits, steam pipelines, heating plants for industrial sites, power lines, railway approaches, sewage plants, business incubators, industrial zones, etc.). Relatively small amounts of funding are budgeted for increasing the skills of entrepreneurs (through entrepreneurship and business management training) or improving the performance of SMEs and entrepreneurs (through advice, consultancy, training and other support for productivity enhancement, meeting quality standards, technology development, marketing, etc.).

Figure 4.3. Allocation of total spending projected in the Business Road Map 2020, by type of policy support, 2015-2019

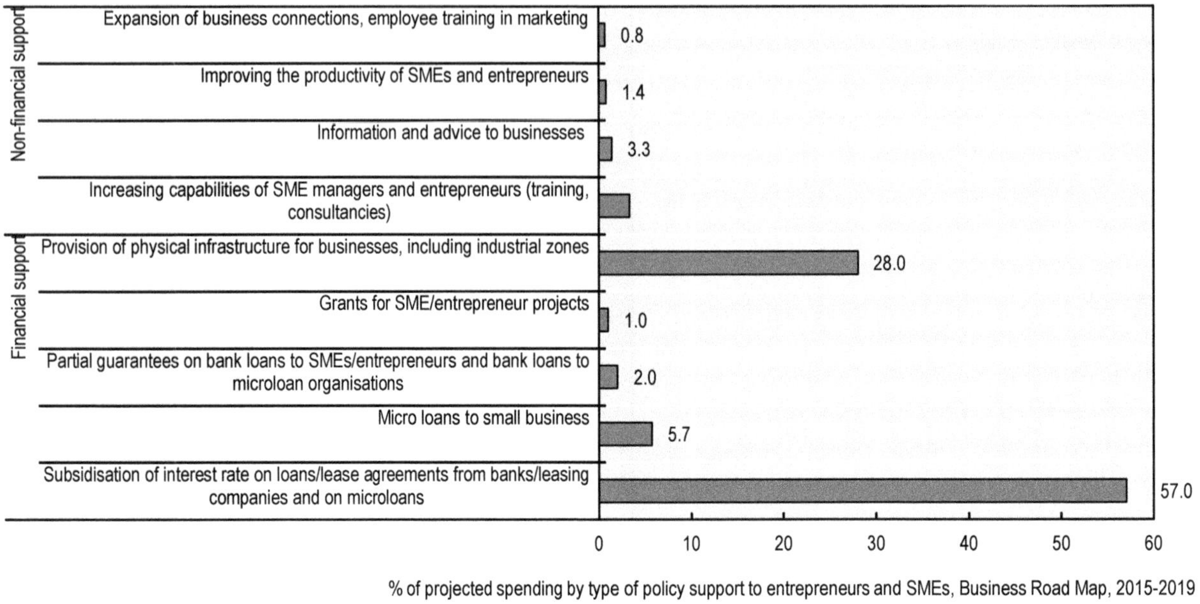

Source: Based on categorisation of budget data in: Republic of Kazakhstan (2015), "Resolution No. 168 of the Republic of Kazakhstan dated the 31st of March, 2015 on Approval of a Unified Business Support and Development Programme 'Business Road Map 2020'", pp. 53–60.

StatLink http://dx.doi.org/10.1787/888933827783

A further analysis shows the distribution of the BRM 2020 budget across the ten policy objectives listed in the programme, of which 9 were associated with direct budget allocations, as shown in Figure 4.4. This shows that the objective of increasing local output of SMEs in priority economy sectors and manufacturing has been given the majority of the funding, as it is allocated approximately 57% of the projected budget (Figure 4.4). Just over a quarter of the projected budget is allocated to the objective of creating new competitive enterprises in the priority economic sectors and manufacturing. Some 7% of the budget is allocated to access to financing in rural settlements, mono-industry towns, and small towns and 4% to enhancing entrepreneurship competences. By contrast, less than 1% of the budget is allocated to each of the policy objectives to expand the number of new business initiatives in rural settlements, mono-industry towns, and small towns, to promote business connections of Kazakh SMEs with foreign partners, and to enhance the productivity of entrepreneurs.

Figure 4.4. Allocation of total projected spending by policy objective, 2015-2019, Business Roadmap 2020

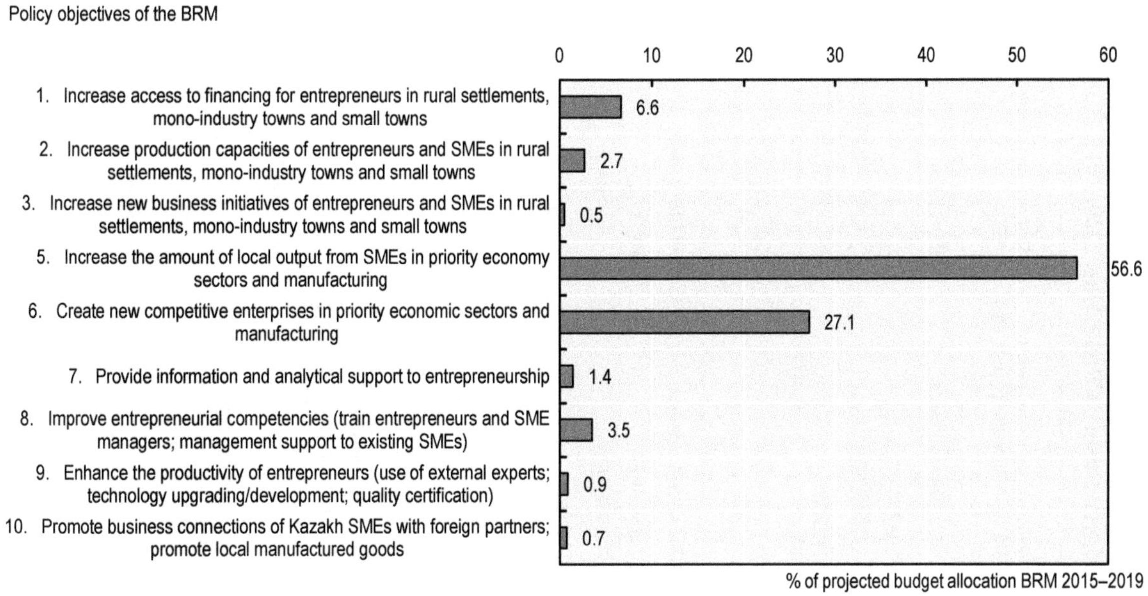

Note: There is no budget line in BRM 2020 for objective 4 'reducing currency risks'.
Source: Based on list of policy statements and budget figures from: Republic of Kazakhstan (2015), "Unified Program of Business Support and Development 'Business Road Map 2020'", Section 4 and Section 8. Summarised in Table A.1 annexed to this OECD report.

StatLink http://dx.doi.org/10.1787/888933828239

Table 4.2 sets out additional information on numbers of projects and budgets of BRM 2020 with respect to the policy objectives above.

Table 4.2. Policy measures, projected number of projects, and projected budgets, Business Road Map 2020, 2015-2019

Policy focus area	Policy objective	Policy instrument	Cumulative projected interventions 2015–2019 (number of projects, etc.)	Total projected budget (KZT)	Projected average cost per assisted project/ SME/ entrepreneur (KZT)
1-3: Supporting new business initiatives of entrepreneurs located in mono-industry towns, small towns and rural settlements	Increase access to financing for entrepreneurs	Interest rate subsidies for bank loans through second-tier banks and leasing companies	1 000 subsidised projects	KZT 6 billion	KZT 6 million
		Credit guarantees	304 guarantees		
		Microloans	3 103 microloans	KZT 13.7 billion	KZT 4.4 million
	Increase production capacities of entrepreneurs and SMEs	Provision of production infrastructure for new business initiatives	45 projects	KZT 8 billion	KZT 177 million
	Increase new business initiatives of entrepreneurs and SMEs (could include adoption of new technologies)	State grants (not exceeding KZT 3 million) for new business projects	100 grants	KZT 1.5 billion	KZT 15 million
5-6: Sector-based support to entrepreneurs in priority economic sectors and in manufacturing industries	Increase the amount of local output from SMEs	Interest rate subsidies for bank loans through second-tier banks and leasing companies	8 392 subsidised projects	KZT 161.6 billion	KZT 19.3 million
		Credit guarantees	3 400 guarantees	KZT 5 billion	KZT 1.47 million
		State grants	400 grants issued	KZT 1.5 billion	KZT 3.75 million
	Create new competitive enterprises	Provision of production infrastructure for new business initiatives	274 projects	KZT 80.7 billion	KZT 270.7 million
		Provision of infrastructure in industrial zones	24 industrial zones supported		
7-10: Provision of non-financial support services	Informational and analytic support to entrepreneurship	Develop and release informational and analytical reference books, and training and methodological aids	13 000 information documents	KZT 4.2 billion	n.a.
			80 organised TV programmes in mass media featuring information		
			112 organised lectures, seminars and master classes		
	Improve entrepreneurial competencies	Provide training in the basics of entrepreneurship; skills enhancement courses for specialists and top SME managers	Train 75 000 entrepreneurs	KZT 2.2 billion	KZT 29 800
			Reimbursement of employee training and foreign expert attraction costs - 9 projects		
			Reimbursement of costs for skills improvement - 50 enterprises		
		Provide service support to entrepreneurs/ SMEs	150 000 entrepreneurs	KZT 8.1 billion	KZT 53 344
		Consultations to existing enterprises on permits and technical documents	2 000 entrepreneurs		

	Enhance productivity of entrepreneurs	Provision of external consultants on issues of new managerial methods and introduction of production technologies (senior experts), enhancement of productivity and energy saving (European Bank of Reconstruction and Development SME support), and technological development	420 external consultants attracted (covering all issues)	KZT 517.4 million	KZT 1.23 million
			50 entrepreneurs reimbursed for costs of development and/or expertise on investment project plans	KZT 1.5 billion	
			15 entrepreneurs reimbursed for costs of upgrading technological processes	n.a.	n.a.
			15 entrepreneurs reimbursed for costs of enhancing work organisation efficiency	n.a.	n.a.
			117 entrepreneurs reimbursed for costs of product and quality management systems certification in accordance with international standards (ISO, etc.)	KZT 562 Million	KZT 4.8 million
	Promote business connections of Kazakh SMEs with foreign partners; promote local manufactured goods	Support for entrepreneurs foreign travel (Business Connections Programme)	150 entrepreneurs	KZT 1.2 billion	KZT 8.14 million
		Training of SME employees involved in the promotion of products and services to foreign markets	236 SMEs reimbursed for costs of training employees in the management of promotion of local manufactured goods, and promotion of domestic products and services	KZT 1 billion	KZT 4.24 million
Prevention of currency risks for entrepreneurs having revenue in foreign currency (and bank loans) due to fluctuations in foreign currency exchange rates	Prevent transformation of currency risks to credit risks	Interest rate subsidies for bank loans in national and foreign currencies through second-tier banks and leasing companies	280 projects	Not identified as a separate budget item (included in total budget amounts for interest rate subsidies)	n.a.
Other actions		Payment for services of financial agencies/organisations authorised to render microloans under the BRM Programme	n.a.	KZT 4.06 billion	n.a.
		Payment of subsidies of Damu Fund to second-tier banks on projects to improve and strengthen entrepreneurs' capacities	n.a.	KZT 910 million	n.a.

Source: Information from: Republic of Kazakhstan (2015), "Unified Program of Business Support and Development 'Business Road Map 2020", Section 4, Tables 1-11, and Section 8.

The Figures and Tables above give an impression of the distribution of the budget allocation of BRM 2020 by policy objective, type of policy support and policy action area. At first sight, the distribution that is revealed may not be fully adjusted to the different relative needs, although further analysis would be needed to confirm this. In particular, in order to meet the government's higher-level objectives for expanding the economic contribution of SMEs and entrepreneurship to the economy, more attention is likely to be required to expanding the number of new businesses in underdeveloped regions, creating new competitive enterprises, and providing non-financial support to increase the capabilities and productivity of SMEs and entrepreneurs.

A more formal portfolio approach to budget and impact assessment would help inform policy

It is not straightforward to gain an overview of the distribution of policy effort across different types of programme and target enterprise, as presented above. This is because the relevant data for BRM 2020 are spread across various documents, certain key information for BRM 2020 is not available (notably expenditures on reducing currency risks) and various programmes with SME and entrepreneurship development activities operate outside the scope of BRM 2020, thus requiring drawing information from other government departments. The latter include activities for innovative start-ups in the strategic plan of the National Agency for Technological Development (NATD), and various self-employment and SME development measures in government strategies for employment, agriculture and regional development for example.

However, such information should be gathered, presented and discussed regularly. This would facilitate assessments of the extent to which the distribution of SME and entrepreneurship policy effort matches the needs, and whether there are policy gaps or duplications. All government ministries and agencies should be required to keep a tally of their expenditures on policy measures targeted to SMEs and entrepreneurship and to report this budget to the Entrepreneurship Development Department of the Ministry of National Economy for collation and presentation. Ideally, this exercise would include reporting of expenditures by the main type of SME and entrepreneurship development barrier that the expenditure addresses (or type of policy intervention – innovation, training, financing etc.) and the main type of enterprise or entrepreneur targeted (start-ups, growth firms etc.).

In a further step, it is useful to compare the utilisation of policy support and the impacts achieved across these categories of intervention and enterprise types, as a guide to making decisions on how to reorient expenditures to where the most benefits can be achieved in relation to costs. This implies undertaking comparable, robust evaluations of the impact of different measures and assessing how value for money varies across different categories of interventions.

Box 4.3. Developing policy portfolio information for SME and entrepreneurship policy – a basic model and explanation

The portfolio approach to presenting and examining the distribution of SME and entrepreneurship programme expenditures and impacts allows an overview of relative policy efforts and their effectiveness and efficiency across different types of programme and support for different stages of enterprise development.

The precise categories of programme intervention to be included in the portfolio depend on the nature of the SME and entrepreneurship challenges in the country and the structure of existing SME and entrepreneurship programme support. The Table below sets out a generic framework that can be adapted to different country contexts.

A number of typical programme focus areas are set out – which can be thought of in terms of the principle barrier or market failure that each programme seeks to address. Some programmes may cover more than one programme focus area. In these cases, the programme can be attributed to the main focus area it relates to or be split if feasible according to components falling in different focus areas.

A number of typical enterprise development stages are also set out. These reflect the path taken by entrepreneurs from conception of the business idea (pre-nascent), through feasibility assessment (nascent), to start-up, and through to operating the business, or moving into growth or internationalisation or seeking to restructure. Again, the categories are not always mutually exclusive, and some attribution to main enterprise development stage or division across enterprise development stages may be required.

Focusing on different categories of programmes and the enterprise life cycle allows an integrated set of support to be developed that can take "would-be" entrepreneurs, over a number of years, from the pre-nascent stage to start-up, expansion and internationalisation, with business support systematically addressing market failures in key areas of each life cycle stage, such as education and training, information and advice, and finance.

The appropriate distribution of funding is not likely to be equal across all cells of the table, because some types of intervention are likely to be more relevant for some enterprise development stages. For example, entrepreneurship training or information, advice and mentoring are more likely to be needed by pre-nascent entrepreneurs or someone in the process of getting a new business started, while an established SME is more likely to warrant strategic government interventions to promote productivity and growth improvements through technology improvement and adoption.

What is important to establish, is rather whether there is adequate expenditure for each of the key market failure areas and enterprise development stages, and whether evidence on utilisation of the support by companies and the impact that it has confirms or calls into question the current mix of policy effort.

A generic portfolio framework for SME and entrepreneurship programme intervention

		Programme Categories (focus areas)					
Enterprise Segments (A-G) (enterprise development stages)		1 Education, training	2 Information, advice, mentoring	3 Access to finance	4 Market access/ development	5 Technology, innovation	Total by business stage
A	Pre-nascent	1A	2A	3A	4A	5A	
B	Nascent	1B	2B	3B	4B	5B	
C	Start-up	1C	2C	3C	4C	5C	
D	Operation	1D	2D	3D	4D	5D	
E	Growth	1E	2E	3E	4E	5E	
F	International	1F	2F	3F	4F	5F	
G	Adjust / exit	1G	2G	3G	4G	5G	
Total by programme category							

In the case of Kazakhstan, figures to fill the cells would be based on the list of projects and budgets from all programmes and interventions, including those in the BRM 2020, the ERM 2020, the NATD, and others. Based on a description of the programme, it would be allocated:

- A programme focus category, and (if applicable and feasible in terms of budget breakdown) additional programme focus categories; and
- A stage of enterprise development (or stages of enterprise development), which the policy measure appears to address.

Information can then be allocated to each cell on the total budget and the total number of assisted entrepreneurs/SMEs. For example, the total for cell 1A would represent the total budget for all programmes/projects which provide education or training to pre-nascent entrepreneurs. If possible, the table could be expanded to include the number of assisted entrepreneurs and impact evaluation results for that programme focus area (on, for example, job creation, business start-up rates, SME growth, increases in productivity, etc.). When completed for all focus areas and target enterprise groups, the tables would provide comparative information on intervention spending, usage, effectiveness and efficiency.

An analysis of the completed table(s) would help to identify where there are relative gaps in programme activity, and where a reallocation of resources could improve the performance of the whole portfolio of the government's budget investments.

The comparison has to recognise that there are different objectives of different interventions and that it is not possible to compare all interventions on a single measure. It also has to recognise that, according to the priorities of government, certain objectives may merit greater spending than others. However, it is only by clearly setting out expenditures and impacts that informed decisions can be made about the balance of effort across the portfolio.

The policy portfolio categorisation facilitates the assessment of the mix of SME and entrepreneurship policy efforts because it permits more precise identification of the target segments that need to be addressed. It also makes the allocation and management of the entire budget portfolio more transparent. In the longer term, including both budget and evaluation information on different programmes, it would be much clearer as to which market failures policy funds are being invested in, and what sort of return on investment might be achieved.

The Government of Kazakhstan has gone some way towards a portfolio assessment. The BRM 2020 and other relevant programmes contain target indicators on impacts to be achieved by key economic sectors and there is monitoring against these targets. The various SME and entrepreneurship development institutions, as independent entities, also have targets and monitoring plans. Furthermore, the Government of Kazakhstan has to some extent recognised the staged approach to SME and entrepreneurship development in its policy measures. This basic framework can be developed into a more systematic approach. This would set out all expenditures by types of target enterprise (e.g. nascent entrepreneurs, micro enterprises, small enterprises, medium-sized enterprises, high-growth potential enterprises, entrepreneurs and enterprises in manufacturing and priority sectors, and entrepreneurs and enterprises in under-developed regions etc.) and programme type (e.g. access to finance, innovation, workforce training support, business advice and management development, entrepreneurship skills etc.). It would eventually include the results of systematic evaluation of impacts of different types of interventions in order to signal which types of interventions and enterprise targets deliver the greatest returns to public investment.

The Entrepreneurship Development Department of the Ministry of Economy could start by making an inventory of all government-supported policy measures (programmes, projects) in support of SME and entrepreneurship development including those managed by other ministries and agencies. The second step would involve categorising each of those measures according to the main policy focus and stage of the enterprise life cycle. An illustrative example of how the current policy measures in Kazakhstan could be categorised in a portfolio framework is provided in Table 4.3 The third step could involve would be attaching budget expenditures to each of the programmes and totalling the amount in each cell, and calculating the totals across life-cycle stages and across policy focus areas. The final step would be to add monitoring and evaluation data across the portfolio to determine the comparative impact of expenditures allocated to each of the policy focus areas.

Table 4.3. Illustrative example of a potential policy portfolio framework for SME and entrepreneurship policy interventions in Kazakhstan

Policy and programme categories (1-7)		Enterprise segments (A-F)						
		A	B	C	D	E	F	
		Pre-nascent/ nascent entrepreneurs	Business start-ups	Self-employed/ microenterprises	Established SMEs	High-growth firms	Exporters	Total funding allocation (KZT)
1	Education training, skills development	Business Advisor programme; School of Young Entrepreneurs, etc. (BRM); Atameken Startup	Damu-Komek programme (Damu); Atameken Startup	Entrepreneurship training (ERM)	Retraining of SME workers (ERM)		Business Connections programme (BRM)	
2	Information/ knowledge	Awareness campaigns (BRM)	Analytical information and promotion of state support programmes (BRM)	Analytical information and promotion of state support programmes (BRM)	Analytical information and promotion of state support programmes (BRM)		Analytical information and promotion of state support programmes (BRM); informational and analytical support for exporters (National Chamber of Entrepreneurs)	
3	Finance		Microloans (Damu); Micro-credit (ERM); Partial loan guarantee programme (Damu); Start-up grant (Damu)	Microcredit (ERM); Micro-lending for women entrepreneurs (Damu)	Microloans (Damu); Interest rate subsidies (Damu); Partial loan guarantees (Damu)	Venture capital programmes	Export credit insurance/ financing (KazExportGarant); 50% reimbursement of costs for promotion of products abroad (BRM)	
4	Market access & development				Business Connections programme (BRM); Procurement and supply chain initiatives (World Bank SME Competitiveness Project)		Reimbursement of product promotion activities (BRM) and participation in trade fairs (National Chamber of Entrepreneurs);	

							Study abroad component of Business Connections Programme (BRM)	
5	Upgrading/ productivity enhancement				Senior Experts Programme (BRM); Subsidisation of costs for foreign experts (BRM)			
6	Technology/ innovations		Technology business incubators (NATD); Commercialisation Centres (NATD); Innovation grants (NATD)		Commercialisation support (Commercialisation Centres-NATD); Industrial design offices (NATD); projects supported by the SECs in region; Centres for Technological Development (Autonomous Cluster Fund)	KazINNO Program of Accelerated Development of Innovation Projects (NATD); venture capital funding (Autonomous Cluster Fund); R&D financing (Autonomous Cluster Fund)	Incubation and acceleration activities for world-class, export-oriented services companies (Autonomous Cluster Fund)	
7	Counselling, advice, consultancy	Entrepreneurship Support Centres (NCE)	Entrepreneurship Support Centres (NCE)	Entrepreneurship Support Centres (NCE)	Consultation services (8 topics) (BRM); BAS programme (EBRD)	BAS programme (EBRD) (cost of EGP component)	Export Service Support (National Chamber of Entrepreneurs)	
Total funding allocation (KZT)								

Note: Each cell would be populated with the main relevant policy measures covering all measures across government including from the Business Road Map (BRM), Employment Road Map (ERM), the National Agency for Technology Development (NATD), the Damu Entrepreneurship Development Fund (Damu), the National Chamber of Entrepreneurs, and projects funded by the Government of Kazakhstan in collaboration with the European Bank for Reconstruction and Development (EBRD) and the World Bank SME Competitiveness Project (World Bank SME Competitiveness Project). For each measure, the portfolio analysis would include information of the expenditure, the number of assisted entrepreneurs and SMEs and outcomes (e.g. start-up rates, jobs created, improvements in productivity, gains in sales/exports, etc.).
Source: OECD categorisation of programmes using information from the Ministry of National Economy.

Programme delivery arrangements

A range of organisations manage business support to SMEs and entrepreneurs

A number of public support programmes are delivered to SMEs and entrepreneurs in the form of finance, advice, training and so on. Effective arrangements for delivering these programmes will be critical to ensuring policy success. In Kazakhstan, the main delivery organisations include the Damu Entrepreneurship Development Fund, the National Chamber of Entrepreneurs (NCE), the National Agency for Technological Development (NATD) and the Autonomous Cluster Fund. Figure 4.5 maps the role of these and other actors in the delivery of SME and entrepreneurship support programmes. The nature and appropriateness of these delivery arrangements are discussed below.

Figure 4.5. Schematic of the main organisations delivering support to SMEs and entrepreneurship in Kazakhstan

Entrepreneurship and business development support infrastructure

- 18 Entrepreneurship Service Centres
- 188 Entrepreneurship Support Centres, including 27 in mono-industry towns
- 14 Mobile Entrepreneurship Support Centres servicing rural areas
- 21 business incubators (2011 data)
- 16 DAMU regional offices (deliver some business support components of the BRM)
- Network of partner universities (deliver entrepreneurship and SME management training in partnership with DAMU and the NCE; some student incubators)
- Network of private consultancy firms (deliver business development services to SMEs)
- Call centre and business portal
- 16 Socio-Entrepreneurial Corporations (SECs) (support business projects in the regions)
- National Chamber of Entrepreneurs (support for exporters)
- 10 Special Economic Zones (sites and premises and incentives for new business initiatives)
- Youth Business Kazakhstan (MOST)
- Public Fund for Youth Entrepreneurship "Atameken Startup"
- Junior Achievement Kazakhstan (entrepreneurship education)

Business innovation support infrastructure

- National Agency for Technological Development (NATD) (support to innovative start-ups and enterprises)
- 43 Centres/Offices of Technology Commercialisation in universities and scientific research institutes
- 21 Commercialisation Offices in universities and research institutes
- 5 regional Innovation Development Centres
- 5 International Technology Transfer Centres
- 5 Industrial (engineering) Design Offices
- 8 Technology Parks
- 2 Innovation Clusters (Park of Innovative Technologies and innovation cluster at Nazarbayev University)
- Joint centres for technological development with multinational enterprises (Autonomous Cluster Fund)

Financing for SMEs and entrepreneurs

- DAMU Entrepreneurship Development Fund (concessional loans, guarantees, start-up grants, microloans)
- Ministry of Healthcare and Social Development (microcredit)
- Development Bank of Kazakhstan (NBK) (mostly financing large enterprises but some support for SMEs; some lending to second tier banks for non-energy industrial enterprises).
- JSC Fund of Financial Support to Agriculture
- Partner banks and leasing companies delivering DAMU financing products
- KazMicroFinance (KMF)
- KazAgroFinance (micro lending to agricultural SMEs and rural businesses, interest rate subsidies for credit/lease agreements to acquire agricultural machinery)
- 1 643 microcredit organisations (only 740 of which are active)
- KazExportGerant (responsible for financing of trade export operations)
- Kazna Capital Management (Fund of funds to promote an efficient private equity market)
- State-funded venture capital funds
- Joint venture capital funds supported by multinational enterprises (Autonomous Cluster Fund)
- National Network of Business Angels of Kazakhstan
- 16 Socio-Entrepreneurial Corporations (SECs) (co-financing for SME investment projects)

Source: OECD based on information supplied by the Ministry of National Economy and from official documents and reports.

National Chamber of Entrepreneurs (NCE)

The NCE plays the key role in entrepreneurship and business development support. It was created in 2013 as the official representative organisation for SMEs and entrepreneurs in Kazakhstan, replacing the former National Chamber of Commerce and Industry. By law, registered and active SMEs and private entrepreneurs are obliged to become members of the NCE. The NCE is designated in BRM 2020 as the main channel for delivering government information, training, and consulting services to SMEs and entrepreneurs through a network of Entrepreneurship Support Centres (ESCs). Exceptions are delivery of the component "co-financing of consulting projects to leading enterprises using external consultants" (a programme run independently by EBRD) and the SME management training delivered by the Damu Entrepreneurship Development Fund.

The ESCs are generally hosted by the NCE in major cities, mono-industry towns and small settlements, but may also be hosted in the Damu regional offices and those local governments that have a budget to host centres. The first ESCs opened in 2013 in the regional offices of the Damu Entrepreneurship Development Fund but there has been rapid expansion of the network since then. In 2015, there were 206 fixed ESCs across the country (18 in the regional centres and Astana, Almaty, Semey and Turkestan, and 188 in other regional centres, small towns and mono-industry towns). In addition, there were 14 Mobile Entrepreneurship Support Centres (MESCs) to meet the needs of SMEs and entrepreneurs located in rural areas.

The ESCs provide a full range of free information services, training courses, and consulting services. Each ESC is staffed with a number of expert consultants offering advice in eight areas: the creation of a business, accounting and taxation, marketing and business planning, information technology, legal regulation, customs procedures, the implementation of quality management systems, and public procurement. In addition, the ESC consultants accompany the client through the entire process of obtaining state support from the BRM 2020 programme and other programmes, including consideration of applications for training programmes. The NCE worked with 57 private consultancies (through a competitive process) to provide these advisory services to existing SMEs across the country. The quality and capacity of private sector trainers and consultants benefited considerably from capacity building efforts of the USAID-funded Kazakhstan Small Business Development Project (2006–2010) and continues to be enhanced by the EBRD's Small Business Advisory Service.

The ESCs are designed to work through a "one-window" integrated approach offering a range of training, counselling and information support through single points of service delivery. This significantly increases the efficiency and stability of the activity, and reduces the time and cost for SMEs and entrepreneurs to access appropriate support. The decision to establish the ESC network with extensive regional coverage was an important policy action because it has led to the elimination of a large gap in the business support infrastructure. Before the advent of this network there was no uniform and centralised business support infrastructure, consulting services were unregulated and costly, and coverage of SMEs and entrepreneurs was negligible outside of the main cities (Toxanova and Zhakupova, 2011).

One of the limitations of the approach to business consulting is that in order to obtain support, individual entrepreneurs and Limited Liability Partnerships must provide copies of their certificate of state registration, identity card/charter, and tax return, together with an application form, a seal and a service agreement. Such requirements are not typical for an organisation which operates on the "one-window" principle and should be simplified to make the service more accessible.

Damu Entrepreneurship Development Fund

The Damu Entrepreneurship Development Fund is the main co-ordinator of state financial support to SMEs and entrepreneurs. It works through relationships with second-tier banks, leasing companies, and micro-credit organisations and does not engage in direct lending to SMEs. Through well-trained staff operating in a branch in each region of Kazakhstan, it manages relationships with its partner financial institutions and monitors the allocation financing to SME projects against targets. It operates under the basic principle of non-interference in the internal procedures of partners for allocating financing to specific SME and entrepreneurship projects. Previously, it was involved in selection of applications from individual SMEs and entrepreneurs for the loan guarantee programme, but this is now performed only by banks. In general, the Fund no longer provides non-financial services to SMEs and entrepreneurs since their transfer to the NCE in 2015, although it still delivers SME management training through partner universities.

Damu has used a set of financial instruments which have acted directly in the financial market and, in a more normal financial situation, would have caused real distortion. These interventions, in particular a heavy reliance on interest rate subsidies, have been necessary in a period when the commercial banks have been restructuring their balance sheets and where inevitably "commercial" interest rates have been excessively high. Nonetheless, this situation will not last indefinitely and Damu needs to have a strategy for withdrawal from the market by emphasising targeted instruments which address specific market failures. Damu's current development strategy uses general SME support agencies with a full range of services as benchmarks (SRING Singapore, PARP Poland, KOSGEB Turkey, SBA USA etc.) and possibly as an aspiration for the sort of organisation it can become. However, this strategy was written before non-financial SME support programmes were transferred to NCE and it would seem appropriate that Damu should revisit it in this light, considering how it can develop as a specialist SME financial institution in the future, making comparisons with specialist SME finance institutions (such as NAFIN in Mexico, KfW in Germany, and SME Bank in the Russian Federation).

National Agency for Technological Development (NATD)

The NATD, under the direction of the JSC Holding Company Baiterek, is the main operator of instruments of state support for business innovation. Its mandate is to support innovation projects and promote the transfer of technologies in priority sectors. In this role, it provides financing (*e.g.* matching grants) for innovation projects (*e.g.* proof of concept, prototype development, patenting, technology adaptation, training, etc.).

It is also responsible for establishing innovation infrastructure. In 2010, it launched a network of 8 science and technology parks and technological business incubators, and in 2012 it introduced new instruments to support innovative start-ups. It operates 21 Commercialisation Offices (located in universities and research institutes), 5 regional Innovation Development Centres, 5 international technology transfer centres, and 5 Industrial Design Offices and venture funds. It also supports the creation of innovation clusters to encourage industrial innovation, such as the Park of Innovative Technologies (coalition of 12 universities and 16 scientific research institutes), and the innovation cluster at Nazarbayev University. It also supports venture capital funds. The NATD aims to expand this innovation support infrastructure further by 2023, including the creation of innovation workshops, fab-labs[5], and co-working centres.

These interventions may be important in supporting innovative start-ups. Commercialisation projects are a top priority for the NATD, which has established a target of increasing their share from 15% of all projects in 2014 to 30% in 2023, although targets for the number of innovative start-ups from incubation and acceleration support appear to be modest (NATD, 2014).

The Autonomous Cluster Fund

The Autonomous Cluster Fund implements the Start Up Kazakhstan programme to attract high-tech SME entities to Kazakhstan and provide incubation and acceleration support.

The delivery structure is well-constructed but young

A significant part of the current business support system has been established relatively recently, for example the ESCs were first established in 2013, the technological incubators in 2011 and the NCE in 2015. It will take more time for these organisations to build capacity and experience in delivering a full range of efficient and effective services. Investing in the professional development of managers and staff, developing performance standards, and monitoring impacts of support on clients will continue to be necessary.

In particular, attention needs to be paid to improving the quality of the entrepreneurship and SME advice and training by, for example, certifying consultants and trainers. At present, state programmes, primarily through the ESCs, employ several hundred "Business Advisors" of varying levels of competency and quality, who are tasked with providing free services to SMEs throughout the country. Each Centre has a number of stations staffed by the advisors, each limited to a certain area of competence, for example marketing, business planning, legal and regulatory requirements, or accounting and finance. When the Centres were launched, the business advisors participated in a three-day training course provided by the EBRD. However, this is a limited amount of professional development to ensure all advisors have the competence required. One area of specialisation per station may also cause some frustrations for potential and existing entrepreneurs who need advice in a number of areas.

Business incubation services should be boosted

According to USAID (2012), there were only 21 business incubators in Kazakhstan in 2011, only some of which were functioning as proper spaces for the incubation of promising start-ups with the full range of advisory and mentoring support required as well as access to seed capital. Compared to the United States, where the density of business incubators was one incubator per 280 000 persons (Ernst &Young, 2010), the density in Kazakhstan was only one incubator per 780 000 persons, suggesting that there is further room for their development.

Although the NATD supports technological incubators at universities and the Socio-Entrepreneurial Corporations (SECs) run 5 incubators, the concept of general or sector-specialised business incubators (e.g. for media, food processing, crafts, design, arts, or consulting) is not yet well developed in Kazakhstan. This type of incubator could be supported by BRM 2020. They would include incubation environments to support promising non-technological start-ups and to play a role in promoting and supporting entrepreneurship in a broad sense, for example acting as centres to facilitate exporting and internationalisation activity or the development of productive clusters.

Many OECD governments have developed a national business incubator policy and subsequent programmes including support for non-technological projects. In Kazakhstan, the government could start with an assessment of the demand for incubation support in different sectors and the associated services required, leading to further support to start-ups in the manufacturing and service sectors that are not necessarily high technology driven. The policy should also seek to strengthen the involvement of private sector companies in investing in and managing business incubators.

Business support should be more integrated

SMEs and entrepreneurs frequently require a mix of different business supports to effectively meet their challenges. However, the business supports available in Kazakhstan tend to be delivered individually. Mechanisms are therefore needed to provide more holistic responses that treat the needs of each client in a comprehensive way.

At the same time, the accessibility of the relevant business support programmes to businesses is complicated by the need to deal with a number of disparate government agencies to obtain assistance on a programme-by-programme basis. There were more than 140 programmes and tools of state support for SME and entrepreneurship development being implemented by various departmental institutions in 2013[6]. Transparency and ease of access to information about the programmes has been somewhat improved by the creation of the single-window business portal www.business.gov.kz, but SMEs and entrepreneurs may still have difficulty identifying the most relevant programmes to them and still need to complete separate applications to each programme. More integrated support would help address these problems. This will require coordination and cooperation between the agencies responsible for different programmes, in particular between the Damu Entrepreneurship Development Fund and the NCE.

An effort to increase integration across programmes was undertaken in 2013 by putting the Damu Entrepreneurship Development Fund, the NATD and eight other state organisations involved in economic development programmes under the strategic management of the JSC National Holding Company Baiterek. SME support is one of the five strategic directions of Baiterek. In this role, Baiterek aims to ensure the effective and complementary functioning of this group of organisations. It has responsibility for introducing centralised approaches to planning, budgeting, corporate governance, establishing and monitoring key performance indicators, and raising the quality and productivity of staff. It also plays a role in raising the level of client orientation of the organisations under its umbrella and increasing awareness among target audiences about their work.

Baiterek has also begun to introduce "package offers" in SME support, whereby a number of the tools of the different Baiterek subsidiaries will be integrated to form coherent product lines, depending on the needs of clients (Republic of Kazakhstan, 2014a). A "support for SMEs" package will combine the various financial supports available (including NATD grants) with entrepreneur competences programmes and innovation support. Another "support for innovative companies" package will combine the NATD grants, venture capital, NATD competency development programmes, and support for business infrastructure. Furthermore, a "support for exporters package", targeting export-oriented enterprises, will include credit insurance, conditional funding through second tier banks, leasing and advisory support (Table 4.4).

Table 4.4. Description of packaged instruments enabling SMEs to access a full range of services according to their needs

Package	Support for SMEs package	Support for innovative companies package	Support for exporters package
Instruments	Co–financing of credits with second tier banks (Damu) Conditional financing (Damu) Guarantees (Damu) Subsidies (Damu) Leasing (DBK–leasing) Leasing of domestic equipment (DBK–leasing) Interbank crediting (DBK) Grants (NATD) Development of entrepreneur competences and innovation support (Damu, NATD)	Grants (NATD) Venture capital (Kazyna Capital Management) Competency development programmes (NATD) Providing business infrastructure (NATD)	Credit insurance (KazExportGarant – KEG) Conditional financing through the second tier banks (KEG) Leasing of domestic equipment (DBK–leasing) Advisory support for exporters (KEG, KazNexInvest)

Source: The development strategy of National Managing Holding 'Baiterek' joint stock company for 2014-2013.

There will be some issues for Baiterek to address in implementing this new approach, specifically regarding how to organise the entry point for SMEs and entrepreneurs. Nonetheless the attempt to integrate programme interventions is very promising and could be extended in other ways. The NCE for example could also increasingly package some of its services.

Monitoring and evaluation of SME policies, strategies and programmes

Monitoring and evaluation arrangements are clear

Legislation in Kazakhstan provides for a relatively sophisticated system for monitoring and evaluation of government plans, strategies and programmes. Ten-year strategic plans are evaluated every five years, taking into consideration the outputs and outcomes of all lower level programmes. State programmes and action plans are subject to annual monitoring, evaluation three years after launch, and a final evaluation at the end of the implementation period. For the most part, these monitoring and evaluation reports are prepared by the implementing ministry or agency. Additional monitoring and evaluation of state programmes is conducted by the Accounts Committee of the Office of the Public Prosecutor. Sectoral programmes, including the BRM 2020, follow similar timelines for monitoring and evaluation, although a central agency in government is responsible for the three-year evaluation rather than the implementing ministry.

Monitoring is strong but impact evaluation is limited

The BRM 2020 programme specifies that monitoring and evaluation is to be carried out on three levels: (1) reporting on the number of assisted entrepreneurs/SMEs and number of services provided (by type and category of entrepreneur; number of subsidised projects, etc.; (2) assessment of the quality of the implementation of the programme tool, determined from satisfaction surveys completed by clients at the end of the intervention (sufficiency, relevance, usefulness, etc.); and (3) subjective assessment of the influence of the state support tool on the level of quality and productivity of the assisted beneficiary (information collected from post-intervention surveys of the client).

Monthly reports are prepared on statistical indicators of programme take-up; quarterly reports on the results of satisfaction surveys with assisted SMEs and entrepreneurs; and annual reports based on telephone or direct surveys with no less than 5% of all persons who accessed support measures during the year. This information is supplemented with input from seminars/consultations with entrepreneurs on the impacts of the programmes. For some programme components, the assisted entrepreneurs are asked to report on the nature of any post-intervention changes to the performance of the firm (jobs created, increases in sales, etc.) and to indicate what percentage of that change they consider could be attributed to the intervention.

This is a systematic approach that builds monitoring and evaluation into all programmes. However, the approach to monitoring the allocation of budgets, outputs, quality of services and quality of co-ordination, is stronger than the evaluation of impacts. There are three key issues that need to be addressed.

Firstly, although some evidence is obtained on programme impacts from enquiries to certain beneficiaries, who are asked to identify how the programme affected their business performance, to determine the "true" impact would require a more systematic and robust evaluation of changes in the performance of assisted firms compared to a control group of similar SMEs that did not participate in the programme.

In its framework for the evaluation of SME and entrepreneurship policies and programmes, OECD (2007) draws a distinction between "monitoring" and "evaluation" (see Box 4.4). Monitoring relies exclusively upon the views of the recipients of the policy (Steps I to III), and Evaluation (Steps IV to VI) seeks, by some means, to contrast recipient views about performance results with the performance of non-recipients in order to account for the "counter factual", *i.e.* what would have happened without the intervention. More attention is needed in Kazakhstan to the use of these Step IV to Step VI techniques of evaluation.

Box 4.4. Methods for monitoring and evaluating SME and entrepreneurship policies and programmes

Monitoring

Step I	Assessment of degree of take-up of schemes
Step II	Recipients' opinions on the quality and relevance of the schemes
Step III	Recipients' views of the difference made by the assistance

Evaluation (contrasts performance of recipients with those of non-recipients to identify the impact after accounting for the "counter factual").

Step IV	Comparison of performance of assisted with "typical" SMEs (e.g. changes in sales, employment, productivity)
Step V	Comparison of assisted with "matched" firms (non-assisted SMEs with similar size, sector, geography, etc.)
Step VI	Comparisons that take account of selection bias

Higher steps give the policymaker greater confidence in being able to attribute changes in supported businesses to participation in the programme.

Source: OECD (2007), OECD Framework for the Evaluation of SME and Entrepreneurship Policies and Programmes, p. 106.

An example of a robust (Step VI) approach to evaluating programme impact is given in Box 4.5.

Box 4.5. Impact evaluation of innovation support programmes for Danish businesses

Description of the approach

The Danish government is committed to undertaking high quality impact evaluations of its support programmes. In carrying out an assessment of Danish innovation support programmes, the Danish Agency for Science, Technology and Innovation (DASTI) aimed to estimate the impact on the growth of productivity in participating firms. The evaluation included observations for firms participating in a number of innovation support programmes, including Innovation Agents (subsidising consultants that help firms identify barriers to innovation by performing an "innovation check"), Innovation Consortia (connecting researchers and firms via research networks), Innovation Networks (support to establish innovation and cluster networks), Innovation Vouchers (supporting firms to purchase consultancy from specialists), Innovation Assistants (incentives for firms to hire highly-qualified persons), and the Industrial PhD Programme (funding internships for PhD students in private sector firms). The approach compared the productivity growth performance of assisted firms to a control group of non-assisted firms. Although firms of all sizes may qualify for participation in the various innovation support programmes, the assessment was restricted to two sets of firms, those with less than 500 employees and those with less than 100 employees.

The Innovation Denmark database identified all the firms that had received innovation supports (8 300 firms). The control group of non-assisted firms was sourced from the Statistics Denmark business registry database (1.3 million firms). Because the two databases use a common business registration (identifier) number, DASTI was able to match programme participants to similar firms in the registry database, including on firm revenue, value-added, number of employees, full-time employment equivalents, skills of employees, and industry classification. The control group sample was further fine-tuned to eliminate firms in industries where there were no programme participants, firms with more than 500 workers, and any firms that could not be observed for at least four years. A further estimation sample was restricted to only firms with less than 100 employees with the objective of assessing the performance impact on smaller versus larger firms. Because the evaluation sought to observe differences in productivity growth for two years and to control for historical productivity growth, the only participant firms included were those that did not receive support in the two years before and after the evaluation. After controlling for other variables such as these, the final evaluation sample included data for 1 140 assisted firms and 87 719 non-participating control group firms.

The evaluation applied a well-formulated firm level production function and linear regression model (ordinary least squares estimation with fixed effects) to the data. A two year time period was selected for measuring the productivity growth (2005 to 2007), primarily because one year is too short to allow for impacts and longer periods led to the loss of too many observations. Key control variables in the regression equation were: 1) initial share of workers holding a bachelor degree (as a proxy for labour skills, an indicator of a firm's ability to absorb new technology); 2) industry specific trends in productivity growth and time varying trends in productivity affecting all firms; 3) lagged productivity growth in the firms, to deal with the possibility that participating firms could have already been growing at a faster pace than non-participating firms prior to receiving the support, 4) a firm size variable to account for the possibility that large firms may increase productivity at a slower pace than smaller, low-productive firms that are catching up, or that large firms may increase productivity faster because they are well-established and better able to absorb new knowledge and technology.

Results revealed that compared to non-assisted firms, firms participating in innovation support programmes grew an average of 2.5-2.9 percentage points faster per year over a two year period following initialisation of the project. However, the results varied by type of programme. No differences with the control group were found for firms participating in the Industrial PhD and Innovation Agents programmes. The Innovation Consortia increased productivity growth rates by 2.7 to 4.1 percentage points, Innovation Networks by 3.6 to 4.0 percentage points, Innovation Vouchers Scheme by 3.5 percentage points and Innovation Assistants by up to 4.1 percentage points. Finally, the impacts on productivity growth were estimated at 2.7 to 3.2 percentage points for firms with less than 100 employees compared with 2.5 to 2.9 percentage points for firms with up to 500 employees.

Factors for success

Critical to the success of this evaluation approach was the availability and quality of a programme database with good information on key variables (sector, size, output, employment etc.) for the programme participants before and during and after the intervention. DASTI set out in advance the required data to be collected for programme participants in terms of firm characteristics, programme inputs, and firm performance levels. In addition, the availability of information from the business register was critical to identifying a control group of similar non-assisted firms and comparing their performance over time with the assisted firms.

Obstacles and responses

By developing the Innovation Denmark database and using a common business identifier number, DASTI was able to work with Statistics Denmark to construct a rigorous sample of assisted and non-assisted firms. However, in other circumstances a database providing information for matched control group firms may not be available. Options for evaluation in these circumstances may include comparing the results for assisted firms with those of comparably similar firms that applied to the programme but were rejected (the non-treatment control group). This would require collecting data on all firms that applied to the programme and monitoring their performance over time.

Relevance to the Republic of Kazakhstan

The impact evaluation approach of the Ministry of National Economy in Kazakhstan is largely based on follow-up surveys with assisted SMEs and entrepreneurs, including their use of the programme, their satisfaction and certain outputs. More robust evaluation methodologies using control groups of non-assisted entrepreneurs and SMEs could increase the accuracy of the evaluation evidence. The Economic Research Institute has the capacity to perform such control group based evaluations. To assist such an effort it would be important to develop a database covering key characteristics of SMEs and entrepreneurs accessing support public programmes (the Damu Entrepreneurship Development Fund, the NCE Entrepreneurs Support Centres), the NATD, business incubators, etc), and their performance over time.

Further information

For a detailed description of the approach and econometric methods used in the programme evaluation, see: DASTI (Danish Agency for Science, Technology and Innovation) (2014), The Short-run Impact on Total Factor Productivity Growth of the Danish Innovation and Research Support System, Copenhagen, Ministry of Higher Education and Science. Online at: http://ufm.dk/en/publications/2014/the-short-run-impact-on-total-factor-productivity-growth-of-the-danish-innovation-and-research-supports-system.pdf/.

More general guidance is available through the Central Innovation Manual on Excellent Econometric Evaluation of the Impact of Public R&D Investments (CIM 2.0), a manual developed by the Danish government to set the standards and requirements for econometric impact studies of public research and innovation programmes and policies.

Secondly, independent experts and organisations are not always responsible for evaluation in Kazakhstan, although this is important for the accuracy of impact results. For example, the monitoring and evaluation of BRM 2020 programmes is generally carried out by the delivery agencies themselves: in the case of financial supports, by the Damu Entrepreneurship Development Fund, and in the case of the entrepreneur competences programmes, by NCE, the organising body for the ESCs. The agencies are required to allocate qualified specialists to carry out the monitoring and evaluation but it is not clear how far independent and external specialists are used.

Thirdly, there is an issue of lack of co-ordination of monitoring and evaluation activity across government. A more systematic approach is important to providing comparative results that could assist in making choices on how to allocate resources across the SME and entrepreneurship policy portfolio. If one programme has a considerably greater impact than another, this would suggest that a resource transfer between the programmes would produce a better overall result. However, to make this comparison would require robust evaluation of the individual programmes on a broadly comparable basis and clarity about the strategic objectives that each programme seeks to achieve, for example creating new enterprises, enhancing the performance of existing SMEs, or creating high-growth enterprises.

The Economic Research Institute (ERI) (in the MNE) has a mandate for collecting and analysing information on the take-up of programmes and the level of satisfaction of recipients with the quality and usefulness of these programmes, but other implementing agencies also have their own analysis departments that collect information on their policies and programmes. This results in a fragmentation of monitoring and evaluation systems and inconsistent approaches and methods across the SME and entrepreneurship policy area. The World Bank (2015) recommends that a single unit be empowered to co-ordinate the monitoring and evaluation of SME and entrepreneurship policies and programmes across these institutions to address the existing fragmented efforts, a role that could be assumed by the ERI.

Notes

1. These conditional funds are allocated from the National Fund of Kazakhstan as well as from international financial institutions, such as the Asian Development Bank (ABD), the European Bank for Reconstruction and Development (EBRD), and the World Bank.
2. See: http://www.akorda.kz/kz/executive_office/presidential_councils/kesipkerler-kenesi/.
3. Membership is automatic and free for SMEs; only large businesses have to pay membership dues.
4. 14 priority economy sectors (56 sub-sectors) are defined in the BRM 2020: agriculture; mining; light industry and furniture production; production of construction materials and other non-metal mineral production; metallurgy, metalworking and machine building; other industry sectors (e.g. energy, waste disposal); transport and warehousing (including maintenance, servicing and repair of vehicles); tourism; information and communication; professional, scientific and technical activity; education; health care and social services; arts, entertainment and recreation; and rendering of other services (computer repair, personal services, cleaning of textile products and furs).
5. A fab-lab is a small-scale workshop generally equipped with an array of flexible computer controlled tools that provides a technical prototyping platform for innovation and invention by local talented people, including entrepreneurs.
6. http://www.business.Damu.kz/ru/.

References

DASTI (Danish Agency for Science, Technology and Innovation) (2014), The Short-run Impact on Total Factor Productivity Growth of the Danish Innovation and Research Support System, Copenhagen, Ministry of Higher Education and Science, http://ufm.dk/en/publications/2014/the-short-run-impact-on-total-factor-productivity-growth-of-the-danish-innovation-and-research-supports-system.pdf/.

EIM and Dutch Ministry of Economic Affairs (2006), "Entrepreneurship in the Netherlands: High growth enterprises, Running fast but still keeping control", Zoetermeer, Netherlands, EIM Business & Policy Research.

Ernst&Young (2010), "Survey of Russian Business Incubators", Ernst&Young, Moscow.

Lilischkis, S. (2011), "Policies in support of high-growth innovative SMEs", INNO-Grips Policy Brief No. 2, Brussels, European Commission, http://www.proinno-europe.eu/innogrips2/.

Ministry of Economic Affairs (2015), "Working Together on Growth: Enterprise Policy on Track – Progress Report on Enterprise Policy 2014", The Hague, Ministry of Economic Affairs, https://innovationpolicyplatform.org/system/files/Progress%20Report%20on%20Enterprise%20Policy%202014%20The%20Netherlands%20(vertaling%20voortgangsrapportage%20bedrijvenbeleid%202014)_0.pdf/.

Ministry of Economic Affairs (2014), "Ambitious Entrepreneurship: An agenda for start-ups and growing businesses", Letter to Parliament about ambitious entrepreneurship, The Hague, https://www.government.nl/binaries/government/documents/parliamentary-documents/2014/07/28/letter-to-parliament-about-ambitious-enterpreneurship/letter-to-parliament-about-ambitious-enterpreneurship.pdf/.

MTI (Ministry of Trade and Industry) (2007), High-Growth SME Support Initiatives in Nine Countries: Analysis, Categorization, and Recommendations, Helsinki, Ministry of Trade and Industry Publications.

NATD (National Agency for Technological Development) (2014), "Development strategy: JSC 'National Agency for Technological Development' 2014–2020", Astana.

OECD (2007), *OECD Framework for the Evaluation of SME and Entrepreneurship Policies and Programmes*, Paris, OECD Publishing, https://doi.org/10.1787/9789264040090-en.

OECD (2013), *An International Benchmarking Analysis of Public Programmes for High-Growth Firms*, OECD LEED Programme, OECD Publishing, Paris.

Republic of Kazakhstan (2014a), "The development strategy of National Managing Holding 'Baiterek' joint stock company for 2014–2013", Astana.

Republic of Kazakhstan (2014b), "The State Program of Industrial-Innovative Development of Kazakhstan for 2015–2019", Approved by the Decree of the President of the Republic of Kazakhstan dated August 1, 2014 No. 874, Astana.

Republic of Kazakhstan (2015a), "Unified Programme of Business Support and Development '*Business Road Map 2020'",* Approved by Resolution No. 168 of the Republic of Kazakhstan dated the 31st of March, 2015, Astana.

Republic of Kazakhstan (2015b), "Entrepreneurial Code of the Republic of Kazakhstan", No. 375-V, 29 October, Astana, Republic of Kazakhstan.

Suddle , K., and S.J.A. Hessels (2007), "High-Growth Support Initiatives", SCALES paper H22706, Zoetermeer, Netherlands, EIM Business & Policy Research.

Toxanova, A., and S. Zhakupova (2011), "Challenges and development prospects of SMEs in the Republic of Kazakhstan", Almaty, Economy Research Institute.

USAID (United States Agency for International Development) (2012), "Needs Assessment and recommendations regarding the implementation business incubators in Kazakhstan: Technical Assistance relating to the Implementation of the Business Road Map 2020", USAID Macroeconomic Project in Kazakhstan, Washington, DC.

World Bank (2015), "Kazakhstan - Small and Medium sized Enterprise (SME) Competitiveness Project", World Bank Group, Washington, DC.

Chapter 5. National programmes for SMEs and Entrepreneurship in Kazakhstan

This chapter examines national programmes for SMEs and entrepreneurship. It assesses national programme measures related to building the skills of entrepreneurs and SME managers; business advisory and consultancy services; raising the level of workers' skills in SMEs; improving access to finance; supporting innovation-related activity in SMEs and innovative start-ups; supporting SMEs exporting and innovation; involving SMEs in public procurement; and providing opportunities for women, youth, people with disabilities and the unemployed in entrepreneurship. Recommendations are offered for programme improvements.

Key messages and policy recommendations

There are two key programmes offering entrepreneurship training to potential entrepreneurs – Business Advisor and School for Young Entrepreneurs. These are important tools, but they currently generate few business start-ups. Actions that can be considered to help increase the conversion rate of entrepreneurship training to business start-ups include introducing tighter screening of participants (in order to focus on those with the greatest start-up motivations and talents), extending the duration of the training courses, providing trainees with complementary advisory and mentoring support, and making start-up financing more accessible to trainees.

The SME Top Management Training and the Business Connections training programmes play valuable roles in raising management competences in existing SMEs. They appear to be performing well in enabling the assisted SMEs to modernise and upgrade their business and production processes and increase their sales and employment. However, not many more than 1 000 SMEs have been participating annually. Consideration should therefore be given to scaling up these programmes.

A network of Entrepreneurship Support Centres (ESCs) offers information, advisory and consultancy services to SMEs. Their approach could be strengthened by the introduction of a business diagnostic tool that seeks to identify areas of competitive strength and weakness in SME clients. The advice and consultancy support of the ESCs could then be focused on assisting individual SMEs to address the key challenges identified. The advice and consultancy support could also focus more strongly on helping SMEs to develop a growth plan as well as to improve their productivity and efficiency. There is a programme gap in advice and consultancy and other types of assistance to high growth potential enterprises. The Enterprise Growth Programme of the European Bank for Reconstruction and Development (EBRD) is one of the few programmes that have the specific objective of fostering high-growth SMEs. An expanded programme such as this should be considered to encourage the development of more high growth potential enterprises.

The majority of the employers involved in offering placements to vocational education students in the new dual training system are large businesses. Efforts are needed to increase the involvement of SMEs. This could involve an initiative to encourage the formation of SME training consortia to support smaller firms in participating in the dual training system.

To improve access of SMEs and entrepreneurs to financing, the Damu Entrepreneurship Development Fund provides lines of credit and loan guarantees to second-tier banks for SME lending. This is very important support that could usefully be scaled up. Access to finance would also be improved by a streamlining of the number of programmes to focus on the most effective instruments. Attention is also needed to simplifying the operating procedures in order to encourage more participation in the initiatives by banks. Non-financial support should also be more systematically offered to those SMEs obtaining credit, for example advice and consultancy on issues such as innovation and internationalisation. Additional measures could also be considered to increase the range of financing options to SMEs and entrepreneurs, including expanding microfinance, factoring and leasing and equity investment finance opportunities. Developing financial literacy skills should not be neglected.

The National Agency for Technological Development (NATD) plays an important role in supporting SME innovation in Kazakhstan through grants for SME innovation projects and creating Technology Parks, Innovation Clusters, Industrial Design Bureaus,

Commercialisation Offices, and International Technology Transfer Centres. It is important to provide sufficient resources for further expansion of this innovation support infrastructure, concentrating on the structures that are most useful to SMEs, including innovation workshops, fab-labs and co-working centres. The Ministry of Education and Science plays a complementary role in supporting technology-oriented start-up businesses through grants for applied research and for spin-off enterprises from universities and research centres. An R&D tax credit is also in place, although it contains no SME-specific element. There is a need to expand the reach of these initiatives. There is also a need to fill gaps in support for innovation capabilities in SME managers (such as innovation consultancy, training and mentoring schemes), supporting SME digital technology adoption and supporting non-technological innovation.

The National Chamber of Entrepreneurs (NCE) offers a range of export promotion support, including training, online information and financial support. However, the main beneficiaries are large companies. For SMEs, some export information services are offered through the BRM 2020. However, more intensive export promotion support should be provided. This could involve consulting and coaching support to SMEs in areas such as quality, productivity and marketing, targeted to SMEs identified as having export potential. Aspects of the export support infrastructure for SMEs should also be reinforced, such as in product standards and certifications.

Important measures have been undertaken to facilitate the engagement of SMEs in public procurement. Measures introduced in 2014 include dividing public procurement contracts into smaller lots and introducing a set-aside for SME contracts. As a result, the share of SMEs in public procurement is very high, at 85%. Some further opportunities could be exploited for developing SMEs through public procurement. These include building the awareness of public procurement opportunities for SMEs that have not been involved in procurement before and introducing a certificate for SMEs that have already performed successfully in government contracts to assist them in winning further contracts.

The BRM 2020 includes targets for the participation of women and youth in mainstream entrepreneurship support programmes and there are various dedicated support programmes for these groups. For example, the Damu Entrepreneurship Development Fund operates the Women's Entrepreneurship Microlending Programme and the NCE's Council of Businesswomen offers mentoring and networking through branches in every region of the country. For youth, training is offered through the School for Young Entrepreneurs, although few receive financial support, and financing and coaching programmes are offered through the Atamaken programmes. Basic training in self-employment is available for people with disabilities through the Employment Road Map 2020 (ERM 2020) and the Komek programme, and funding for assistance equipment is organised through charitable contributions from banks. The unemployed can also receive basic training and micro credit for self-employment from the ERM 2020. This broad set of action demonstrates strong recognition of the importance of widening the opportunities for entrepreneurship to all sections of the population. At the same time, however, Kazakhstan's inclusive entrepreneurship policy could be strengthened by introducing a more systematic combination of training, advice, financing and networking support and a clear focus of support on developing stronger businesses rather than on increasing the numbers of people creating subsistence businesses.

The key recommendations of the report on improving national programmes for SME and entrepreneurship development in Kazakhstan are set out below.

Key recommendations on SME and entrepreneurship programmes

Entrepreneurship training and SME management training

- Identify and address barriers to business creation by graduates of the Business Advisor I and Business Advisor II training programmes as well as barriers to progression between the programmes. This may include making changes to the screening and selection process for applicants, the length of the training, the balance of theoretical versus practical training, the level of guidance and mentoring of the trainees, and the linkages between the training programme and sources of start-up financing.
- Increase the number of trainees supported by the School for Young Entrepreneurs and increase the level of mentoring, coaching, incubation, and post-start-up support services attached to the training.
- Increase the number of participants in the Top SME Managers Training and the Business Connections programmes by increasing the number of delivery partners and locations. Segment the training in order to create more uniform cohorts of SME managers in each training group, grouping trainees on the basis of the size and sector of their firms and their level of existing management expertise and ambitions.

Business advice, consultancy and mentoring

- Develop a business diagnostic tool to enable consultants in the Entrepreneurship Service Centres and other business support infrastructures to assess more systematically the performance of client companies, and to identify strengths, weaknesses, and areas for improvement. Use the diagnostic results to target advice, consultancy and mentoring services to the identified needs. Offer a basic online version of the diagnostic tool to enable SMEs to undertake self-assessments and obtain online guidance.
- Identify and select a group of start-ups and existing SMEs with high-growth potential and offer them a dedicated package of advice and financing aimed at addressing the challenges of high growth.

SME workforce skills development

- Introduce publicly financed SME training facilitators to support local networks of SMEs that agree to work collectively on training initiatives in co-operation with vocational education and training institutions. The role of these training facilitators should be to: encourage the voluntary formation of the networks of SMEs; help the networks to assess the joint training needs of their SME members; develop joint training plans for the networks; enter into dialogue with colleges to secure training courses tailored to the needs of the networks; encourage the SMEs to offer work placements and apprenticeships to students taking the courses; and monitor the quality of the training plans implemented, according to training standards for the occupations concerned.
- Offer grants to SMEs to cover some of the training costs of hosting apprenticeships and work placements for vocational education and training students and university students, for example by adapting the 'youth practice' component of the Employment Road Map 2020 to finance SME work placements.

Access to finance

- Undertake regular surveys, interviews, focus group discussions and programme evaluations to collect evidence on the range of financing needs and problems of SMEs and entrepreneurs and the performance of financial institutions and financial instruments in supporting access to finance. Use this information to guide development of a more diverse and balanced set of financial instruments, including a wider range of microcredit, factoring and leasing and business angel financing opportunities, in line with the OECD-G20 High-Level Principles on SME and Entrepreneurship Financing.
- Strengthen microfinance provision through the creation of an apex institution to help channel finance to microfinance institutions and support for developing skills and capabilities in microfinance organisations.
- Pilot an initiative to support leasing and factoring mechanisms for SME and entrepreneurship financing.
- Stimulate the development of a venture capital sector that finances innovative start-ups. For this purpose, provide well-designed time-limited public financing for venture capital funds, explore the feasibility of a medium-term tax incentive for investing in venture capital funds and eliminate the requirement for repayment of all public finance invested in funds. Ensure that exit strategies for venture capitalists are in place by developing a secondary market of the Stock Exchange with simplified issuing requirements for SMEs.
- Explore the feasibility and potential of tax incentives to angel investors to stimulate the development of early-stage private finance, and create awareness of angel investments through media campaigns, seminars, disseminating success stories, and founding an operational business angels' network.
- Develop information, guidance and awareness events and implement training and consultancy programmes for strengthening the financial skills of SME managers and entrepreneurs.

Support for innovative start-ups and SME innovation

- Carry out intensive and targeted actions (such as seminars, innovation fairs, innovation awards, media campaigns, etc.) to raise awareness of the importance and opportunities for innovation and digital technology adoption among SMEs.
- Expand the support infrastructure for innovation in SMEs by expanding the activities of innovation clusters, industrial design bureaus, and incubators as well as smaller structures including innovation workshops, fab-labs and co-working centres.
- Extend training, consultancy and mentoring schemes aimed specifically at developing innovation skills and capabilities among SME managers (including non-technological innovation). Such schemes should be targeted specifically towards innovation and should complement general management support.

- Expand early-stage growth funding for innovative business start-ups from universities and research institutions.

Support for SME internationalisation

- Develop a dedicated internationalisation programme for SMEs targeting the specific problems of SMEs in export readiness. This should identify companies with high export potential and provide targeted consultancy and coaching to improve productivity and quality, as well as giving general information and basic export promotion support to a wider range of SMEs.
- Strengthen the infrastructure for SME export development, including support for product testing, product standardisation and product standards certification.

Public procurement

- Further develop awareness among SMEs of procurement opportunities with public authorities through campaigns and communication strategies and consider introducing a certificate for SMEs that have already performed successfully in government contracts.

Entrepreneurship programmes for special target groups of the population

- Expand existing programmes for women, youth, people with disabilities and the unemployed and offer combined packages of access to finance, training, advice and networking support.
- Establish Women's Enterprise Centres or women's desks in the Entrepreneurship Support Centres in regions where the needs appear to be the greatest. Provide resources to enable the National Chamber of Entrepreneurship's Council of Businesswomen and its regional branches to provide a comprehensive package of training, consulting, and financial support services to women on a regional level. Implement regional pilot actions to test levels of demand, satisfaction and impact for dedicated women entrepreneur streams of the Business Advisor, Top SME Managers Training, and Business Connections programmes.
- Develop a comprehensive approach to the development of youth entrepreneurship, guided by the OECD principles for youth entrepreneurship policy, involving co-operation between the Ministry of National Economy Entrepreneurship Development Department, the Council for the Development of Youth Entrepreneurship, the National Chamber of Entrepreneurship and other relevant stakeholders.
- Strengthen support for entrepreneurship by people with disabilities by establishing a development fund to provide financing for the launch of businesses including financing for assistance technologies. Provide sensitivity training to staff of the Entrepreneurship Support Centres on how to adapt advisory and other services to better serve entrepreneurs with disabilities. Encourage the National Chamber of Entrepreneurs to facilitate the formation of an "Entrepreneurs with Disabilities Network" to promote mutual support and sharing of experience, using the Entrepreneurship Service Centres as a framework to reach the whole country.

Entrepreneurship training and SME management training

Training programmes to promote entrepreneurship skills and competences in Kazakhstan are of two main kinds: entrepreneurship training for potential and nascent entrepreneurs; and training to enhance the skills of existing SME managers. The main entrepreneurship and SME management training programmes, as provided for in the Business Road Map 2020 (BRM 2020), are:

- The Business Advisor courses (targeting potential and fledgling entrepreneurs in the first phase and individuals with existing entrepreneurial initiatives in the more advanced second phase).
- The School of Young Entrepreneurs (targeting 18-29 year olds).
- The SME Top Management Training Programme (targeting the top and medium level managers in SMEs operating in priority economic sectors).
- The Business Connections programme.

In addition, there are actions to offer entrepreneurship education to students in the formal education system, as discussed in the human capital section of the business environment chapter of this report.

Entrepreneurship training is relatively recent in Kazakhstan

The initial steps in developing entrepreneurship training in Kazakhstan were taken through the USAID-funded Kazakhstan Small Business Development Project (KSBDP) during 2006 to 2010. This enabled the introduction of the 128-hour Business Essentials course module and the ILO Start Your Business and Business Management Training modules. The project enabled training of trainers (in consulting and training companies) who then delivered the training to entrepreneurs and SMEs on a commercial basis, commonly with subsidies to the SMEs and entrepreneurs (USAID, 2010).

The Kazakhstan government then continued the initial support for entrepreneurship training by funding actions through the BRM 2020 and Employment Road Map 2020 (ERM 2020). Under BRM 2020, approximately 20 000 potential and new entrepreneurs were trained in business matters under the Business Advisor programmes and the School of Young Entrepreneurs, and about 1 000 existing SMEs received management training through the SME Top Manager Training and Business Connections projects in 2014 (Table 5.1). These programmes are described and assessed below.

Table 5.1. Number of clients served by BRM 2020 entrepreneurship and management training programmes, 2014

BRM 2020 Programme	Total participants by training programme, 2014	Number of beneficiaries in each programme that participated in other BRM 2020 programmes, 2014					Net participants (total less the beneficiaries participating in more than one programme)
		Business Advisor I	Business Advisor II	Training Top Management of SMEs	Business Connections (stage 1)	Business Connections (stage 2)	
Business Advisor I	19 238						19 238
Business Advisor II	3 236	674					2 562
School of Young Entrepreneurs	1 077	140	66				871
Subtotal for entrepreneurship training	*23 551*	*814*	*66*				*22 671*
Training Top Management of SMEs	423	77	64				282
Business Connections (stage 1)	586		117	46			377
Business Connections (stage 2)	111				65		46
Subtotal for management training in existing SMEs	*1 120*	*77*	*181*		*65*		*705*
Column totals	*24 671*	*891*	*247*	*46*	*65*		*23 376*

Note: The first column of figures indicates the number of participants in each programme. The following four columns report on the number of participants of each programme that also benefited from other training programmes. For example, 674 of the 3 236 Business Advisor II participants had also taken the Business Advisor I training.

Source: Data from the Performance Report on the BRM 2020 programme (Republic of Kazakhstan, 2015).

Start-up rates from initial Business Advisor training are low and transitions to deeper support are limited

The Business Advisor training is conducted by professional lecturers and trainers in 209 locations across Kazakhstan and managed by the Entrepreneurship Service Centres (ESCs) of the National Chamber of Entrepreneurs (NCE). It is group-based and consists of two levels. Business Advisor I focuses on the basics of entrepreneurship, and Business Advisor II provides more in-depth training on the functional areas of business. Both courses are offered according to a quarterly schedule of training dates and are short-term in nature. They are offered as sequential programmes. According to the BRM 2020, participants are supposed to present their certificate of completion of the Business Advisor I training course before participating in Business Advisor II.

The Business Advisor I basic training consists of a short course over two days covering how to identify business ideas, how to do market research, the basics of a business plan, samples of documents necessary to obtain financing, administrative requirements for business creation, etc. Over the four years 2011-2014, over 71 000 potential and fledging entrepreneurs had received this training. Over 95% of the trainees were satisfied with the training received. However, only 12% reported that they could start a new business as a result of taking the course.

Two days does not allow for a very in-depth coverage of the issues and is likely to leave many of the potential entrepreneurs frustrated in terms of taking the next steps. This is evident in the low business creation rate reported for Business Advisor I graduates: 2% in 2011, 5% in 2012, 8% in 2013 and 12% in 2014[1] (Republic of Kazakhstan, 2015, p. 49), which means that only about 5 000 of the 71 297 participants enrolled in the programme from 2011 to 2014 managed to start their own business. Although the business creation rate has been increasing over time, it does not compare well with international experience. For example, results from a tracer study of participants in the ILO's Start Your Business training programmes globally indicate that one-third of the trainees who did not already have a business were able to start a new business after the training, and on average created two jobs additional to the entrepreneur (van Lieshout et al., 2012; ILO, 2011). One of the reasons for these better outcomes may be the longer duration of the training compared to Kazakhstan's Business Advisor I. The Start Your Business training lasts up to eight days, and in addition provides trainees with at least one group counselling session to provide guidance on development of their business plans.

On the other hand, those completing Business Advisor I can register for a second phase under Business Adviser II. This starts with a 2-5 day course, depending on the topics covered. Entrepreneurs completing this course can then continue to a longer group-based training programme with online seminars and access to mentoring services. The training provides in-depth coverage of a list of topics approved by regional authorities, and includes assistance with the development of a market feasibility study and a business plan. Mentors include specialists and consultants experienced in mentorship identified by the regional authorities. They provide lectures, seminars, information and consulting to training participants. The mentoring process takes place over a period of three to eight weeks depending on the nature and needs of the eligible projects.

Business Advisor II is a more in-depth programme than Business Advisor I, with components ideally suited to training and supporting new entrepreneurs. All of the trainees indicated that the training met their expectations. However, participation in this programme is relatively low. In 2014, there were only 3 236 participants. Furthermore, only 674 had completed the Business Advisor I training, accounting for 20.8% of the Business Advisor II participants. One of the reasons for the low rate of transition between the two courses may be the excessive application procedures for Business Advisor II: for example, existing entrepreneurs must provide a copy of their tax return for the last reporting period.

A significant increase is required in the numbers of Business Advisor I trainees that start a business in order to help meet the targets set by the government for increased employment and value added in SMEs. Business creation rates could be improved by encouraging a much larger number of certificate completers from the Business Advisor I programme to enrol in the second phase for enhanced learning and development of a business plan. The barriers to transition between Business Advisor I and II should be examined and efforts made to encourage more of the Business Advisor I completers to participate in the second phase of training. In addition, more support in accessing finance could be offered to entrepreneurs creating businesses after completing the training, including direction towards available interest rate subsidies and loan guarantees.

The School of Young Entrepreneurs also results in few new enterprises although it is appreciated

The School for Young Entrepreneurs (SYE) is a BRM 2020 programme aimed at building the entrepreneurial capacity of young people between 18 and 29 years old in Kazakhstan. The first project was implemented in the autumn of 2012 in South Kazakhstan State University in Shymkent with the support of the regional government. Within three months, the project had trained 400 young people and thereafter expanded. Since 2015, the SYE is implemented by the National Chamber of Entrepreneurs (NCE) in partnership with a range of universities in the regions. It involves a two-week training course on the basics of entrepreneurship and the theory and practice of business management. The young entrepreneurs are also offered consulting services on business plan development and the opportunity to present their completed business plans at the "Fair of Ideas" competitions held in the regions, where the most successful SYE business plan projects are presented and winners are assisted in attracting funding. Achieving the SYE Training Completion Certificate also allows participants to compete for grant-based funding within the BRM 2020 (a start-up grant of up to Kazakhstan Tenge (KZT) 3 million) or to apply for Damu Entrepreneurship Development Fund guarantees for start-up loans from development and second-tier banks. Applications for funding are submitted through the Regional Co-ordinating Councils.

In total, over the three-year period to the end of December 2014, 2 109 young people had received training under the SYE project; of whom 29% were university students. The reach of the programme is expanding: from 400 participants in the Shymkent region in 2012 to 1 077 from regional centres and the cities of Astana, Almaty and Semey in 2014, with delivery through 17 NCE Entrepreneurship Service Centres (ESCs). The 2014 training resulted in 638 business plans (developed by 936 of the young people who completed the training) and the selection of 18 best projects at 17 "Fairs of Ideas".

However, although programme monitoring and impact assessment reveals that the majority of participants are satisfied with the training they receive, only about 6% of the trainees indicated that they could start a new business as a result of taking the course. Of the 2014 cohort of SYE trainees, only 57 new enterprises were created, representing 6% of the individuals trained (Republic of Kazakhstan, 2015), or about 9% of the business plans developed. This is a very low percentage relative to youth entrepreneurship training in other countries. For example, Adie CréaJeunes in France has realised a 30% start-up rate, and may offer some inspiration for further youth entrepreneurship policy development in Kazakhstan.

Box 5.1. Adie CréaJeunes youth entrepreneurship training and start-up support programme, France

Adie CréaJeunes is a youth entrepreneurship training and support programme targeting 18-32 year olds that is offered in all major cities of France (20 sites) by the Adie Association, a non-governmental organisation. From the introduction of this system in 2008 to the end of 2012, more than 4 000 young people participated in the programme, 30% of whom started their own businesses. Information sessions on the programme are held every week in all of the sites and new training programmes start every 4 to 6 weeks. The selection of participants is based primarily on the level of motivation of the applicant towards pursuing a project and their availability and commitment to participate in all of the training classes.

The programme consists of practical and interactive group-based training modules focused on building confidence and practical business knowledge. The courses are delivered over a period of two to four months with classes held during 3-5 half days per week. In parallel with the group workshops, participants receive individual coaching at least once a week to provide guidance on developing their project and putting into practice the learning elements shared in the training modules. This coaching support may continue after the launch of the business for up to 18 months. During and following the programme, regular meetings of the young entrepreneurs are facilitated to promote sharing of experience and create a learning network. Finally, participants can apply for micro-credit of up to EUR 10 000 from the programme to aid financing of their start-up, or will be directed to an appropriate financial partner.

Source: http://www.adie.org/nos-actions/Creajeunes-et-les-programmes-jeunes/.

An examination of the reasons for the low conversion of SYE trainees to business creation is therefore needed. This could be done by holding focus groups or roundtable workshops with young people who completed the training and with the training providers to assess the limitations of the programme. Based on the review, options to improve business start-up rates from SYE trainees may include using more stringent criteria for selecting applicants to the programme, lengthening the period of training, or allocating extended mentorship services to participants during the preparatory stage of refining their business idea and developing their business plan. Furthermore, the SYE programme could introduce continuing mentorship, business coaching and monitoring through the start-up phase and during the first one to two years of the start-up, a practice that is becoming increasingly common in other countries because of evidence that this contributes to a higher level of survivability and growth of supported businesses. Greater links could also be made for participants with promising projects to support available in business incubators.

The SME Top Management Training programme is effectively supporting ambitious SME managers

The SME Top Management Training programme provides business education and support to entrepreneurs and senior managers in SMEs who want to grow their business significantly. The objectives are to enable participants to:

- Undertake a sound assessment of potential new business ideas and to consider which ideas have the greatest commercial potential;
- Understand the management, marketing, financing, operating and planning components of growing profitable businesses;
- Reflect on the challenges facing SME leaders in Kazakhstan by networking and learning from other participants;
- Interact with legal, financial and investment experts from within the Kazakhstan business community;
- Undertake the development of a market feasibility plan and receive feedback; and
- Access materials and templates to develop a comprehensive business plan.

It has three components: (1) a 3-day residential module at Nazarbayev University on how participants can grow their businesses, taught in English by professors from Duke University; (2) a series of three on-line interactive webinars (one per week over a period of three weeks, each lasting approximately 75 minutes), which allow participants to ask questions to a Kazakhstan business expert on such topics as the legal issues of entrepreneurship, raising capital, and pitching a business plan; and (3) guidance in the development of a market growth plan to enable participants to test the potential of their business growth ideas, followed by development of an in-depth business plan (receiving feedback from programme faculty on each plan).

The programme is funded through the BRM 2020, supported by Damu Entrepreneurship Development Fund, which makes the final selection of training participants from the applicants, and delivered through the Nazarbayev University in Astana from April to November each year. The objective is to train 420 participants a year, through 14 cohorts of 30 participants. During 2011-2016, 2 104 senior SME managers participated in this training. The programme is attracting the intended target group of SME managers. Figures to 2014 showed that about 40% of the managers employed fewer than 20 workers, 30% over 20 workers, and 3% over 100 workers. Although participants came from all sectors of economic activity, the greatest number had businesses in the agribusiness industry (19%) and light industry (18%).

The impact of the programme on the performance of participating SMEs appears to be very positive. Following the programme, approximately two-thirds of the trainees reported increasing the annual turnover of their businesses and 58% reported creating new jobs as a result of the programme, totalling 3 300 additional SME jobs (Republic of Kazakhstan, 2015). Approximately two-thirds of participants reported developing new products or services, 60% increasing their profitability, half improving their production efficiencies, and one-third entering new markets, either domestic or foreign.

This therefore appears to be a very successful programme in terms of impact on assisted SMEs, which merits scaling up to accommodate more SMEs. At the same time, there may be scope to increase impacts by paying more attention to the make-up of each cohort of

SME managers. Currently, the level of sophistication and capability of SME managers in each cohort can vary considerably, depending on the referred list of SME managers provided by the Regional Co-ordinating Councils. If the total size of the programme were larger, the SME managers could be grouped into more coherent training groups based on the size of their businesses (managers of small versus medium businesses), the level of sophistication of the SME managers, and perhaps on a sector basis. This would allow adjustments to the training to better respond to differences in the developmental needs of different SME manager groups.

Business Connections also shows positive impacts for existing SME managers

The objective of the Business Connections programme is to enhance the capacity of SME managers to develop contacts with foreign partners with the aim of transferring technologies, acquiring equipment, organising mutual delivery of goods, works and services, acquisition of franchises, and creating joint ventures. Targeting senior and middle managers of SMEs in priority economic sectors, the opportunity is provided for free training in Almaty or Astana on modern management models, as well as for an internship in Germany or the USA. This programme is divided into two stages.

The first stage is three weeks of business training at a university in Astana or Almaty under the supervision of foreign and domestic business trainers and consultants (training participants must cover their own transport and living costs in Astana or Almaty). The first two weeks deal with topics related to modern methods of conducting business, managerial competence and competence in the field of foreign relations. The third week consists of online seminars and consultations and development of a business plan.

The second stage consists of a four-week internship in Germany or a three-week internship in the USA in an enterprise with a similar profile to their own. Selection of internship participants is made jointly by Kazakh-German and US-Kazakhstan Commissions. To receive the second stage training, the entrepreneurs need to show a clear purpose for the internship, have information about potential partners and suppliers (in the USA or Germany), have the authority to negotiate and sign contracts and have a certificate of completion of the first phase of the Business Connections programme or the SME Top Management Training programme. In the second phase of the project, all travel and accommodation costs are covered by the state.

As of the end of December 2015, 2 795 entrepreneurs had participated in the first stage of Business Connection training, of whom 361 went on to the second stage. An evaluation showed positive impacts from participation for the SMEs involved in terms of improvements in business management (marketing and sales, finance, manufacturing/production and strategic management), modernisation of equipment and business processes, increases in number and geographical spread of customers and contracts, and increases in turnover (Republic of Kazakhstan, 2015).

Business advice, consultancy and mentoring

NCE-delivered business development services would benefit from introduction of a business diagnostic tool

SMEs and entrepreneurs in all sectors of the economy can access free-of-charge individual business advice consultations through the network of Entrepreneurship Service Centres (ESCs) operated by the National Chamber of Entrepreneurs (NCE) (and formerly by the Damu Entrepreneurship Development Fund). The Damu Entrepreneurship

Development Fund had planned to increase the number of clients to be served by the ESCs from approximately 130 000 in 2014 (Damu, 2015, p. 30) to 190 000 in 2023 (Damu, 2014). In addition, the number of customers receiving remote services (online/phone consultations) was to increase from approximately 40 000 in 2014 to 150 000 in 2023 (Damu, 2014, p. 36). Although there is no confirmation that the NCE has adopted the same or similar targets, an expansion of this kind is likely to require more promotion and awareness of the availability of services among SMEs and entrepreneurs, an expansion in the number of service windows in the existing 188 ESCs, and opening of more ESCs in circumstances of strong demand.

Existing SMEs in priority sectors can also access consultancy through the BRM 2020 project "Service Support to Existing Business Activities". Consultations are provided by qualified consultants and companies selected through a competitive procurement process (28 suppliers in 2015) and by staff employed by the NCE. Table 5.2 shows the types of consultation services offered under the project and the numbers of clients that used each service in 2015. During 2011-2014, when the service was implemented by the Damu Entrepreneurship Development Fund, 166 600 services were taken up by 49 700 existing SMEs (Republic of Kazakhstan, 2015). In 2015, when the service was implemented by NCE, the numbers increased to 35 174 clients accessing 56 640 services (NCE, 2016). Approximately 71% of the 2015 clients were individual entrepreneurs, 16% were limited companies and 13% were farm enterprises. Some 42% were in the wholesale and retail trade sector, and only 6% in the manufacturing sector, but this usage closely reflects the sector distribution of SMEs in the economy.

Table 5.2. BRM 2020 Consultancy Support SMEs – Distribution of Clients by Type of Service Used, 2015

Type of consultancy service	Number of clients using each service	% of all services used
Legal advisory services (*e.g.* on preparation of business registration documents, drafting of contracts, review of documents for compliance with legislation)	16 748	29.6%
Services related to accounting and taxation, record-keeping, the preparation of financial statements and reports	14 611	25.8%
Marketing counselling services (*e.g.* advice on pricing policies, business plan preparation, development of marketing strategies and promotion of goods and services, competitive environment analysis, trade mark development and advertising campaigns)	10 687	18.9%
Customs legislation, procedures and clearance-related services	4 461	7.9%
Consulting in the field of information technology (*e.g.* advice on the development and support of Internet resources, website development, development and management of an online business, automating financial and operational activities)	3 338	5.9%
Services related to public procurement, procurement of national companies and subsoil users (*e.g.* guidance on preparation of tender documents, advice on improvements to be made to meet the requirements of government suppliers)	2 902	5.1%
Consulting and support regarding implementation of quality management systems (*e.g.* pre-certification audits, preparation of documents for certification in accordance with international standards, training of staff in quality systems, development and implementation of integrated management systems)	2 245	4.0%
Services involving management issues (*e.g.* advice on organisational management structures, financial analysis and planning, personnel record management and remuneration of employees, elaboration of a strategic plan for business development, corporate governance and policies, economic feasibility studies, development of international market entry strategies)	1 648	2.9%
Total	*56 640*	*100.0%*

Source: NCE (2016).

The availability of publicly-supported consultancy for SMEs in priority sectors is an important measure, because few of the users could afford to have qualified staff to tackle problems in the areas covered or to pay for the services of private sector consultancy firms or experts. Building a business diagnostic tool into the service approach could increase its effectiveness and efficiency as well as reach out to more SMEs with generic support.

Under the current approach, clients currently self-select the service(s) they think they need from a menu of eight services. They may therefore use the support as a short-term fix for pressing issues rather than as a solution to perhaps more significant performance issues. A diagnostic tool used at the outset of service support would help the SME managers and consultants to identify other major challenges that their businesses face and help ensure that the firms are offered the most appropriate support, including more integrated packages of service advice recognising interconnections in the issues faced by companies. The tool could also be used to identify firms that could benefit from further more intensive support, including the more integrated learning and development programmes offered through the Top SME Managers Training and Business Connections training.

Such a diagnostic tool could be operated as part of the business development service support offered, in the form of a self-assessment tool or an assessment tool used by an external consultant based on information provided by the company and reported back to the company.

A number of SME support agencies make use of this diagnostic approach; Box 5.2 profiles the SCORE and M-CORE tools in use in Malaysia.

Box 5.2. The SCORE and M-CORE SME Diagnostic Tools, Malaysia

SME Corporation Malaysia (SME Corp.), the SME support agency in Malaysia, has developed diagnostic tools to assess the capabilities, performance and development needs of SMEs. It operates two major tools – SCORE and M-CORE – as discussed below.

SCORE

The SME Competitiveness Rating for Enhancement (SCORE) tool enables the assessment of the competitive performance of an SME across a number of aspects of business operations to identify areas where development actions would improve competitiveness.

Individual SMEs are given a 1-5 star rating to reflect their overall performance and ratings against seven individual assessment criteria: financial strength, business performance, management capability, human resources, innovation (technology acquisition and adoption), quality/certification, and market presence.

The tool can be used directly by SMEs accessing an online version: http://myescore.smecorp.gov.my. This enables the SMEs to identify areas where they need to make improvements in order to enhance their business performance. The tool can also be used for an external assessment undertaken by an SME Corp. consultant through onsite visits. They can use the tool to establish a first diagnosis or to validate or adjust a prior self-diagnosis.

SME Corp. will focus on improving the capabilities of SMEs with an overall star rating of 3 or below through its business advisory and other support programmes. This can include specialised on-site consultancy provided by the Malaysia SME Expert Advisory Panel on issues such as technology improvement, production capacity, engineering, automation, machinery and equipment, materials technology, productivity improvement, process improvement, financial management, quality assurance, information and communications technologies, business systems and logistics, inventory management, international standards, or lean production systems.

The 4- and 5-star rated SMEs are considered to have the highest potential and to merit more intense support. In addition to the standard consultancy offer, these SMEs may be targeted to join international trade missions and other industrial networking programmes and supported with linkages to successful multinational companies.

As well as assisting SMEs to identify their business development needs, the tool has facilitated a more structured, focused and efficient approach to the provision of business development services by SME Corp. based on prior identification of the specific support services (technical/production expertise, better market access, financial controls etc.) that are best matched to the needs of the SMEs.

M-CORE

SME Corp. uses a separate diagnostic tool – the M-CORE (Micro-enterprise Competitiveness Rating for Enhancement) – to assess the competitive performance of microenterprises (less than 5 full-time employees or less than RM 300 000 in turnover).

If a (registered) microenterprise is successful in passing the M-CORE assessment with a qualifying rating of Level 1 and above, it can participate in capacity building components of the Microenterprise Enrichment and Enhancement Programme. This programme, using an integrated approach, includes short-term training courses, access to advisory services from business counsellors and the SME Expert Advisory Panel, and facilitation of access to financing.

Source: http://www.smecorp.gov.my/vn2/node/48; http://www.score.gov.my/.

Other business advice and consultancy programmes could be scaled up

In addition to these programmes, the government of Kazakhstan has made an agreement with the European Bank of Reconstruction and Development (EBRD) to offer its Business Advisory Service (BAS) programme in national priority sectors as part of the BRM 2020. BAS covers 50% of the costs of intensive consultancy support to SMEs for improving manufacturing processes and developing markets. An initial agreement in 2013 provided USD 30 million of funding to support 300 SMEs with services over three years. A further agreement extended the programme until 2020, with at least 800 SMEs to be supported. It is delivered through EBRD offices in cooperation with the NCE, the Damu Entrepreneurship Development Fund and regional government offices, which offer promotion and referral activities for the programme. The EBRD programme is helping to strengthen and build business development services capabilities in Kazakhstan. This could permit a gradual transfer of the service approach to Kazakhstan government authorities and private sector companies.

The Senior Experts Programme is a further significant BRM 2020 programme providing subsidised consultancy support to SMEs in priority economy sectors or manufacturing industries. It subsidises the costs of bringing in senior, highly qualified foreign specialists to help individual SMEs to solve a technical or organisational problem, for example related to implementation of new management techniques, production technology or equipment, or training of personnel. The programme assists the SMEs in making contact with the foreign specialist. While the programme covers the cost of the specialist's fees and transport to Kazakhstan, the SME must assume the expert's local travel and subsistence costs. In 2013 and 2014, only 62 SMEs benefited from these foreign consultations. Approximately half of them reported that they led to increases in production efficiency, growth in annual turnover, or market expansion (Republic of Kazakhstan, 2015). Greater efforts could be made to promote the use of the programme among SMEs that could benefit in order to spread these positive impacts further across the economy.

Further strengthening of the pool of local consultants is needed

One of the main challenges for strengthening business development services in Kazakhstan is to increase the number of domestically-based consultants who can build client demand and deliver good quality services. EBRD (2013), for example, highlights the lack of depth in SME consultancy in Kazakhstan, particularly outside the main cities. The Kazakhstan government and international donors have been active in seeking to build a larger body of business development consultants within the country. In addition, the Kazakhstan Chamber of Management Consultants (KCMC) has been working on initiatives to promote the use of international standards in the domestic consultant sector. Recently, the agreement between the government of Kazakhstan and the EBRD to deliver the BAS programme until 2020 included EBRD support to train 250 additional consultants. These are important measures to build the long-term capabilities of the business development services sector in Kazakhstan.

Consultancy support for growth-oriented firms should be extended

The only dedicated consultancy and mentoring programme for growth-oriented SMEs in Kazakhstan is the Enterprise Growth Programme (EGP) operated by the EBRD. The target is medium-sized enterprises, which receive advice over a 12-18 month period to internationalise their products and link with international buyers and distributors or to develop their potential for import substitution and become major suppliers for the domestic market. This usually means addressing their main impediments: low quality of products and manufacturing, lack of transfer of technologies to reach international standards, poor management and marketing skills, and lack of access to markets. The longer-term nature of the intervention makes it unique in the Kazakhstan business support landscape.

The EBRD programme is a first step in the direction of supporting high-growth potential companies in Kazakhstan. However, experience from other countries suggests that those companies with the greatest potential for growth need targeted and flexible support from a variety of sources, including advice and finance and access to other public supports. One approach to addressing this need is illustrated by Scotland's Companies of Scale Programme (see Box 5.3).

Box 5.3. Companies of Scale Programme, Scotland

Description of the approach

Companies of Scale is operated by Scottish Enterprise, the main economic development agency for Scotland. It provides specialist support, targeted at a small number of companies with a turnover that exceeds GBP 10 million and with ambitions to grow to GBP 100 million-plus businesses. The programme provides an intensive form of advice to help these businesses to accelerate their growth by responding effectively to transitional growth "triggers", including ownership changes (e.g. management buy-outs), new product development or the entry into a new market.

The combination of past performance and future growth ambitions are key criteria used for assessing the suitability of companies to take part in the programme. There are obviously potential limitations in using historical performance as guide to future growth potential, and a large part of the selection process involves a qualitative and subjective assessment by agency staff (based on their own extensive business experience) of the likelihood that the firm will be able to achieve their growth targets. Another subjective assessment is that firms are chosen on the basis of their willingness to engage in the programme and to closely interact with other companies on the programme.

Companies of Scale is unlike normal business development programmes as it is not a "fixed" offering which has a universal package of support tools for all of the programme's participants. Rather it is more of an "account management" approach in which Scottish Enterprise works with the participating firms to help identify the specific and bespoke types of support which are needed to achieve growth and how they can be obtained from within the broad package of Scottish Enterprise services, such as support for innovation, internationalisation and organisational development, or undertaken by external providers, procured by the companies and supported financially by the programme. Often these external services are provided to a group of companies participating on the programme.

The programme is extremely focused, giving intensive support to only 22 firms in the first 5 years of operation.

Factors for success

Key success factors in the design of the programme include:

- Using a team of programme managers with strong business experience and understanding, who work very closely with participating companies, often attending company board meetings and other meetings of a strategic nature;
- Tailoring support to the needs of the individual firm and taking a holistic approach that links target firms to a wide variety of different types of business development support;
- Providing rapid responses to company challenges at points where there are "growth triggers"; and
- Organising interactions with peers, including other entrepreneurs participating on the programme.

Relevance for Kazakhstan

Support for SMEs with high growth potential will be important in addressing the shortage of medium-sized, high-productivity enterprises in Kazakhstan. This approach targets a small number of high-potential firms and focuses on points in the companies' evolution where mentoring advice and tailored support could make a difference. Such an approach in Kazakhstan could combine intensive advice, coaching and mentoring with privileged access to existing financial and other SME supports. It also shows how small groups of high growth potential SMEs could be created in Kazakhstan for peer learning and common supports.

Source: Mason and Brown (2010), OECD (2013a).

Workforce skills development

SMEs should be encouraged to participate in the dual training system

As of 2017, all vocational education and training colleges are involved in the emerging dual training system in vocational education in Kazkahstan, whereby students receive a mix of classroom training in vocational training colleges and work placements in employers. However, the majority of dual training relationships between colleges and businesses have so far been with large employers. More deliberate policy strategies and incentives will be needed to enable SMEs to benefit substantially. Studies in Germany and the United Kingdom reveal that one of the main reasons why smaller enterprises are less engaged in offering job placements than large firms is because they are more resource and time constrained, for example lacking a qualified and dedicated person in the company to be responsible for dual training (BIBB, 2015; British Chambers of Commerce, 2011).

One way for the government to respond to this constraint would be to encourage the formation of SME training consortia. The approach would seek to form groups of SMEs in particular regions and sectors that have certain common skill needs and are willing to co-operate with other SMEs in developing training. The SMEs in each consortium would make agreements to work with specified vocational colleges in the development of relevant training programmes. Each SME within a consortium would commit to providing work placements for a specified number of trainees in the dual training system. Support could be provided to each consortium through the assignment of an external trainer to help develop and monitor the training plans of its SMEs. SMEs could also be offered subsidies to cover some of the training costs of the work placements and even some of the costs of the subsequent employment of graduates for a limited period. To finance the subsidies, the government could consider expanding the ERM 2020 "youth practice" initiative to include employment of vocational education and training students.

Efforts could also be made to encourage SMEs to hire university graduates

SMEs in Kazakhstan tend to have low rates of recruitment of university graduates, although the integration of young, highly educated people into the enterprise can provide a significant stimulus to SME innovation. The barriers reflect both lack of understanding of the opportunities among SME managers and university students and a lack of channels to connect these two worlds. There are various initiatives in other countries that seek to stimulate the employment of university graduates in SMEs and adoption of such a programme in Kazakhstan could help promote greater employment of universities graduates in SMEs.

One approach is to organise course work or course projects in which university students work with selected SMEs to develop solutions to certain technical or management challenges facing the businesses, working under the supervision of their university teacher. This type of approach, such as the Knowledge Transfer Partnerships in the UK, can help solve SME business development problems while increasing the relevance of course work. It can also be important in helping create connections and familiarity among university students and SMEs, favouring future employment offers by SMEs and their greater acceptance by students. Another approach is to offer co-operative work terms or internships in SMEs as part of the learning programme, similar to the example of the UK Shell Technology Enterprise Programme (STEP) profiled in Box 5.4

To help secure the employment of university graduates in the SMEs on completion of the university projects or placements, financial support from the ERM 2020 Youth Practice direction could be made available, for example in the form of a full wage subsidy for the employment of a university graduate for six months. In 2014, 17 500 graduates were supported with youth internships, with half ending up employed in a permanent job. However, there is no data on the share of the graduates going to work with SME employers.

Box 5.4. The Shell Technology Enterprise Programme, United Kingdom

The Shell Technology Enterprise Programme (STEP) is a highly selective 8-week (summer or term-time) internship in smaller, growth-oriented businesses for undergraduate students approaching their final year sponsored by the Shell company as part of its corporate social responsibility strategy. The programme has been operating in the UK for over 20 years.

The objective is two-fold: (1) to give undergraduate students the opportunity to obtain exposure to relevant business projects and acquire workplace skills, thereby increasing their employability, and (2) to enable small enterprises to discover the benefits of a skilled labour force for business productivity and innovation and, in doing so, convince them of the value of hiring university graduates in the future. The undergraduate work placements are designed to tackle a problem or a new opportunity which a smaller business may not have the time, resources or in-house skills to deal with.

The small business is supplied with an intern who has the relevant skills and knowledge to work on the specific project. The most common projects have to do with setting up information technology systems, creating websites or databases, creating new designs, or carrying out market research (projects that small businesses may not have the necessary resources to put in place), although they may also deal with solving a technical, production or new product development problem.

Approximately 1 000 students are recruited into the programme annually, with an admissions rate of only 1 in 8 of the student applicants. The selected applicants tend to come from science and technology programmes rather than the arts and humanities. The interns are paid a training allowance of GBP 185 a week, free of income tax and national insurance. Since its inception, the STEP has delivered more than 21 000 projects in small businesses across the UK.

The Kazakhstan government could sponsor such an initiative itself or work with a major company operating in Kazakhstan to support such a programme. The benefits could include stimulating innovation around the projects that interns undertake in SMEs and increasing the propensity of SMEs to employ university graduates.

Source: http://www.step.org.uk.

Training and retraining initiatives for existing SME workers should be expanded

In 2013, only 3.4% of employed workers in Kazakhstan had undertaken any training, retraining or upgrading of their qualifications during the previous 12 months (World Bank, 2015). This indicates a weak propensity among Kazakhstan SMEs to invest in formal workforce training (i.e. both continuous employee training and apprenticeship training) compared to their counterparts in OECD countries (OECD, 2013b). Furthermore, there is only limited public support for continuous workforce training in SMEs. In view of the fast changing economic and technological environment and low SME productivity and innovation rates in in Kazakhstan it would be beneficial to increase the emphasis on the training of existing SME workforces.

The most significant public programme to support SME workforce training is the Enterprise Competence Enhancement Component of the BRM 2020. This offers support to SMEs in priority sectors to train staff, including top managers, in productivity enhancement. It involves a partial reimbursement (40%) of third party costs for the training, not to exceed KZT 2 million per employee and limited to no more than 15 staff per enterprise per year. The Component also offers SMEs support to hire experts who can implement best production practices through a partial reimbursement of the costs borne by the SMEs to hire senior experts, not to exceed KZT 9 million per expert per year and no more than three experts per enterprise per year. In addition, the BRM 2020 can reimburse up to 50% of the costs of training and consultancy for exporting and product promotion activities in SMEs with industrial and innovating activities, including participation of employees in seminars, internships, and courses in foreign countries and visits of foreign consultants to SMEs in Kazakhstan. Applications are processed through the ESCs.

The number of SMEs and employees participating in these training programmes were not reported in the 2014 BRM 2020 performance report, and it is important to ensure monitoring of these training in the future. In addition, enhanced efforts should be made to increase the number of SME beneficiaries, especially small enterprises, through more aggressive promotional efforts.

The ERM 2020 also includes some support for SME workforce training. However, as opposed to BRM 2020 initiatives, it focuses principally on labour market integration objectives rather than increasing SME competitiveness. ERM 2020 can provide a wage subsidy for the employment of unemployed workers in SMEs and other firms, worth up to 50% of the salary for the first six months (but no more than KZT 26 000), reducing to 30% of the salary for the next three months and 15% of the salary for a final three months. It can also finance up to six months of retraining or 12 months of training support to match the unemployed workers to SME skill needs. In 2014, the ERM 2020 supported 35 700 unemployed people to take this training.

Access to finance

Damu supports SME lending through credit lines and loan guarantees to banks

The Damu Entrepreneurship Development Fund is the main public institution running access to finance programmes to support SME lending. One its major activities involves providing lines of credit to second-tier banks to enable them to make long-term loans to SMEs. The main programmes concerned are the Stabilisation Programme, the Regions Programme, the Target Regions Programme, the Ondiris Programme and Support for Manufacturing SMEs.

The Stabilisation Programme was established in 2007 with support from the Asian Development Bank. It allocated a total of KZT 1 671 billion in the period 2007-2017, and financed approximately 35 500 projects and 10 000 SMEs. The loans could be made for capital investment, refinancing of outstanding loans, or working capital. The maximum loan amount per SME was set at KZT 440 million in the first phase and KZT 550 million in the second phase while the interest rate could be set by the participating banks. In the third phase, the maximum loan size was set at KZT 750 million and the maximum annual effective interest rate was set at 12.5%; maximum loan terms and grace periods were also set.

The Regions Programme was launched in 2008 to support banking to SMEs across all the regions of the country. It was furnished with KZT 28 billion from the national budget and KZT 6.7 billion from regional government administrations. In the first phase the average loan size was KZT 44 million, the average annual effective interest rate was 13.55% and the average loan term was 38 months. The second and third phases were launched in 2010 and 2012. A total of KZT 168.8 billion was disbursed to 3 054 SMEs as of 2016 under the second and third phases of the programme, with average annual effective interest rates of 10.65% and 14.69% respectively. A further 411 SMEs were provided with a total loan amount of KZT 20.3 billion in an additional programme initiated in 2010 for SMEs in priority sectors in the regions of Almaty, Akmola, and South Kazakhstan.

The Ondiris Programme was established in 2009 to take a sector-based approach targeting manufacturing SMEs. Government financing is provided from a "Stress Assets Fund" established in 2008 to ensure stability of the financial system, with participating banks contributing 30% of the funds. As of 2016, 359 SMEs had been funded for a total loan amount of KZT 111.2 billion. In 2014, a parallel programme allocated KZT 100 billion to 13 partner banks to provide loans to SMEs for a maximum amount per borrower of KZT 1.85 billion, a maximum period of 120 months and a maximum nominal interest rate of 6%. As of 2016, 1 572 projects had been financed with KZT 317 billion.

Through the BRM 2020, the Damu Entrepreneurship Development Fund also operates an interest rate subsidy programme and a credit guarantee programme. The interest rate subsidies can be provided on loans of up to KZT 4.5 billion for a maximum period of 3 years, with a subsidy rate of between 7-10% according to the location and sector of the SME. They can be used for investments, the acquisition and/or refurbishment of fixed assets and/or expansion of production, and up to 30% of the loan amount can be used for financing of current assets. At the beginning of 2017, KZT 146.32 billion of subsidies had been provided, supporting 9 060 projects for a total investment of KZT 1 716.53 billion. The main beneficiaries have been in the manufacturing and transport sectors (31% and 25% of all projects, respectively).

The credit guarantee programme offers guarantees of up to 50% of the loan amount for a maximum amount per SME of KZT 180 million. The loans can be used for investments or for acquisition of new and/or refurbishment of fixed assets, and up to 50% of the loan amount can be used for current asset financing, up to a maximum of KZT 60 million. At the beginning of 2017, guarantees of KZT 40.3 billion were in place, supporting 2 626 projects and an investment of KZT 93.4 billion. Again, the manufacturing and transport sectors have been the main beneficiaries (41% and 14% of total projects, respectively).

The efforts of the Damu Entrepreneurship Development Fund are important in helping to fill the gap in SME lending. However, the numbers of SMEs reached and the total budgets and loan amounts of the programmes are insufficient to fully address the financial needs of SMEs, which Damu has estimated to be USD 118 billion in 2015[2]. One of the issues that needs to be addressed is limited willingness of banks to make use of the lines of credit, guarantees and subsidies available. The participation of banks is held back by complex programme administration procedures, limited bank experience in lending to SMEs and limited bank access to SME credit history information (KODIT and KDS, 2012). Avenues to bring greater bank participation would include simplification of application procedures for banks, support to develop the skills of bank staff to assess SME loan applications and support for the reporting of SME credit history information.

Another issue is that the range of Damu financial instruments appears to have grown organically over time, based on meeting short-term demands and concerns rather than on long-term research into the needs of SMEs. Table 5.3 shows how often new programmes have been introduced, even though the purposes and conditions of some of these programmes overlap. A more streamlined and coherent approach should be considered based on a review of effectiveness, relevance and synergies across the different programmes. This should be accompanied by active promotion of the retained programmes to SMEs and simplification of procedures for SMEs and banks.

Table 5.3. Overview of Damu Entrepreneurship Development Fund financial instruments

Name of the Programme	Starting year
Stabilisation Programme	2007
Regions Programme	2008
Ondiris Programme	2009
Leasing support for manufacturing sector SMEs	2009
Target Regions Programme (for SMEs located in Almaty, Akmola, and South-Kazakhstan)	2010
Interest rate subsidies and loan guarantees under BRM 2020	2010
Leasing support for SMEs	2011
Support for manufacturing sector SMEs	2014

Source: OECD interview programme in Kazakhstan and Damu operating reports.

Furthermore, financial support to SMEs and entrepreneurs tends to be most effective when combined with non-financial supports for example in the form of business advice and consultancy and support for innovation and internationalisation. Responsibility for the provision of public business development services to SMEs has recently been transferred from Damu to the NCE while Damu retains responsibility for the financial instruments. Strong links should be maintained between Damu and NCE to co-ordinate these two types of support. The government could also encourage greater non-financial support from banks themselves. Box 5.5 shows an example from Turkey of bank provision of non-financial services in co-ordination with its financial products.

Box 5.5. The combination of lending and non-financial support to SMEs by Türk Ekonomi Bankasi (TEB), Turkey

Since the early 2000s, banks in Turkey have been very active in designing and implementing SME-specific loans often with public support from regional development agencies, public banks, and the Small and Medium Enterprises Development Organisation (KOSGEB). The Türk Ekonomi Bankasi (TEB) is one of the most successful banks in SME banking products and services. One of the keys to its success is the provision of non-financial support to help SMEs to improve their business practices and achieve growth.

TEB has developed eight different credit products specifically designed for SMEs. Alongside these products it offers a wide range of training, consulting and information-sharing services for SMEs. TEB's main services are grouped under three categories:

(1) TEB SME Academy, which delivers training sessions to SMEs all over the country; (2) TEB SME Consultants, where specifically trained 'Relationship Managers' of the bank provide one-on-one consulting services to SMEs, (3) TEB SME TV where information, success stories and news, as well as interactive sessions on the topics which concern SMEs are broadcasted. TEB has invested in staff development as well as physical infrastructure to support the effective delivery of these services.

This non-financial support has helped TEB to develop a 360-degree understanding of its customers, not only with respect to their financials, but also regarding their business strategy, production, sales, marketing, human resources and organisation. This knowledge supports the bank in its SME lending, leading to lower credit risk, improved cross-selling and strong loyalty amongst the SME client base.

TEB's SME client numbers increased from approximately 20 000 when these services were launched in 2005 to over 700 000 in 2011; its SME loans as a share of total loans grew from 25% in 2006 to 48% by 2015; and loan delinquency rates in its SME portfolio decreased. Driven by the success in Turkey, BNP Paribas (one of TEB's larger shareholders) replicated some of TEB's non-financial services in Algeria and is looking to further replicate this model in various European markets.

Relevance to Kazakhstan

Providing non-financial support to SMEs alongside financial products would help financial institutions in Kazakhstan to decrease their SME lending credit risk and increase the reach of their financial instruments to SMEs. Public bodies such as the Damu Entrepreneurship Development Fund could offer capacity building support and financial incentives to banks to promote the development of their non-financial services to SMEs.

Source: http://www.teb.com.tr/about-teb/contribution-to-smes/; IFC (2012) Providing Comprehensive Non-financial Services to SMEs in Turkey: A Success Story for Both Bank and Clients.

Non-bank financial instruments are in their infancy

The G20/OECD High-Level Principles on SME and Entrepreneurship Financing stress the importance of enabling SMEs to access diverse non-traditional financing instruments and channels. These instruments are growing in Kazakhstan but there is nevertheless strong scope to develop them further.

Microfinance

The emergence of non-bank financial institutions is only recent in Kazakhstan. Of its different forms, microfinance is the most developed. There were 1 505 registered microfinance institutions in Kazakhstan in January 2017, although at September 2016 only 331 were listed as active and their granted microcredits totalled only KZT 65.1 million.

The Damu Entrepreneurship Development Fund has been one of the major players in supporting the emergence of microfinance institutions. Between 2009 and 2014, it made a conditional placement of funds with partner banks for lending to microfinance institutions. This financed eight microfinance institutions for a total amount of KZT 1.74 billion. The average loan size was KZT 217 million, with an average term of 55 months, and an average effective annual interest rate of 13.96%. It also provided credit lines to microfinance organisations (directly from the Fund or under its guarantee arrangements with banks) between 2016 and early 2018 that financed approximately 10 000 projects. In 2017, it launched the State Programme for the Development of Productive Employment and Mass Entrepreneurship, placing funds in short term banking and microfinance organisations for micro lending to entrepreneurs.

In addition, the government's Kazagro group of companies operates two funds offering microcredit in rural areas, although these funds are small in scale (OECD, 2013d). The Fund for Financial Support of Agriculture (FFSA) supports a network of rural microfinance institutions that aim primarily at supporting agricultural production but also offer small loans for rural entrepreneurship (such as agro-tourism, rural points of sale, food processing etc.). The Agrarian Credit Corporation can also provide microcredit for agricultural purposes and for rural entrepreneurs.

There has been significant support for microcredit institutions in Kazakhstan through these initiatives. However, more is needed to reach the scale required to meet government targets for SMEs and entrepreneurship. Some further initiatives are already under consideration. In particular, the Damu Entrepreneurship Development Fund is considering a new initiative to support microcredit and there have been proposals for collaboration between the government and the ADB to create an apex institution for the existing micro-lending institutions in order to enable them to access cheap finance. These initiatives should be pursued.

Factoring

Factoring services started in Kazakhstan in 2009. There are six factoring companies with total transaction volume of USD 30 million[3]. However, there is still a general lack of awareness among SMEs of factoring as a financial product. In collaboration with the World Bank SME Competitiveness Project, the government is conducting a strategic assessment of how to develop the factoring industry in Kazakhstan in order to support SMEs in local supply chains. The project also aims to help to increase institutional capacity to implement and supervise a factoring development programme in Kazakhstan.

Leasing

The Damu Entrepreneurship Development Fund provides leasing finance support to SMEs by placing financial resources in second-tier banks and leasing companies for leasing transactions with SMEs. It established an initial leasing programme in 2009 dedicated to the manufacturing sector. In 2011, it established a second leasing programme for SMEs from all sectors. Both programmes finance only new leasing transactions and have a maximum lease term of 84 months. The conditions of the former programme are more favourable than those of the latter (e.g. the maximum interest rate is 8% in the first programme and 14% in the second, and the maximum period for repayment of principal is 24 months in the first programme and 12 months in the second). As of January 2017, only 431 SMEs were financed with KZT 15.6 billion under these initiatives.

Private equity, venture capital and business angel investments

There have been several government initiatives to help develop a fledgling venture capital industry in Kazakhstan. One of the earliest attempts involved creation of eleven venture capital funds between 2004 and 2009 by the National Innovation Fund, now the National Agency for Technological Development (NATD), in collaboration with domestic and foreign investors. The funds aimed at financing companies in information and communication technologies, new building materials, pharmaceuticals and other sectors with export potential. However, not all the funds have been successful, and six had made a combined loss of USD 7.5 billion by the end of 2009. Further support for venture capital investment was provided under the SPAIID 2010-2014. This enabled the creation of four domestic venture capital funds with total fund size of KZT 12 billion. The main focus of these funds appears to have been on the expansion and restructuring of existing businesses rather than on innovative start-ups.

The government has also worked on developing a stronger infrastructure around venture capital and private equity. In 2007, it established Kazyna Capital Management to operate as a fund of funds aimed at developing a private equity market in the country. Currently operating under Baiterek Holding Company, Kazyna has invested in eleven private equity funds. It has also been active in the creation of professional associations and networks to carry out lobbying, promotion and awareness-raising activities for equity investment. In 2013, the NATD and Kazyna Capital Management helped set up the Kazakhstan Association of Venture Capital and Private Equity. Earlier government support was provided for the establishment of a National Network of Business Angels of Kazakhstan (OECD, 2011a).

Several constraints to the further development of the venture capital industry in Kazakhstan still need to be addressed, however. Awareness of equity investment opportunities and mechanisms remains low, both among potential investors and investees. No secondary stock market yet exists in Kazakhstan to provide an easy exit route for venture capital investments, although the Kazakhstan Stock Exchange has been considering the development of a junior market for SME stocks (ADB, 2015). Furthermore, although the government is making investments in the equity capital of venture capital funds, government agencies are expected to provide full repayment of the budget funds invested despite the very risky nature of venture capital investments (World Bank, 2015). In addition, there are few tax incentives available to encourage private investors to become active in venture capital, private equity and business angel investments.

Financial literacy

Most of the focus of the government of Kazakhstan in seeking to increase the use of alternative financial instruments to debt has been on seeking to develop finance supply. Additional actions should be take on the demand side to strengthen financial literacy amongst entrepreneurs and SME managers, in terms of their ability to understand the range of financing options available to them, how to structure their finance projects, and how to approach different potential investors and present their investment projects to them effectively. Training initiatives with entrepreneurs would be very valuable in seeking to address limited financial skills among SMEs and entrepreneurs. Capacity building could also be supported with operational staff in financial institutions responsible for assessing financing opportunities for SMEs and entrepreneurs.

Support for innovative start-ups and SME innovation

The NATD offers grants for SME innovation and invests in business innovation infrastructure

The National Agency for Technological Development (NATD) is the main state operator on technological development and innovation, working under the responsibility of the Ministry of Investment and Development. As set out in the NATD's strategy 2014-2023, it plays a major role in supporting business innovation in Kazakhstan by providing innovation grants to manufacturing enterprises, building the supply of business incubation facilities, and building links with technology organisations in other countries. Sixteen sectoral areas are prioritised for the support[4].

The main activities of the NATD involve providing innovation grants, ensuring the stimulation of innovation activity, defining technological tasks and finding the solutions through international technology transfer networks, providing technological forecasting information and analytical activities, supporting the development of business incubators under the BRM 2020 programme, and developing venture financing.

Table 5.4 indicates the key performance indicators and targets set for these support interventions. The content of each area of intervention is discussed further in the paragraphs below.

Table 5.4. Key performance indicators for NATD financial support for innovative projects

Key performance indicators	Unit	Baseline (2016)	Target (2023)
The volume of products produced by business entities that received support (with accumulation from 2014)	KZT billion	90.7	228.1
Number of new projects and projects for the modernisation and expansion of existing production facilities, taking into account the increase in labour productivity and expansion of sales markets (with accumulation from 2014)	Projects	155	267
Number of foreign partner organisations for technology transfer	Partners	1	No more than 7
Number of technical requests processed within the framework of a pilot project on technological brokering in the event of the availability of financing within the framework of the implementation of state tasks (with increasing effect)	Requests	-	7
Number of technologies implemented in production, the number of projects aimed at solving technological tasks of industry and commercialisation of technologies (units) (incremental)	Projects	13	81
Number of projects supported by a grant for technological development of enterprises (per year)	Projects	2	4
Number of projects supported by a grant for the technological development of industries (per year)	Projects	2	4
Number of projects supported by a grant for the commercialisation of technology (per year)	Projects	0	4
Support for the operation of technology incubators (per year)	Incubators assisted	-	5
Number of incubated projects	Number of projects (start-ups)	-	Up to 25 per year

Source: NATD.

Strategic Area 1: Financial support for innovative projects

NATD financial support for innovative projects is offered in three main forms: grant for technological development of existing enterprises, grant for technological development of industries and grant for commercialisation of technologies. Table 5.5 shows the activities for which the innovation support grants can be awarded and the maximum grant amounts. Its innovation grants to SMEs supported 126 projects in 2015-2017.

Table 5.5. Innovation grants provided by NATD

Purpose of the grant finance	Maximum amount of grants (KZT)
Grant for technological development of existing enterprises	Up to 70% of the justified costs under the license agreement and (or) up to 50% of the reasonable costs for the acquisition of equipment, but not more than KZT 400 million
Grant for technological development of industries	Up to 70% of the justified costs under the license agreement and (or) up to 50% of the justified costs of acquiring the equipment and up to 85% of the justified costs of increasing technological competencies, but not more than KZT 500 million
Grant for commercialisation of technologies	Up to 50% of reasonable declared costs, but not more than KZT 200 million

Source: NATD.

Strategic Area 2: Innovation infrastructure

The NATD has developed eight Technology Parks, which contained 18 080 square meters of usable space in 2015, of which 93% was occupied, 67% by innovative companies (NATD, 2016). Five of the parks provided incubation infrastructure and services, hosting 131 companies in 2015, of which 89% were SMEs. The other three parks did not have their own business incubation infrastructure.

The NATD also supports two Innovation Clusters, which aim to encourage industrial innovation through sharing of existing capacity, knowledge and experience across partners. One of the clusters is managed by an independent cluster foundation called the Park of Innovative Technologies, whose members include 12 major universities and 16 scientific research institutes in Almaty. Some 150 companies are hosted on the park, of which more than 60% are SMEs operating in information technologies, and knowledge exchanges are encouraged among the businesses and the research partners. The other Innovation Cluster was established by the Nazarbayev University and operates on the same principles.

The NATD has also established four Industrial Design Bureaus to assist innovative industrial companies to develop design-technology documentation. The bureaus have assisted domestic companies to launch production of 177 new products (World Bank, 2015). In 2015, they developed 88 sets of documentation and produced 93 product prototypes, 12 of which went into production.

The NATD has also established 21 Commercialisation Offices in universities and research institutes. They offer finance as well as information services and methodological support for all stages of the technology transfer process, from the identification of technologies for commercialisation at universities and research institutes to licensing or start-up creation. Between 2011 and 2012, they received 222 applications, of which 56 were selected for proof of concept support and 27 were selected for further commercialisation support (World Bank, 2015). In addition, the NATD supported the establishment of five Regional Commercialisation Centres in the most innovation-active regions of Kazakhstan (Almaty, Astana, Karaganda, Uralsk, Ust-Kamenogorsk). Operational agreements have been secured between these centres and five technology parks.

Finally, the NATD supports 5 International Technology Transfer Centres. They include the Kazakh-French Centre for Technology Transfer, established with a French company, and the Kazakh-Korean Technology Transfer Centre, established with the Innopolis Fund of Korea. Other centres have been developed with partners in the Russian Federation, the USA, and China. At the end of 2015, 18 joint projects were being implemented in the centres.

In the future, the NATD aims to expand the innovation infrastructures that it supports, and focus more strongly on the creation of innovation workshops, fab-labs and co-working centres. As part of this transformation, the technology parks and industrial design centres will be privatised. The NATD also plans to launch a new type of grant funding programme for the industry design offices and offer public support to accredited private industrial parks and regional innovation offices established by regional government authorities.

The emphasis on more targeted innovation infrastructures is likely to lead to increased policy efficiency and effectiveness. The keys to success will be ensuring a sufficient scale of resources for expanding the infrastructure, making an appropriate allocation of resources across the different elements of the infrastructure system and ensuring networking and specialisation in the system. Table 5.6 provides the example of how the Basque Technology Park Network has succeeded in steering and co-ordinating such an innovation infrastructure system.

Box 5.6. Basque Technology Park Networks, Basque Country, Spain

Description of the approach

The Basque Country Technology Park Network co-ordinates the actions of the four technology parks in the region – the Bizkaia Technology Park, the Alava Technology Park, the San Sebastian Technology Park and the Garaia Innovation Pole. The network is supported by the Basque government and the Basque economic development agency, SPRI.

The parks seek to: attract technologically-advanced businesses; promote knowledge exchange and co-operation among universities, R&D centres, other innovation support actors, and businesses; support the creation of new technology-based companies, including with business incubators; and encourage the diffusion of technology and innovation culture throughout the region, including through facilitating the access of local companies to national and international networks, providing advice and training to entrepreneurs, and offering training to local firms in technologies and advanced management.

The network helps secure a shared strategy among the parks that promotes distinct orientations for each park and steers them towards complementary technological areas. The network has also introduced a telecommunications system that permits the interconnection of all the businesses operating in the parks.

Factors for success

The success of the technology parks is founded on:

- Attraction of R&D investment, ensuring that companies are genuinely innovative and that the locations are more than business parks;
- Promotion of internationalisation and international contacts in innovative fields to ensure that innovation is not just local;
- Specialisation of each park; and
- Offering training and advice for firms on and off the parks with relevant specialisations.

Relevance for Kazakhstan

This network demonstrates the potential for technology parks to operate in synergy though specialisation and making connections with each other and the wider international R&D community. Kazakhstan has developed a network of technology centres, but they could be more effective if they were more clearly specialised as part of a national strategy, on a larger scale, and networked to each other and to international innovation networks.

Source: http://www.parke.eus/bizkaia/?page_id=29&lang=en.

Strategic Area 3: An international partnership network

The NATD also promotes international cooperation in technology development by establishing links with technology support organisations in countries with advanced innovation systems. It has targets in this area for the period 2014 and 2023 to increase the number of Kazakhstan technological cooperation centres abroad from 5 to 6; the number of major foreign technology companies in Kazakhstan from 12 to 120; the number of Kazakhstan companies implementing technology transfer activities from 50 to 2 750; and the amount of finance for projects implemented in cooperation with foreign partners from KZT 50 million to KZT 500 million. However, there is no clear public action plan which shows how these targets could be reached with the resources available.

Strategic Area 4: Information and analytical support for innovation processes

This measure aims to raise awareness among businesses of the innovation support that is available, monitor the implementation of innovation support programmes, and design new initiatives in line with global trends in innovation. The target is to increase the number of applications to NATD support programmes by 20% from 2014 to 2023.

The Autonomous Cluster Fund is active in high-technology start-up support

The Autonomous Cluster Fund works to attract high-tech start-up projects within the framework of Start Up Kazakhstan. Foreign subsoil users are committed to making local expenditures amounting to 1% of their annual revenue, and this has enabled it to attract financing of KZT 3.6 billion. The activities of the Fund include development of incubation and acceleration facilities for high technology start-ups, creation of joint venture capital funds, including the GVA Alatau Fund, opening of new joint centres for technological development with multinationals in order to localise production and finance R&D, and investments in start-ups. The initiative has financed 70 projects.

The Ministry of Education and Science supports technology commercialisation

The Ministry of Education and Science is co-operating with the World Bank in implementing the "Fostering Productive Innovation Project", which aims to stimulate the commercialisation of research in Kazakhstan. The project will run from 2016 to 2020, financed by a loan from the World Bank of USD 88 million and a Kazakhstan government budget of USD 22 million (World Bank, 2015).

One of the components of the project is directed to fostering high quality R&D with commercialisation potential in Kazakhstan and the development of human capital in R&D. It offers grants of up to KZT 230 million for Senior Research Staff and KZT 180 million for Junior Research Staff. The selection of projects for financing and monitoring is carried out by the International Council for Science and Commercialisation, consisting of scientists and experts in the field of technology commercialisation.

The second component supports technology business start-ups and spin-offs, including through the creation of the Venture Fund for Early Financing. Some 43 start-ups are currently supported under this initiative. In addition, technology brokers can accompany selected supported R&D projects to encourage innovation activities. Measures are also being undertaken to strengthen the functioning of technology commercialisation offices in Kazakhstan universities.

The project follows on from the Technology Commercialisation Project operated by the government of Kazakhstan and the World Bank from 2008-2015. That project included provision of research grants to scientists for research with commercialisation potential and financial support for technology start-ups and spin-offs in the form of grants for proof of concept and prototype development activities. This project delivered satisfactory results overall (Guimon, 2013) and demonstrated the relevance of activities in this area.

R&D tax incentives could be better targeted towards SMEs

The Kazakhstan government operates an R&D tax incentive to support innovation in businesses. Key features of the incentive are as follows:

- Research and development expenses are fully deductible from corporate income tax;
- An additional tax deduction of 50% is applied to expenses related to commercialisation of inventions, utility models and industrial designs;
- Corporate income tax exemption is applied if at least 90% of the income is generated from R&D, innovation activities and scientific research works;
- VAT exemption is applied for scientific research conducted on the basis of state contracts;
- Tax exemptions are available for companies located in the Park of Innovative Technologies; and
- Losses from entrepreneurial (and R&D) activities are carried forward for ten years.

The approach makes no specific provision for SMEs. However, a higher rate of tax credit to support SME innovation could be considered, responding to the greater financing constraints often faced by SMEs and the government's stated objective of encouraging additional SME activity. Furthermore, a simplification of application procedures and carry-forward or carry-back arrangements for the use of the tax credit would facilitate the participation of SMEs in the programme. The SkatteFUNN R&D tax credit in Norway has adopted these types of SME-friendly measures (Box 5.7).

Box 5.7. R&D tax credit and SMEs, Norway

Description of the approach

The SkatteFUNN scheme in Norway offers an R&D tax credit against business R&D expenditures, using the definition of R&D provided by the OECD Frascati Manual. The scheme has been designed in such a way as to facilitate the participation of SMEs:

- There is a higher incentive rate for SMEs, which obtain a 20% credit against R&D project costs compared with 18% for large enterprises.
- The application procedure is simple: it is based on self-declaration, firms can apply online, the online application form provides explanations for all questions, an example of a completed application form is available online and guidance notes are provided. Innovation Norway also offers a pre-assessment of whether the project qualifies for support or not.
- If the tax credit for the R&D expenses is greater than the amount that the firm is liable to pay in tax, the remainder is paid in cash to the firm. If the firm is not liable for tax, the entire allowance is paid as a cash grant. This helps resolve a problem whereby new firms sometimes have not made sufficient corporate income to qualify for tax credits.

Sources:
http://www.skattefunn.no/prognett-skattefunn/English/1253989461805?lang=en
http://www.forskningsradet.no/en/Funding/SkatteFUNN/1210046495447
European Commission (2014), A Study on R&D Tax Incentives: Final report; OECD (2011b), Business Innovation Policies: Selected Country Comparisons, OECD Publishing.

Current business innovation support programmes need to be extended

The government has been developing and strengthening its programmes to support innovative start-ups and SME innovation in recent years. Its support includes innovation grants, innovation infrastructures, research commercialisation programmes and business R&D tax credits. However, the numbers of SMEs and start-ups that benefit are still relatively low and largely concentrated in technology-based activities. It would be useful to expand programmes to serve more firms and to place a greater emphasis on support for innovation in non-technological areas. Furthermore, the main thrust of the existing programmes is on providing financial incentives to companies, whereas some other important types of interventions are weak or absent. In particular, innovation consultancy, training and mentoring schemes could be developed, focused on strengthening innovation skills and competencies among SME managers and employees. A dedicated intervention to support SMEs to adopt digital technologies would also be beneficial. In addition, a complementary programme could further reinforce the access of innovative start-ups to early-stage venture capital and consultancy assistance for growth.

Support for SME internationalisation

There is various support for export promotion but impact is limited

Until very recently, the National Export and Investment Agency (KAZNEX Invest) operated the government's export support activities, under the jurisdiction of the Ministry for Investment and Development. KAZNEX Invest was responsible for both export development and FDI attraction. Its export promotion programmes were implemented within the framework of SPAIID 2015-2019, which foresaw a budget of KZT 38.3 billion for export promotion in that period. As of 2018, the provision of export support has been transferred to the National Chamber of Entrepreneurs.

The export promotion activities include training and international study tours for export-oriented firms, an interactive online information resource (www.export.gov.kz) that offers information about becoming an exporter, the organisation of trade missions abroad, and the publication of an export directory and other literature. There is also a range of financial support available to businesses to help them export, for example for promotion of trademarks, presentations at international exhibitions (on a single national stand), company participation in international exhibitions, and developing packaging for export. In addition, offices operate in the Russian Federation and China to assist exporters in the marketing of their products in those countries.

Although these initiatives could be of particular benefit to SMEs, the main beneficiaries appear to be large companies and the number of interventions is relatively modest. For example, between 2010 and 2014, only 31 trade missions were organised and only 170 enterprises participated in foreign exhibitions. In 2017, the export directory had only 1 059 company entries and 859 products. Over the period 2009 to 2014, only 200 people from 100 enterprises received training in exporting.

In addition to these activities, the BRM 2020 aims to provide information services to SMEs planning to carry out international cooperation and export activities in the markets of Eurasian Economic Union. In addition, the Strategy 2020 announces incentives to establish science-intensive high-tech export-oriented enterprises and diversify Kazakhstan's exports towards higher value added products that meet international quality standards. Nonetheless, overall, this does not amount to a major SME-oriented exporting and internationalisation strategy.

Programmes for business internationalisation need to be scaled up and better targeted towards SMEs

Across countries, there are commonly four major barriers to SME internationalisation (OECD, 2009):

- Shortage of working capital to finance exports;
- Limited information to locate/analyse markets;
- Inability to contact potential overseas customers; and
- Lack of managerial time, skills and knowledge.

Against this framework, the current SME internationalisation programmes in Kazakhstan are underdeveloped. Other countries have developed more integrated, intensive and SME-targeted programmes, such as the example given in Box 5.8. This type of model could be used to develop a reinforced set of support interventions for SME internationalisation in Kazakhstan. Key elements of a renewed approach would involve identifying companies with export potential and providing targeted consultancy and coaching to these firms, encompassing support for management upgrading, productivity increases and quality improvements. At the same time, the government should invest in further developing the infrastructures needed for SME export development, such as those related to product testing, standardisation and standards certification.

Box 5.8. TradeStart Network, Australia

Description of the approach

In 2002, the Australian government set the goal of doubling national exports by 2006. To support this goal it developed the TradeStart network to offer a range of export advice and coaching services alongside the longer-established financial assistance available from the Export Market Development Grants Programme. An initial amount of AUD 21.5 million was committed for the period 2002-2006.

The TradeStart network is managed by Austrade, the Australian Government's trade and investment development agency, in partnership with state, territory and local governments and industry bodies and with other government ministries. It aims to flexibly address the needs of individual businesses by drawing on the combined resources of its partner organisations, focusing on coaching and action learning using experienced advisors.

Export hubs have been established in key locations to provide local businesses a one-stop blend of export assistance from Austrade, and industry development support from AusIndustry, the specialist programme delivery division of the Department of Industry, Innovation and Science. Of 27 TradeStart locations, 21 are in non-metropolitan areas.

The number of new exporters supported by the programme increased from 600 to 2 266 in five years between 2005 and 2010. The total amount of exports by these exporters increased from AUD 200 million to AUD 1.3 billion over the same period. The number of SMEs assisted reached approximately 4 500 in 2013.

Relevance to Kazakhstan

TradeStart emphasises coaching and action learning with firms. This type of service would help complement the financial support for SME export development that currently dominates in Kazakhstan. TradeStart has also been successful in reaching out to SMEs by operating offices outside of metropolitan areas and working in partnership across agencies and levels of government. It is also important in Kazakhstan to increase the numbers of SMEs engaged in internationalisation including in rural and remote regions.

Sources:
http://www.austrade.gov.au/Australian/How-Austrade-can-help/Trade-services/TradeStart
http://www.budget.gov.au/2013-14/content/ministerial_statements/download/Regional_MS.pdf
Snyder, J.D., et al. (2012) A Global Review of Innovative Practices in Regional SME Exporting Strategies & Foreign Direct Investment Attraction, MSU.

Public procurement for SMEs

Measures have been introduced to facilitate the access of SMEs to public procurement

Public procurement is a large market. In Kazakhstan, government current expenditures for purchases of goods and services were estimated to amount to some 10.3% of GDP in 2006-2010[5]. Governments in many countries operate measures to overcome the barriers that SMEs and entrepreneurs often face to accessing this market, with the aim of helping SMEs to grow, improve their productivity and innovate by supplying government and meeting government standards. This includes increasing the awareness of procurement opportunities, addressing barriers in the procurement process, such as minimum contract sizes, and allocating quotas of procurement values that must go to SMEs. Such measures have been put in place in Kazakhstan, and are expressly allowed by the Treaty on Eurasian Economic Union. Notably, an amendment of the public procurement law in 2014 introduced provisions for dividing public procurement contracts into smaller lots to facilitate the participation of SMEs in tenders and introduced an SME set-aside or quota. Furthermore, the Kazakhstan government operates a National Agency for the Development of Local Content that helps domestic producers improve their competitiveness with the aim of increasing the percentage of local content in goods, works and services sold on the domestic market.

Further opportunities exist to increase the awareness and capacities of SMEs to participate in public procurement processes

The government procurement office estimates that approximately 85% of the state procurement value is now delivered by SMEs. However, some further opportunities exist to remove barriers to SME access to public procurement. A USAID project implemented between 2006 and 2010 recommended implementation of an electronic procurement system, including creating an SME database, and introducing a pre-certification "green zone process" for SMEs that have performed successfully on government contracts (USAID, 2010). These suggested steps could still be taken into practice, for example under the management of the NCE. Box 5.9 gives the example of an integrated programme to support SME access to public procurement in Korea and Box 5.10 gives the further example of a national training and awareness programme for SMEs in public procurement operated in Ireland. These types of actions could be put together in a comprehensive system of support for SME participation in public procurement in Kazakhstan.

Box 5.9. Promoting SME Access to Public Procurement in Korea

The Korean Public Procurement Service Authority (PPS) has introduced several initiatives to increase SME participation in government procurement:

- An electronic procurement platform – the Korea On-line E-Procurement System (KONEPS) – improves transparency and minimises costs for the public sector in dealing with SMEs and provides easy access to SMEs on tender information and broader bidding opportunities;
- Advance payments of up to 70% of the purchase price are provided to qualifying SMEs in advance of delivery of the goods;
- An SME network loan programme is implemented with selected financial institutions enabling qualifying SMEs to obtain bank loans for up to 80% of the relevant contract price to cover the costs of contract execution;
- Fees for various bidding procedures are waived for SMEs.
- An Excellent SME Product award is made each year acknowledging high quality performance and innovative technology products provided by SMEs. The products are highlighted in the KONEPS product catalogue accessed by procurement agencies and by other suppliers of goods, works and consulting services that may be looking for subcontracting opportunities; and
- A Multiple Award Schedule (MAS) for SMEs provides a simplified procurement process for recurring, high volume purchases through use of indefinite delivery contracts.

Source: ADB (2012), SME Development: Government Procurement and Inclusive Growth; Seo, K. (2011), Innovating Public Procurement through Korea On-line E-Procurement System.

Box 5.10. Support for SMEs in Procurement – Ireland

Description of the approach

InterTradeIreland operates four programmes that support SMEs to participate in public procurement:

- Go-2-Tender training programme – a two-day introductory tender training programme, followed by a half day of one-to-one mentoring.
- Advanced Go-2-Tender training programme – a two-day tender training programme for experienced tenderers, followed by two days of one-to-one mentoring.
- Consortia Facilitator service – a mentoring service supporting SMEs in bidding collaboratively for contracts that would otherwise be beyond their reach.
- Meet The Buyer events – annual public events where public buyers make themselves available to meet with SMEs.

In order to address the problem of lack of information on the part of SMEs on tender opportunities, legislation requires all supplies and services contracts in excess of EUR 25 000 to be advertised on a single portal (where all transactions are free of charge). The government continues to remind procurement organisations to consider the needs of SMEs in repeated communications (DPE, 2014).

Success factors

The combination of information and training helps offer SME suppliers a level playing field in public procurement.

Relevance to Kazakhstan

Although there is a single portal for public procurement in Kazakhstan, set-aside provisions for SMEs and a relatively high share of public procurement from SMEs, additional training and awareness services could increase further the role of public procurement in strengthening the SME sector.

Source: http://www.intertradeireland.com/.

Entrepreneurship programmes for special target groups of the population

Many countries operate programmes that target specific groups of the population for entrepreneurship development, for example women, youth, immigrants, the unemployed or seniors. These policies seek to respond to an under-representation of these population groups in entrepreneurship or growth-oriented entrepreneurship and to various market failures and institutional barriers that lead to this under-representation (OECD, 2017). In Kazakhstan, women, youth (18-29) and people with disabilities are specifically targeted by dedicated BRM 2020 and ERM 2020 programmes and dedicated support for self-employment among the unemployed is included in the ERM 2020.

Women entrepreneurs

Several of the entrepreneurship development programmes outlined in the BRM 2020 make references to inclusion of women among the entrepreneurs to be supported, while not involving women-specific initiatives. Data on the gender breakdown of business support clients in the various BRM 2020 programmes indicate that women account for anywhere between 28% and 46% depending on the programme (Table 5.6). Furthermore, data from NCE for 2015 shows that 46.7% of clients at ESCs were women, although this figure varies regionally between 33% in Southern Kazakhstan and 61% in Almaty City (NCE, 2016). In 2012, the Damu Entrepreneurship Development Fund reported that women accounted for 32% of its support programme clients overall and set a target to increase the share of women entrepreneurs receiving state support to 40%[6]. As of January 2018, women accounted for 45% of the total number of entrepreneurs supported under the financial programmes of the Damu Entrepreneurship Development Fund.

Table 5.6. Share of women among the clients of various BRM 2020 programmes, 2014

BRM 2020 Programme	Total clients/ beneficiaries	Number of female clients/ beneficiaries	Women's share of all clients/ beneficiaries
Business Advisor I	19 236	7 868	40.9%
Business Advisor II	3 236	1 484	45.8%
School of Young Entrepreneurs (SYE)	1 077	365	33.9%
Training of Top Management of SMEs	423	168	39.7%
Business Connections (phase 1)	586	241	41.1%
Business Connections (phase 2)	111	31	27.9%
Senior Experts	100 (32 missions)	36	36.0%
Service Support for Existing SMEs (individual consultations)	17 344	8 056	46.5%
Business Support Centres in Monotowns	14 845	6 844	46.1%

Source: Republic of Kazakhstan (2015), Performance Report: Unified Programme of Support and Business Development "Business Road Map 2020" (in Russian).

There are two major dedicated access to financing programmes for women entrepreneurs. One is the Women's Entrepreneurship Micro Lending Programme, established by the Damu Entrepreneurship Development Fund in 2010[7]. The lending is delivered through agreements with selected second-tier banks and capped at KZT 30 million per borrower. In 2010-2017, 1 529 women entrepreneurship projects were supported for a total amount of loans of KZT 14.3 billion. The second programme is Women in Business, which was jointly launched by the European Bank for Reconstruction and Development (EBRD) and the Damu Entrepreneurship Development Fund in 2015 with funding from the EBRD and the government of Kazakhstan. It allocates a budget of KZT 3.8 billion for loans to women entrepreneurs and women-led SMEs in order to help them grow to larger businesses[8]. From 2016 to early 2018, 11 927 women's projects were supported, for the total amount of KZT 6.6 billion. The loan clients will receive further business advisory, training and mentoring support through the EBRD's small business support programme, which is expected to benefit between 2 000 and 2 500 women-led SMEs. One of the strengths of this programme is that, compared with the established micro-credit support, it has a greater focus on enhancing the capacity and growth of women entrepreneurs and their enterprises by offering larger loans accompanied by consultancy and mentoring support.

Despite these two dedicated programmes, women are under-represented in the access to finance support of the Damu Entrepreneurship Development Fund overall. As of 1 January 2018, women-owned SMEs accounted for only 30% of the subsidised loan clients and 18% of the subsidised loan value of the Damu Entrepreneurship Development Fund. Similarly, women-owned SMEs accounted for only 35% of loan guarantee clients and 28% of the guaranteed loan value of the Fund.

There have been positive developments in non-financial support for women entrepreneurs in addition. This includes the creation of a Council of Businesswomen within the NCE in 2015. Regional branches have been formed in every region of the country, headed by successful businesswomen. The branches organise awareness-raising activities for women entrepreneurs on the system of SME financing, provide information and consulting services to support promising business ideas and projects brought forward by women, support exchanges of experience among women entrepreneurs, and promote dialogue between women entrepreneurs and economic development bodies. The approach could be intensified by ensuring that the regional branches are adequately staffed by female experts who can provide the support needed by women entrepreneurs, integrating the Council of Businesswomen into the decision-making processes of the NCE, and working more extensively with other stakeholders to ensure that women are being served by financial institutions and ESCs. An interesting model is provided by the Committees for the Promotion of Women's Entrepreneurship established at local chambers of commerce in Italy (Box 5.11).

Box 5.11. Committees for the Promotion of Women's Entrepreneurship, Italian Chambers of Commerce

In 1999, the Italian Ministry of Productive Activities entered into an agreement with the national association of chambers of commerce that resulted in the establishment of 105 Committees for the Promotion of Women's Entrepreneurship (CIFs) located at local chambers in all 20 Italian regions. CIFs are staffed with more than 1 000 female experts who have been delegated by local business associations and trade unions to act as intermediaries listening to the needs of women entrepreneurs, aiming to integrate them into the decision-making processes of the chambers, promoting women-specific support measures, and increasing co-operation with other public and private stakeholders to promote female entrepreneurship.

The CIFs deal with all topics related to women's entrepreneurship, including awareness raising, access to finance, training and mentoring, and innovation. The main instruments used to achieve these goals are seminars, meetings, conferences and working groups. To collect evidence to back their activities, the CIFs carry out surveys to analyse the economic situation and needs of women-owned enterprises in their locality. An important communication tool is the nationwide website which provides comprehensive information on new policy measures and on economic conditions affecting women's entrepreneurship (www.imprenditoriafemminile.camcom.it). For more localised information, the website directs users to the websites of individual CIFs.

Over the years, the CIFs have developed several innovative initiatives in favour of female entrepreneurship. One example is the "Giro d'Italia of women entrepreneurs", an itinerant information and awareness campaign carried out in the form of one-day events organised in co-operation with local stakeholders and successful women entrepreneurs. Each year it promotes a specific theme or motto (enterprise transfer, entrepreneurship education, internationalisation, etc.) using roundtable discussions, role-model testimonials, and theme-specific workshops. The CIFs also co-operate in collecting and sharing good practice examples. For example, in April 2013, they profiled local projects facilitating women entrepreneurs' access to finance. In February 2013, the national government renewed its commitment to support the activities of the CIF network by assigning the national association of chambers of commerce the task of creating 20 regional units for the co-ordination of the 105 local CIFs.

Through the CIF, the Chambers have started up the Observatory of Female Entrepreneurship in 2003 that analyses and presents a gender view of the Italian entrepreneurial environment. Working with the Ministry of Economic Development, the CIF-chamber of commerce initiative has also led to the development of the regular national report "Enterprise in Gender" on women starting a business.

The example of the CIFs, however, demonstrates how the NCE might play a more proactive role in supporting the development of policies and programmes in favour of female entrepreneurship and the growth of their enterprises, especially at the regional level.

Source: OECD (2014), Italy: Key Issues and Policies, OECD Studies on SMEs and Entrepreneurship, p. 150; http://www.imprenditoriafemminile.camcom.it/.

Nevertheless, the provision of women-focused entrepreneurship and business management training courses could strengthened to help overcome the skills and experience barriers and the issues in managing business-family balance that research suggests are holding back women entrepreneurship in Kazakhstan (Sange Research Centre, 2013). In the short term, this need could be addressed by dedicating a number of entrepreneurship training and advice courses to women as part of the Business Advisor, Top SME Managers Training, and Business Connections programmes. Pilots could be run to test demand, satisfaction levels, and impact of women-dedicated courses within these programmes. They could be piloted in particular in regions where women are under-represented among active SMEs, such as in the Zhambyl, Almaty, and South Kazakhstan regions.

To further capitalise on the potential of women entrepreneurs to boost the development of employment and value added in SMEs, the government should also consider launching a more comprehensive women's entrepreneurship development initiative. This would focus on ensuring that women have access to the appropriate training and capacity building to start and develop more growth-oriented enterprises. It could combine actively promoting successful women entrepreneurs as role models through the media, opening training centres for women entrepreneurs, and creating pathways for financing that are combined with mentoring and advisory support to facilitate stronger start-ups and the expansion and growth of women-owned enterprises. Dedicated support programmes and services for women's entrepreneurship have been shown to increase the impact on women entrepreneurship relative to "gender-blind" approaches. Box 5.12 provides an example of such an initiative.

Box 5.12. Women's Enterprise Centres, Canada

Description of the approach

The Canadian government funds networks of Women's Enterprise Centres (WECs) in all of Canada's regions. Across the four provinces of western Canada, a network of WECs is supported by the government regional development agency, Western Economic Diversification Canada (WD), under an initiative called the Women's Enterprise Initiative.

The WECs provide a one-stop shop for existing and potential women entrepreneurs offering advice, business planning assistance, mentoring/matchmaking, networking opportunities, information, and referrals to accountants and lawyers. Although they were set up by WD, a federal government agency, they operate as not-for-profit organisations and are awarded five-year renewal contracts to provide their services. They also deliver loan funds (pools of up to CAD 5 million) targeted to new or existing businesses owned by women with loan values of up to CAD 150 000. These loans may be combined with advice and assistance in the development of a business plan. The WECs are also part of the delivery network for the WEConnect Access to Supply Chains programme, which aims to help prepare women entrepreneurs in accessing global supply chains.

Initially, there was one WEC in each of the four provinces, but there are now eight offices. On average, each WEC employs 11 staff members, and makes use of 178 volunteers and 315 partners in performing its activities. Annual funding to the WECs totals CAD 3.9 million.

Results

The WECs are filling an important gap by offering targeted training, seminars, advisory services and financial assistance for women entrepreneurs and by increasing the profile of women entrepreneurs and encouraging other women to start or grow their businesses.

Over the period 2008–2012, the WECs in western Canada provided services to 17 403 women entrepreneurs. On an annual basis, clients accessed an average of 12 703 business advisory services, 38 501 information services, and 4 496 women received training (WD, 2014). This assistance led to new start-ups and jobs, job retention in existing client firms, increased revenues, and higher survival rates than for the average Canadian SME.

WECs also issued an annual average of 113 loans (50 to new businesses and 63 to existing businesses) totalling approximately CAD 6.4 million annually and leading to the creation of an average of 596 jobs in the funded enterprises. Over the four-year period, the WECs approved CAD 25.6 million in loans that created 2 384 jobs; an average of 5.3 jobs per loan, or equivalent to one job per CAD 10 037 of loan, which compares very favourably with other federal government programmes in terms of efficiency. The total value of the loan fund as of 31 March 2012 was CAD 20.4 million.

The most significant impacts on the women entrepreneurs have been improved development of their business, management and/or personal skills, increased access to other programmes and services, networking with other women entrepreneurs, accessing information for decision-making, and receiving encouragement to start or further develop their own business. An evaluation found that:

- Over half of non-loan clients and 43% of loan clients reported improving their business practices as a result of programme assistance;
- Over two-thirds of the loan clients reported that the assistance enabled their business to survive;
- Approximately half of the non-loan clients reported that the assistance encouraged them to start their business and improve their business practices;

- 18% of loan clients and 16% of non-loan clients reported that the assistance increased the export capacity of their businesses; and
- On aggregate, clients estimated that 44% of their current revenues would not have been generated without the WEC services and assistance.

What is not known is whether, in the absence of WECs, these women clients would have been able to obtain equivalent services from the generic business support organisations, although 74% of the assisted clients reported that they had only received business support services from the WECs.

Success factors

The gender-sensitive approach to the delivery of services and assistance has been important to the success of the initiative, including the emotional and motivational support that women entrepreneurs receive from the WEC staff during the counselling, mentoring and training. The strong capabilities of the staff, the support provided by the Board of Directors and other volunteers, and strong linkages developed with other programmes and services have been critical.

Obstacles and responses

One of the initial problems was meeting the demand for services from women in all parts of each province, which can span large geographic distances. Initially, the WECs used a mobile service (when the initiative was created in 1994, use of the internet was not well developed in Canada), while also seeking to develop partnerships with other service delivery partners in the more rural areas. Eventually, the WECs in three of the provinces opened up one or two branch offices to develop a presence in other key centres.

Funding is becoming a problem for the WECs. There are two issues. First, government funding has remained the same since 2005, and the initiative does not have sufficient resources to develop new programmes, update technology or serve the needs of more women entrepreneurs. To address this issue, some of the WECs have been seeking other funding sources, or leveraging resources of other organisations that would enable them to reach out to underserved groups, such as Aboriginal and rural women. Second, in some recent years the government has approved operational funding to the WECs for only one year at a time, whereas the five-year contribution agreements enabled the Centres to undertake longer-term programming.

Although most clients are satisfied with the WEC services, some clients would like to see better follow-up or follow-on services; more tailored training and seminar programmes to fit with the characteristics of their business or their stage of development; and stronger capabilities of the WEC staff. The WECs are working to be more responsive to the distinct needs of the client base, given that these needs are not homogenous for all women entrepreneurs, and are committed to the professional development and competency of their staff.

Relevance to Kazakhstan

This Canadian experience suggests that targeting women with directed measures can increase the number and quality of women-owned enterprises and the growth of these enterprises. The model would be relatively simple to adopt in Kazakhstan because many of the components of a WEC are already delivered in Kazakhstan, although not targeted specifically to women and not as a cohesive package. Such an initiative could be started by issuing a call for proposals from intermediary organisations to operate a Women's Enterprise Centre or a women's desk within the framework of Entrepreneurship Support Centres in certain regions where the needs appear to be greater. The Women's Enterprise Centres would offer a comprehensive package of support services that include access to financing, counselling, training, mentoring, networking and entrepreneurship awareness.

Sources:

Alberta Women Entrepreneurs: www.awebusiness.com; British Columbia Women's Enterprise Centre: www.womensenterprise.ca/; Manitoba Women's Enterprise Centre: www.wecm.ca/; Women Entrepreneurs of Saskatchewan Inc.: www.womenentrepreneurs.sk.ca/

Evaluation reports can be found at: http://www.wd.gc.ca/;

WD (2014), "Evaluation of the Women's Enterprise Initiative".

Young entrepreneurs

Although large numbers of young people in Kazakhstan are in self-employment, many are in low productivity and informal activities. Youth entrepreneurship policies that provide support in accessing finance with training, advice and networking services could help more of these young people to develop higher value-added entrepreneurship activities. The government has started to develop youth entrepreneurship programmes in recent years, and the President established a Council for the Development of Youth Entrepreneurship to identify and propose solutions to youth entrepreneurship problems in 2013 (Scientific-Research Centre "Youth", 2013).

Overall, monitoring evidence shows that people under 30 make up between approximately 15% and 30% of the beneficiaries of other non-financial support programmes under the BRM 2020 (Table 5.7).

Table 5.7. Share of young people (16-29 years old) among clients of various BRM 2020 programmes, 2014

BRM 2020 Programme	Number of participants 16–29 years of age	Share of all clients/ beneficiaries
Business Advisor I	5 043	30.9%
Business Advisor II	979	30.3%
School of Young Entrepreneurs (SYE)	1 077	100.0%
Training of Top Management of SMEs	131	31.0%
Business Connections (phase 1)	155	26.4%
Business Connections (phase 2)	15	13.5%
Senior Experts	22	22.0%
Service Support for Existing SMEs (individual consultations	3 355	19.4%
Business Support Centres in Monotowns	4 750	32.0%

Source: Republic of Kazakhstan (2015), Performance Report Unified Programme of Support and Business Development "Business Road Map 2020" (in Russian).

There is also a key dedicated entrepreneurship training initiative for young entrepreneurs in the form of the School for Young Entrepreneurs (SYE), which is part of the BRM 2020. Unfortunately, the start-up rate among SYE graduates appears to be low, suggesting deficiencies in the level of support for the business start-up and post-creation stages. Youth entrepreneurship programmes in other countries often provide for a longer period of intervention that includes pre- and post-start-up mentoring and coaching support for up to two years. This may also include opportunities to transfer to a business incubator for additional start-up support. In some cases, the start-up rate of participants in these young entrepreneur programmes can reach 30% or higher.

Access to financing can also be a major constraint to business creation for young people. Graduates of the SYE have the right to apply for a state start-up grant and/or a guarantee for start-up financing from a second tier bank. However, the BRM 2020 programme performance report indicates that very few receive a start-up grant or credit guarantee. Only 53 young people were in the process of applying for a state grant and 35 were collecting documents to apply for a guaranteed loan from a second-tier bank in 2014 (Republic of Kazakhstan, 2015). Youth entrepreneurship programmes in other countries often combine access to financing with training and mentoring. For example, The Prince's Trust Youth Business Scotland (PTYBS) offers both start-up grants of up to GBP 1 000 and small loans of up to GBP 5 000 to support the start-up of businesses, in addition to the advisory and mentoring support (Halabisky, 2012).

In order to increase the accessibility of start-up financing to young entrepreneurs, the Damu Entrepreneurship Development Fund introduced special provisions in 2013 in its "express guarantee" programme for entrepreneurs under 30 years of age and in business for less than one year. This removes the sectoral restrictions normally associated with the guarantee programme and increases the guarantee to 85% of the overall credit amount up to KZT 20 million[9]. A small number of banks are partnering with the Fund in this young entrepreneur guarantee programme. One of the aims of the initiative is to promote the development of youth entrepreneurship in the spheres of trading, catering and other types of activities, which were not previously a priority in the BRM 2020 programme, but which may better align with the types of businesses started by young entrepreneurs. In 2010 to 2017, 816 young entrepreneurs had received loan-related financing under this framework, totalling KZT 9.2 billion.

The government also supports some other promising initiatives to develop young entrepreneurs. The Atameken Startup Public Fund for Youth Entrepreneurship was established in 2012 by the National Economic Chamber of Kazakhstan Atameken Union. This aims to support young entrepreneurs with innovative ideas through coaching, mentoring and potential access to angel financing. In 2013, Atameken Startup Weekends were held in 22 cities, including Almaty, Astana, all oblast centres and five mono-industry towns. In total, about 5 000 people attended the events. The best project teams receive cash awards to encourage the young people to open their own business. This approach to youth entrepreneurship development, which reflects a global trend that has taken root in more than 150 countries and is producing significant impact, should be accelerated in Kazakhstan, and complemented by the creation of start-up accelerators where the most promising teams from the Startup Weekends can be provided with intensive support to refine their business ideas/models, develop prototypes, and prepare their innovative products/services for market entry.

In partnership with Youth Business International (YBI), Youth Business Kazakhstan (MOST) was established in 2015. This is an initiative of the Social Public Fund of Kazakhstani Leaders (SPFKL) and the Young Entrepreneurs Club (YEC). Supported by the Damu Entrepreneurship Development Fund and KazMicroFinance (KMF), MOST provides a free-of-charge integrated package of support to help young entrepreneurs in establishing and developing their own businesses, in accordance with the global approach of the YBI. The YEC undertakes the educational and mentoring parts of the programme, access to finance is provided through cooperation with the Damu Entrepreneurship Development Fund and the KMF, and the SPFKL oversees the programme implementation and provides access to contacts in governmental bodies and other potential partners and supporters. Although data on the performance of the programme in Kazakhstan is not available, the YBI programmes in other countries achieve impressive results[10].

Despite these initiatives, the numbers of supported young entrepreneurs will need to be increased if a significant impact is to be made on increasing youth entrepreneurship in comparison with the scale of this group. The government may be guided in the formulation of a comprehensive approach to the development of youth entrepreneurship by the principles presented in Box 5.13.

Box 5.13. OECD principles for youth entrepreneurship policy

Generic principles:

1. Select beneficiaries of youth entrepreneurship programmes carefully and tailor the support provision to the needs of youth.
   - Extensive support should be low cost and offered widely.
   - Intensive support should be competitive or filtered to select recipients that are motivated and most likely to succeed.
2. Use youth entrepreneurship policies and programmes to promote creativity and innovation.
   - Seek (even low level) innovation in supported business projects (including organisational, marketing, green, social).
3. Recognise that different policy interventions complement and reinforce each other.
   - Offer combined access to finance, training, mentoring, and networking.
   - Ensure education, economic and labour policies are co-ordinated and complementary.
   - Identify gaps and synergies across stakeholders.
4. Consider adapting mainstream programmes as an alternative to youth-specific actions.
5. Engage youth and youth organisations in the design and implementation of youth entrepreneurship policies and programmes.
   - Communicate with youth through appropriate channels.
   - Consult youth organisations in policy design.
   - Leverage stakeholder knowledge and experience.
6. Appraise and evaluate youth entrepreneurship policies and programmes, making adjustments when design or implementation can be improved.
   - Identify intervention needs, targets and expected impacts.
   - Evaluate results and adjust the approach.
   - Seek employability as well as venture creation outcomes.
   - Measure long-term as well as short-term impacts.

Strategy for supporting youth entrepreneurship:

1. Develop a vision for youth entrepreneurship support.
   - Embed entrepreneurship promotion and support within youth employment strategies.
2. Communicate the objectives of youth entrepreneurship policies and programmes to youth, youth organisations and the community.

3. Government actors and other stakeholders have defined, complementary roles in supporting youth entrepreneurship.

Building a supportive institutional environment:

1. Ensure that the regulatory environment does not discriminate or provide disincentives for youth entrepreneurship.
   - Be supportive of youth entrepreneurship in welfare, tax and regulatory systems.
   - Ensure that bankruptcy laws do not prevent young entrepreneurs from having a second chance.
2. Promote positive image of entrepreneurship to build a culture of entrepreneurship amongst youth.
   - Inform youth and society about the potential of youth entrepreneurship.
   - Celebrate young entrepreneurs as role models.
3. Ensure that youth can access information and resources about entrepreneurship.
   - Provide ready information on how to start up.
   - Make business start-up support easily accessible to youth.

Improving entrepreneurship skills:

1. Provide entrepreneurship education in schools, vocational training and higher education.
   - Develop entrepreneurial mind sets as well as new ventures.
   - Provide opportunities to learn through experience (e.g. business simulations and competitions).
   - Include low educational achievers.

2. Provide coaching and mentoring for young people with interest and potential for sustainable projects.
   - Use an appropriate matching mechanism to ensure a good fit between coachee/mentee and coach/mentor.

3. Encourage networking.
   - Create links with other young entrepreneurs, senior entrepreneurs, investors and partners.

Facilitating access to finance:

1. Provide financial literacy education to all youth.

2. Ensure youth can access loans and microfinance.
   - Use grants when loans are not feasible.

3. Encourage alternative financing methods such as guarantees, crowdfunding, peer-to-peer lending, and business angel investment.

4. Complement financial support with business training and mentoring.

Source: OECD (2015), Supporting Youth Entrepreneurship in Lithuania A Review of Policies and Programmes, pp. 11–12.

Entrepreneurs with disabilities

Estimates indicate that there were approximately 557 600 adults with some form of disability in Kazakhstan in 2014, approximately 4.8% of the working age population (Naukenova, 2015). Entrepreneurship can sometimes provide a more suitable option than employment for people with disabilities who are seeking to participate in the labour market. For example, it may provide more flexibility in tasks, hours and place of work and offer an alternative for people faced with discrimination in the hiring practices of established businesses (Halabisky, 2014; Kitching, 2014). However, people with disabilities often face particular barriers to succeeding in entrepreneurship, including limited access to start-up capital, lack of entrepreneurship knowledge, skills and experience, and lack of confidence and aspirations. Furthermore, standard business development support may not always be appropriate for the needs of disabled entrepreneurs, for example if services are not accessible (due to transportation, facility or format issues) or business advisors are not supportive or understanding of the issues facing disabled entrepreneurs (Halabisky, 2014).

There are a number of BRM 2020 initiatives to support people with disabilities in entrepreneurship. The ERM 2020 also includes people with disabilities among the target groups identified for active labour market programmes, including self-employment assistance.

An important step in supporting people with disabilities in entrepreneurship is the monitoring by that the Damu Entrepreneurship Development Fund undertakes of the participation of entrepreneurs with disabilities in the mainstream BRM 2020 programmes. This shows, for example, that at the end of December 2014, 1 680 people with disabilities had taken classes on business basics as part of the Business Advisor course. In addition, all of the Damu Entrepreneurship Development Fund's regional branches provide legal advice and business counselling to entrepreneurs with disabilities. The NCE also mainstreams entrepreneurship support for people with disabilities through giving access to entrepreneurs with disabilities to the advice services of the ESCs, although the number of clients with disabilities supported with business advice is in the low hundreds.

There is also a key dedicated BRM 2020 programme for people with disabilities run by the Damu Entrepreneurship Development Fund called Komek. An important element of the Komek programme is its website: www.Damu-komek.kz. The website offers a video tutorial about the basics of running your own business, distance access to entrepreneurship training programmes and a section on laws, regulations and incentives for entrepreneurs with disabilities. It also contains an online bulletin board that helps connect people with disabilities needing help in starting or running a business with sponsors who can provide equipment, finance and other resources for the business. The Damu Entrepreneurship Development Fund works closely with associations of people with disabilities to promote the website to potential entrepreneurs. As of January 2018, the website had received 2 431 requests for help from entrepreneurs with disabilities and resulted in finding sponsors for 2 068 of them. The sponsorships included providing sewing equipment, computers and office equipment, and equipment for shoe-making and furniture production.

In addition, the Damu Entrepreneurship Development Fund works with various second-tier banks as part of their corporate social responsibility activities to elicit offers of equipment, financing, training and coaching for entrepreneurs with disabilities. Using this approach, Damu also develops specific programmes with partner banks. For example, it operates the Look at the Stars business plan competition with Kuz Zholy, a foundation of the Kazkommertsbank. In a first round, the competition awarded grants of KZT 100 000 to the 60 entrepreneurs (from approximately 140 applicants) with disabilities who were judged to have the best business plans. A second round in 2014 awarded grants of between KZT 100 000 and KZT 200 000 to a further 80 entrepreneurs. A second example is the Better Lives for People with Disabilities project launched in 2014 by the Damu Entrepreneurship Development Fund, the Shyrak Association of Women with Disabilities and BG International Ltd. (Kazakhstan). This is a competition in the cities of Almaty, Astana, Uralsk and Burlinsk District of West-Kazakhstan Region, which selected five entrepreneurs with disabilities from each region to receive training under the Business Advisor I programme, personal consultations on developing a business plan, and grants of KZT 510 000 for business start-up.

These initiatives show that there is clear recognition in Kazakhstan of the potential for entrepreneurship among people with disabilities and motivation to support them in entrepreneurship. However, relatively few people participate in the support available and the funding relies largely on negotiating separate agreements with banks for charitable contributions. Furthermore, loan financing is not one of the specific options offered to this group of entrepreneurs even though they are likely to face difficulty in accessing formal financing channels.

A strengthened set of entrepreneurship support initiatives should therefore be considered for people with disabilities. This could include grants and loans for the launch of businesses started by people with disabilities and financial support for the acquisition of assistive technologies necessary to perform the work by entrepreneurs with disabilities. The financial support could be started up with a dedicated fund established by the government to which banks could be asked to make charitable contributions alongside government. In addition, a range of dedicated advice, mentoring, and training services could be developed for entrepreneurs with disabilities and sensitivity training could be provided to staff of the ESCs on how to appropriately adapt mainstream business advisory and other services to better serve entrepreneurs with disabilities. The NCE could also be encouraged to facilitate the formation of an Entrepreneurs with Disabilities Network to promote mutual support sharing of experience.

Box 5.14 provides an example from the United Kingdom of an integrated and intensive programme of support to entrepreneurs with disabilities that was supported through a small initial government development fund.

Box 5.14. Ready to Start Project for People with Disabilities, United Kingdom

The approach

The Ready to Start project supported people with any form of disability to start a business through the provision of skills training and individual business advisory services, matched with direct financial support. It operated between 2006 and 2009 and aimed to recruit 1 200 eligible people and support 600 participants to start businesses. During this time, the UK government had set a target of transitioning 1.5 million disadvantaged people into work, one million of whom were receiving disability benefits. Self-employment was seen as a viable option for tackling this issue.

Organised and implemented by the Leonard Cheshire Disability charity, a team of regional co-ordinators covering 27 locations across England and Wales recruited clients and developed relationships with partner organisations to gain their support and seek client referrals. Partner organisations provided mentoring and training, as well as one-to-one advice on non-business matters including benefits, housing and self-management. Regional co-ordinators oversaw the support delivery to ensure that clients received the full range of support services needed and organised face-to-face and virtual networking events.

After the project started, direct financial support was added in the form of a small development fund. It aimed to help participants purchase equipment, insurance and marketing materials, and assistive technologies, and cover the costs of a year's membership in the Federation of Small Businesses or similar trade bodies to provide continuing support and networking opportunities. Clients were also provided with a refurbished computer with the appropriate adaptations and software.

Much of the financial support for the project was provided by Barclays Bank (GBP 3 million). Additional funding and support was provided by the Prince's Trust. Other partner organisations such as Action for Blind People and Business Link London (a government business development services organisation) were crucial in recruiting and referring clients. Other partner organisations were important for delivering training and advisory services, including Destiny, Northern Pinetree Trust and Meganexus.

Results

The project recruited 1 382 potential entrepreneurs with disabilities and, of these, 735 established new businesses (274 transitioned into employment or further training). Project evaluations estimated that the project saved the UK Treasury an estimated GBP 3.5 million per annum (approximately EUR 4.3 million) in social benefit payments.

Success factors

The project was successful because it provided intensive support that was tailored to individual clients' needs. This included mentoring support at a distance (online and telephone) alongside face-to-face support. Participants reported that the development fund was the most useful element of the support, followed by the mentoring offer. The availability of a small development fund allowed the project to meet the special financing needs of clients who would have otherwise been prevented from launching their business.

Obstacles and responses

The project required a large amount of financial and human resources. The charity was able to leverage a combination of public and private sector funds and strategically partner with complementary organisations to recruit participants and deliver the services. Media promotion of the project and the role of regional co-ordinators in recruiting and orienting potential regional partner organisations were helpful in securing the commitment of project partners.

Relevance to Kazakhstan

The project serves as a good example of how complementary, non-competitive relationships across a network of partners can successfully reach clients on a proactive basis and deliver a set of integrated support services to a very narrow target base across a wide geographic area. It also demonstrates the importance of creating a development fund to help finance the start-up costs.

Source: Contact: Leonard Cheshire Disability, London, UK, https://www.leonardcheshire.org/sites/default/files/RTS_Closing_Report_FINAL.pdf.

Unemployed people

The ERM 2020 includes a dimension for supporting self-employment for unemployed people considering employment options. Through application to the employment centres, unemployed people can access free training on the basics of entrepreneurship (with the provision of financial support towards the cost of travel and accommodation to attend the training) and assistance in developing a business plan. They can also access consultancy services (marketing, legal, accounting and other services) for up to one year. The ERM 2020 can also provide microcredit (up to KZT 3 million) for start-ups by formerly unemployed people. Up to KZT 3 million can also be provided for the development of infrastructure necessary for the operation of the business (sewage systems, heat and water supply, gas supply, telephone and electricity networks) and/or the acquisition of associated technological equipment.

From January to mid-August of 2015, 2 200 unemployed people received the entrepreneurship training, of whom 1 377 started their own business for the first time. More than 2 000 participants received microloans amounting to KZT 4.8 billion, creating 2 500 additional jobs. This is a better conversion rate from assistance to business creation than achieved by the Business Advisor and SYE programmes, suggesting the relevance of combining access to microcredit with the entrepreneurship training.

However, a major issue for Kazakhstan is that much self-employment activity is unproductive self-employment that people undertake because of lack of better alternatives and that provides only a subsistence income (Kulbosynonova, 2013; Mussurov and Arabsheibani, 2015). This suggests that the emphasis of public programmes for entrepreneurship by the unemployed should not be on increasing the flow of people into self-employment in general. Instead, policy for self-employment should combine two focuses. One strand of the approach should assist the unproductive self-employed to move into paid jobs. A second strand should strengthen the entrepreneurship projects of the self-employed by promoting the formalisation of existing informal activity and the entry of new self-employed into the more productive spheres of economic activity.

One of the targets of the ERM 2020 is to reduce the self-employment rate from the 2010 baseline of 33% to 26% by 2020. Clearly this should be achieved largely by supporting the unproductive self-employed to move into better quality self-employment or into better jobs. To help target support, the Kazakhstan Agency of Statistics has developed a methodology to identify the unproductive self-employed, i.e. those who do not generate sufficient income to meet their subsistence needs or whose average monthly income is less than the living wage of the region where they live. These people are to be targeted for training assistance and other support such as microcredit to help them develop more productive enterprises or have a better opportunity to switch into paid employment.

Notes

1. Kazakhstan has the advantage of being able to match tax authority data on the registration of individual entrepreneurs with information on participants in the programme.
2. Government response to OECD fact-finding questionnaire for this review.
3. http://www.factoring.org/eNewsletter/WebNews.asp?id=89&aid=905.

4. The sixteen areas are: advanced technologies in the exploration, production, transportation and processing of mineral and hydrocarbons; advanced technologies in the mining and metallurgical complexes; advanced technologies in agriculture; biotechnology; innovative technologies of chemistry and petrochemistry; progressive mechanical engineering, including the use of new materials; alternative and renewable energy; information and communication technologies; energy efficiency; advanced technologies in light industries; advanced technologies in the furniture and woodworking industries; advanced technologies in construction, including the use of new materials; advanced technologies in the packaging industry; robotics; nano and space technology; energy.

5. http://data.worldbank.org/indicator/NE.CON.GOVT.ZS.

6. "Lyazzat Ibragimova urged women entrepreneurs to actively participate in programmes realized by Fund 'DAMU'"11 March 2013: http://www.Damu.kz/13339/.

7. For the purposes of this programme, a women-owned enterprise is defined as one in which a women or women own at least 50% of the business and at least 30% of the employees are female (outlined in ADB, 2013, p. 41).

8. "EBRD provides first credit line under new Women in Business Programme in Kazakhstan", EBRD, 22 September 2015 (http://www.ebrd.com/news/2015/ebrd-provides-first-credit-line-under-new-women-in-business-programme-in-Kazakhstan.html/.

9. "Young entrepreneurs can be provided by DAMU Fund's guarantees without constraints on their activity", 15 July 2014 (http://www.Damu.kz/16400/).

10. In 2014 YBI members in over 40 countries provided 65 559 young people with practical skills-based training, and 18 949 entrepreneurs were supported in starting a business (13 059) or growing an existing business (5 890). See: YBI Network Review 2015 at: http://www.youthbusiness.org/wp-content/uploads/2015/07/YBI_networkreview_inside-2015-Art.pdf/.

References

ADB (Asian Development Bank) (2012), SME Development: Government Procurement and Inclusive Growth, Asian Development Bank, Manila, Philippines.

ADB (2013), *Kazakhstan Country Gender Assessment*, Asian Development Bank, Manila, Philippines.

ADB (2015), Asia SME Finance Monitor 2014, Asian Development Bank, Manila, Philippines.

BIBB (Federal Institute for Vocational Education and Training) (2015), "VET Data Report Germany 2014: Facts and analyses accompanying the Federal report on vocational education and training – selected findings", Federal Institute for Vocational Education and Training, Bonn, Germany.

British Chambers of Commerce (2011), "Skills for Jobs: More to Learn?" October, British Chambers of Commerce, London, UK.

Damu ("Damu" Entrepreneurship Development Fund) (2014a), "Development Strategy for 2014–2023", Damu Entrepreneurship Development Fund, Almaty.

Damu (2015a), *2014 Annual Report*, Baiterek, Almaty, Damu Entrepreneurship Development Fund.

EBRD (European Bank for Reconstruction and Development (2013), "Strategy for Kazakhstan", as approved by the Board of Directors at its meeting on 17 December 2013, EBRD, London, UK.

European Commission (2014), A Study on R&D Tax Incentives: Final report, European Commission, Brussels.

Guimón, J. (2013), Research centers of excellence in Kazakhstan: The Technology Commercialization Project, The Innovation Policy Platform Policy Brief, World Bank, Washington, DC.

Halabisky, D. (2014), "Entrepreneurial Activities in Europe - Entrepreneurship for People with Disabilities", OECD Employment Policy Papers, No. 6, OECD Publishing, Paris, http://dx.doi.org/10.1787/5jxrcmkcxjq4-en.

Halabisky, D. (2012), "Entrepreneurial Activities in Europe - Youth Entrepreneurship", *OECD Employment Policy Papers*, No. 1, OECD Publishing, Paris, http://dx.doi.org/10.1787/5jxrcmlf2f27-en.

IFC (2012) Providing Comprehensive Non-financial Services to SMEs in Turkey: A Success Story for Both Bank and Clients.

ILO (International Labour Organization) (2011), "Tracer Studies on the Know About Business Entrepreneurship Education Programme - A synthesis report from eight studies", ILO, Geneva.

Kitching, J. (2014), "Entrepreneurship and Self-Employment by People with Disabilities", Background paper for the OECD Project on Inclusive Entrepreneurship, OECD, Paris.

KODIT and KDS (2012), "Credit Guarantee and Credit Evaluation System for SME Development in Kazakhstan", Ministry of Strategy and Finance, the Republic of Korea

Kulbosynonova, N.K. (2013), "Self-Employed Population in Kazakhstan: Who are these people and what is their income?", M. Aueziv South Kazakhstan University, Shymkent, Kazakhstan, http://old.group.org/en/publication/view/1494/.

Mason, C. and R. Brown (2010), High Growth Firms in Scotland, Scottish Enterprise, Glasgow, UK.

Mussurov, A., and G.R. Arabsheibani (2015), "Informal self-employment in Kazakhstan", *IZA Journal of Labor & Development*, 4(9).

NCE (2016), Report on the implementation of the service support for existing business activity in the fourth direction of the unified business support and development of the program "Business Road Map - 2020" at the end of 2015, National Chamber of Entrepreneurs, Astana.

NATD (2016), Annual report for the National Agency for Technological Development for 2015, NATD, Astana

Naukenova, A. (2015), "Kazakhstan's and developed countries' experience in reforming social policy on employment of people with disabilities", *Economics and Sociology*, Vol. 8(1): 287–297.

OECD (2017), The Missing Entrepreneurs 2017: Policies for Inclusive Entrepreneurship, OECD Publishing, Paris. http://dx.doi.org/10.1787/9789264283602-en.

OECD (2015), Supporting Youth Entrepreneurship in Lithuania A Review of Policies and Programmes, OECD Publishing, Paris.

OECD (2014), *Italy: Key Issues and Policies*, OECD Studies on SMEs and Entrepreneurship, OECD Publishing, Paris. http://dx.doi.org/10.1787/9789264213951-en.

OECD (2013a), An International Benchmarking Analysis of Public Programmes for High-Growth Firms. OECD Publishing, Paris.

OECD (2013b) Skills Development and Training in SMEs. OECD Publishing, Paris, http://dx.doi.org/10.1787/9789264169425-en.

OECD (2011a), "Competitiveness and Private Sector Development: Central Asia 2011-Competitiveness Outlook, OECD Publishing, Paris, http://dx.doi.org/10.1787/9789264097285-en.

OECD (2011b), Business Innovation Policies: Selected Country Comparisons, OECD Publishing, Paris. http://dx.doi.org/10.1787/9789264115668-en

OECD (2009), "Top Barriers and Drivers to SME Internationalisation", Report by the OECD Working Party on SMEs and Entrepreneurship, OECD, Paris.

Republic of Kazakhstan (2015), *Отчет об эффективности Единой программы поддержки и развития бизнеса «Дорожная карта бизнеса 2020»* (Performance Report Unified Programme of Support and Business Development "Business Road Map 2020"), Astana.

Sange Research Centre (2013), "Kazakhstan: Improving Capacity to Support SME Development - SME Survey – A Needs Assessment", May, Asian Development Bank, Manila.

Scientific-Research Centre "Youth" (2013), *Youth of Kazakhstan – 2013 National Report*, Republic of Kazakhstan, Astana.

Seo, K. (2011), Innovating Public Procurement through Korea On-line E-Procurement System (presentation to World Bank conference, April 2010, Istanbul).

Snyder, J.D., et al. (2012), A Global Review of Innovative Practices in Regional SME Exporting Strategies & Foreign Direct Investment Attraction, Michigan State University, East Lansing.

USAID (United States Agency for International Development) (2010), "Kazakhstan Small Business Development Project – Final Report - October 2006–September 2010", USAID, Washington, DC.

van Lieshout, S., M. Sievers, and M. Aliyev (2012), *Start and Improve Your Business Global Tracer Study 2011: ILO's business management training programme*, International Labour Organization (ILO), Geneva.

WD (2014), "Evaluation of the Women's Enterprise Initiative", January, Western Economic Diversification Canada, Edmonton, Canada.

World Bank (2015), Project Appraisal Document on a Proposed Loan in the Amount of US$40 Million to the Republic of Kazakhstan for a SME Competitiveness Project, Washington, DC: World Bank.

Chapter 6. The Local Dimension to SME and Entrepreneurship Policy in Kazakhstan

The overall focus of this chapter is the adaptation of SME and entrepreneurship policies to regional differences in Kazakhstan. It starts by assessing regional variations in the levels and characteristics of SME and entrepreneurship activities and in the obstacles found in regional business environments. It then assesses how regional government authorities and regional co-ordinating committees help tailor national SME and entrepreneurship development programmes to regional conditions and how coherence is achieved between national and regional level SME and entrepreneurship policy actions. Finally, the chapter examines the issue of simplifying regional business regulation. The chapter offers a number of policy recommendations.

Key messages and policy recommendations

Kazakhstan is a large and regionally diverse country. The diversity is very apparent in differences in the rates and characteristics of SME and entrepreneurship activity across regions and in differences in the enablers and obstacles to SME and entrepreneurship development in regional business environments.

Government actions for SME and entrepreneurship development are mainly organised through the national Business Roadmap 2020 (BRM 2020) programme and operate across the whole country. The resources largely come from government ministries and the Damu Entrepreneurship Development Fund, with co-funding contributions from the regional government authorities. However, Regional Coordinating Councils have a significant influence on the mix of the BRM 2020 programmes found in each region, based on their decisions on which BRM 2020 projects to bid for and to co-fund. This helps to adjust the nature of BRM 2020 actions to the economic development priorities of each regional government, for example the relative priorities they place on SME financing compared with developing SME management capabilities or entrepreneurship training.

On the other hand, there are significant regional differences in the numbers of BRM 2020 business subsidies given relative to the scale of the small business base, implying that SMEs and entrepreneurs are under-served in some regions. This uneven level of overall BRM 2020 support results from regional bidding and co-funding decisions and inertia in the arrangements that should be re-examined. Furthermore, BRM 2020 budgets are supplied to regional government authorities only on an annual basis, which makes planning and long-term programming difficult. Key Performance Indicators for BRM 2020 at regional level are also largely focused on outputs rather than outcomes. As a result of these issues, there are difficulties in supplying the scale and quality of services that SMEs and entrepreneurs demand in the regions and in ensuring that regional actions contribute fully to achieving national SME and entrepreneurship development objectives.

A more transparent mechanism needs to be developed for the allocation of BRM 2020 funding across the regions, based on national SME and entrepreneurship development and regional development priorities and the nature and scale of the SME business base. Such a mechanism should provide budgets to the regions for multi-annual periods in order to favour the development of infrastructure and training and capacity-building programmes that need time to get established. Outcome indicators should be included in the Key Performance Indicators collected, in addition to measures of numbers of projects and beneficiaries.

The key reference point for the regional development aspects of the Kazakhstan's sectoral government policies – in particular transport and infrastructure – is the National Strategy for Regional Development. This emphasises the promotion of regional growth poles in five major urban agglomerations. In contrast, the only regional development focus within BRM 2020, the guiding document for SME and entrepreneurship policy, is on supporting rural towns, small towns and mono-industry towns, which are eligible for dedicated support measures. While SME and entrepreneurship policy can make an important contribution to the development of low economic potential areas, making the regional focus exclusively on lagging areas runs counter to the growth pole focus of the national regional development strategy and may reduce the capacity to achieve the substantial national growth in SME value added sought by the government.

An approach to marrying the growth hub objective and the objective of supporting rural areas, small settlements and mono-industry towns would involve continuing the existing basic SME and entrepreneurship supports and their weighting towards lagging territories whilst introducing new dedicated support for high-growth potential enterprises in the five urban growth pole hubs, where rapid growth SMEs and start-ups are most likely to be concentrated.

A potentially important tool for adapting SME and entrepreneurship actions to regional needs is the use of integrated medium-term regional development strategies incorporating SME and entrepreneurship development objectives and measures. Although regional government authorities do currently produce strategy documents, they appear to be updated on an annual basis and relate mainly to budgetary planning and performance monitoring. More genuine regional development strategies would include key objectives and priorities for economic development, including SME and entrepreneurship development, key programmes to be used and key performance indicators to assess success. They could be used to steer multi-annual regional financial allocations from BRM 2020 and combine with regional support from other sectoral programmes. The design and implementation of the regional development strategies, including their SME and entrepreneurship components, could be supported through a national programme of capacity building for policy making at a regional level.

Kazakhstan has made great strides in reducing the burden of business regulations at national level. However, much of the responsibility for the implementation of business regulation is with the regional government authorities and significant regional divergences exist in the quality of regulatory implementation. The Entrepreneurship Service Centres in the regions provide information and support for entrepreneurs starting new businesses with respect to regulation for business registration and creation. This could usefully be extended to regulatory support for existing businesses and the offer of streamlined cross-department decision-making and seamless electronic self-declaration facilities. The recent creation of a national business ombudsman function has provided a further important channel for reducing the burdens of business regulations on SME and entrepreneurship development. This function could be strengthened by creating a formal network of business ombudsman representatives in each region. These regional representatives would seek to define ways to improve regulation with each regional government authority together with SMEs and entrepreneurs in the regions, and act as a channel to deal with complaints from business regarding their treatment by government.

The key recommendations of the report on strengthening the local dimension of SME and entrepreneurship policy in Kazakhstan are set out below.

Key recommendations on the local dimension to SME and entrepreneurship policy

- Create better alignment between the spatial development priorities of Business Road Map 2020 and those expressed in the national regional development vision by introducing a dedicated Business Road Map 2020 programme for high-potential SMEs and entrepreneurship in the five cities designated as national growth pole hubs.
- Introduce a transparent, multi-annual budget framework for the regional allocation of Business Road Map 2020 resources for SME and entrepreneurship development, based on an assessment of the scale and nature of SME and entrepreneurship support needs in each region, and providing for regional monitoring of key performance indicators on associated SME and entrepreneurship programme activities and impacts.
- Increase the information and support available to existing businesses at regional level on compliance with business regulations. Create a mechanism to consult with regional networks of SMEs and entrepreneurs to identify potential areas for regulatory improvement at regional level.

Regional differences in SME and entrepreneurship activity and constraints

Kazakhstan is a very large and heterogeneous country in which there are important regional differences related, for example, to population size, market access, infrastructure availability, and foreign direct investment stocks. The large distances across the country and the low overall population density mean that SMEs frequently serve a regional or local market, rather than national or international markets, and operate within regional business environments, which vary significantly between regions. As a result, there is an important local dimension to SME and entrepreneurship policy, since support for SMEs and entrepreneurship must respond to different local obstacles and opportunities.

Kazakhstan has substantial regional differences in population sizes, industries and incomes

The territory of Kazakhstan is divided into 14 regions plus the two major cities of Astana and Almaty. The regions with the largest populations are South Kazakhstan (2.8 million), Almaty (1.5 million), and Astana (0.8 million), while the smallest regional populations are in North Kazakhstan (0.6 million) and Atyrau (0.6 million). Kazakhstan contains very large rural areas, often lacking key infrastructure, although in most regions more than 40% of the population live in urban settings, and the urban share of population is 57% on a national basis. Economic conditions for SMEs and entrepreneurship in the major cities of Astana and Almaty are qualitatively different to the rest of the country, including the presence of much large numbers of enterprises and enterprises per head and a wider range of available infrastructure.

There are also wide differences in industry sector concentrations across the regions (Table 6.1). For example, whereas manufacturing accounts for more than 15% of gross domestic product (GDP) in five regions of the country, it makes up 5% or less in five other regions. In three regions, primary industries account for more than 45% of GDP, but services account for more than 50% of GDP in Astana and Almaty.

Table 6.1. GDP by sector by region, 2016

Per cent

	Agriculture & Forestry	Primary industry	Manufacturing	Construction	Wholesale and retail trade	Transport	Information and Communication	Real Estate	Other Services	Total
Kazakhstan	5	15	11	6	16	8	2	8	29	100
Akmola	16	5	14	7	11	11	1	11	25	100
Aktobe	6	26	9	6	17	8	1	7	21	100
Almaty	15	3	17	12	9	11	1	7	25	100
Atyrau	1	48	4	9	3	5	0	3	26	100
West Kazakhstan	4	45	4	5	9	7	0	5	22	100
Zhambyl	11	5	14	6	11	15	1	7	30	100
Karaganda	3	16	32	4	12	7	1	6	19	100
Kostanay	12	9	12	6	14	11	1	11	23	100
Kyzylorda	4	31	8	5	9	10	0	7	26	100
Mangistau	1	46	4	7	5	7	1	8	23	100
South Kazakhstan	10	5	19	5	12	9	1	11	30	100
Pavlodar	5	11	29	5	11	11	1	5	21	100
North Kazakhstan	23	3	8	5	15	9	1	12	25	100
East Kazakhstan	8	8	24	6	15	7	1	8	24	100
Astana City	0	1	3	9	24	9	4	9	42	100
Almaty City	0	1	4	2	32	5	5	9	41	100

Source: Ministry of National Economy, Committee on Statistics.

In common with other parts of the ex-Soviet Union, Kazakhstan is host to a number of mono-industry towns – cities which are dominated by a single industry, often in the mining sector, and often in decline. For the purpose of giving special support, Kazakhstan defines mono-industry towns as meeting one of the following criteria:

- The volume of production of the core industry of the city is over 20% of the city's production;
- The core industry of the city employs more than 20% of the total employed population; and
- The enterprises of the core industry of the city have suspended all or some of their activities.

Using this definition, 27 mono-industry towns have been identified. These are concentrated in certain areas of Kazakhstan with eight in Karaganda region, and four each in Kostanay and East Kazakhstan. Five of the mono-industry towns have been analysed by the government as having good economic potential, two as having poor economic potential, and the rest as being of medium potential.

Kazakhstan witnesses large regional differences in GDP per capita. This partly reflects the regional differences in sector structures outlined above – with the high GDP per capita figures in Atyrau, Mangistau and West Kazakhstan relating to dominance of the oil industry and primary industry. It also reflects the success of the more highly developed economies of Astana City and Almaty City (Figure 6.1).

Figure 6.1. Gross Domestic Product per capita at regional level, 2004 and 2015

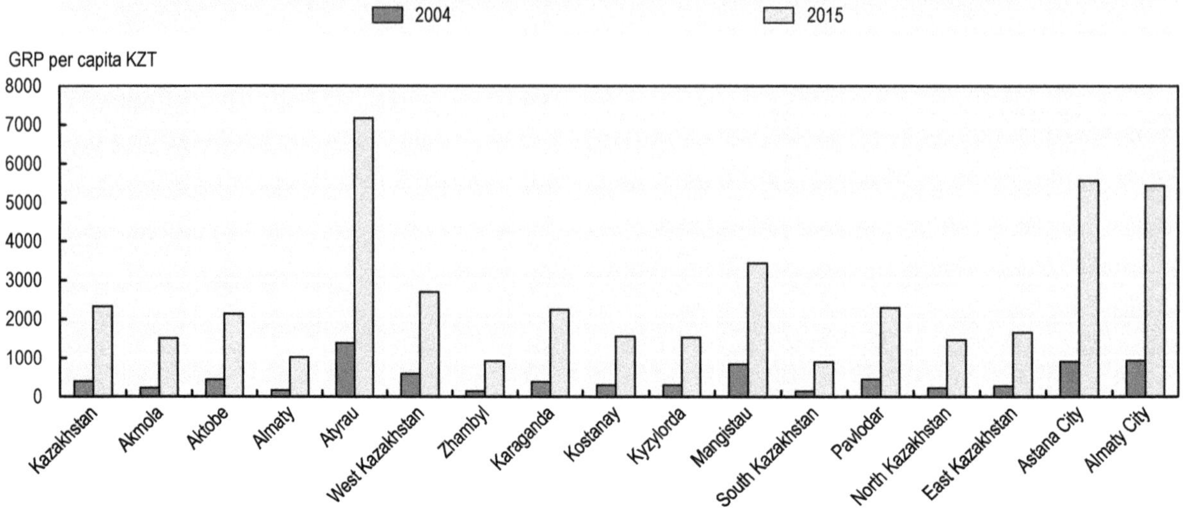

Source: Ministry of National Economy, Committee on Statistics.

StatLink http://dx.doi.org/10.1787/888933828258

SME densities and characteristics vary widely between regions

The density of SMEs, in terms of numbers of SMEs relative to the working population, varies considerably across the regions of Kazakhstan. This is particularly the case for enterprises in the 'small' and 'medium' size classes, while the distribution of independent entrepreneurs varies less dramatically. As shown in Figure 6.2, the largest numbers of SMEs compared with the population are in Astana City and Almaty City.

Figure 6.2. SME density – number of SMEs per 1000 working age population, 2016

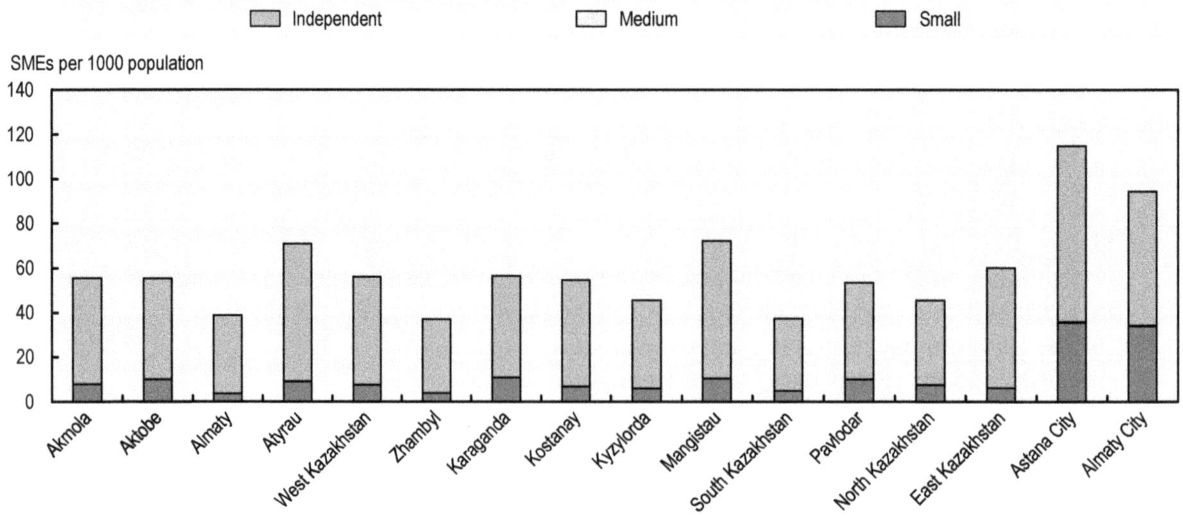

Source: Ministry of National Economy, Committee on Statistics.

StatLink http://dx.doi.org/10.1787/888933827802

The regional density of SMEs correlates well with GDP per head at regional level, and while causation also flows from GDP to levels of SME activity, substantial regional SME activity is likely to be an important contributor to regional prosperity (Figure 6.3). This suggests the importance of increasing numbers of enterprises (particularly those larger than independent entrepreneurs) in the regions as a means of stimulating both regional development and national growth.

Figure 6.3. Comparison of regional SME density and regional GDP per capita, 2015

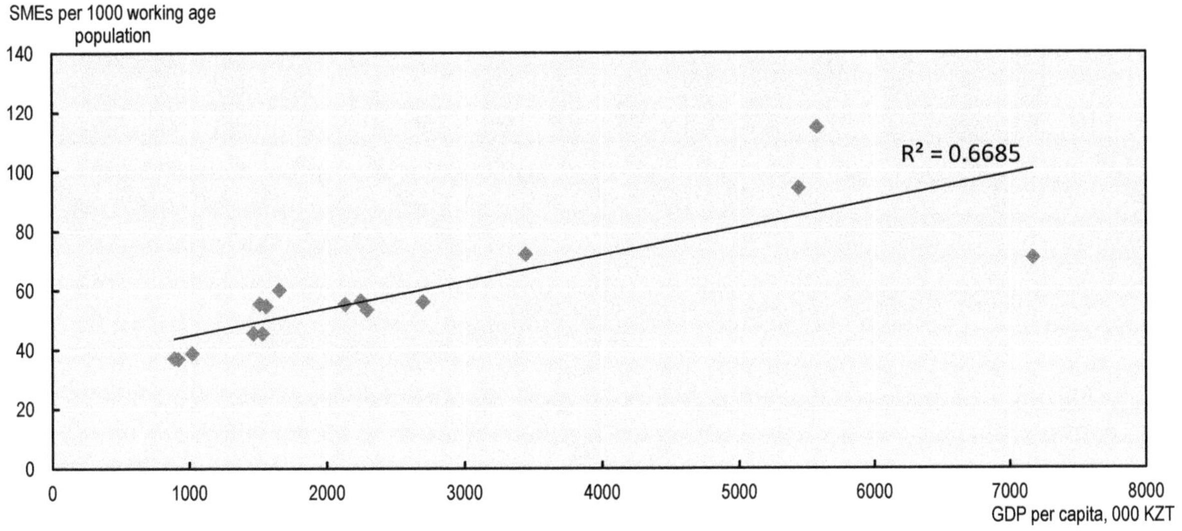

Source: OECD calculations from Ministry of National Economy, Committee on Statistics data.

StatLink http://dx.doi.org/10.1787/888933828277

There are also significant regional differences in the extent to which SMEs are involved in innovation, based on self-reported data from enterprises compiled by the Kazakhstan Committee on Statistics. The highest shares of SMEs involved in innovation are in Kostanay, Astana City, East Kazakhstan, Zhambyl and Kyzlyorda, whereas West Kazakhstan, Mangistau, Pavlodar, and Almaty City have relatively low shares (Figure 6.4). To some degree, this reflects differing sectoral concentrations, with enterprises in Almaty City being disproportionately in the field of trade for example. However, overall, it signals the importance of strengthening regional entrepreneurship system conditions in regions where SME innovation is currently very weak.

Figure 6.4. Level of innovation activity by region, 2015

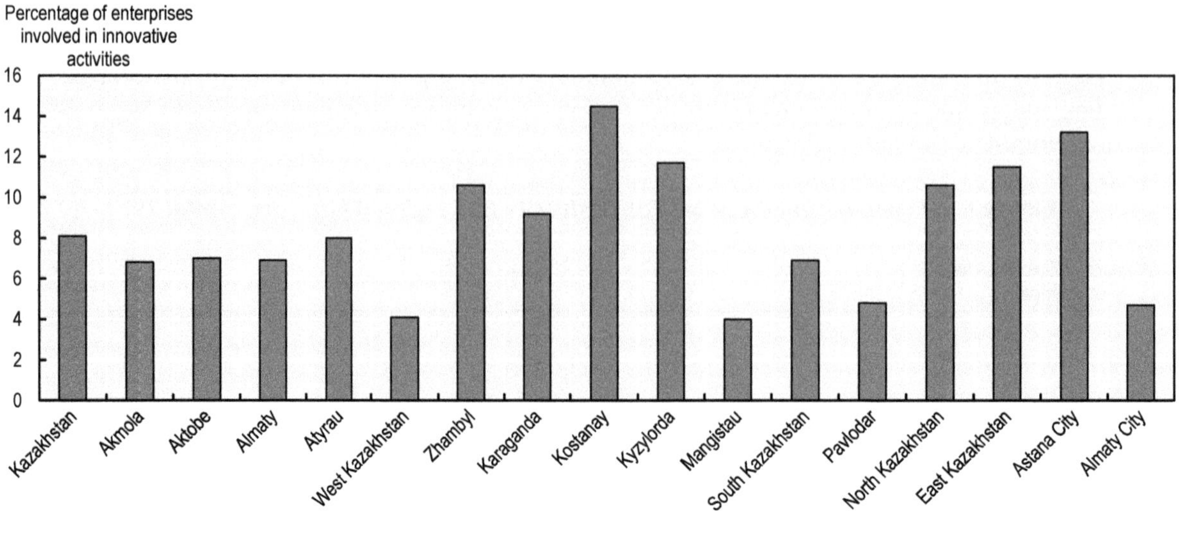

Source: Ministry of National Economy, Committee on Statistics.

StatLink http://dx.doi.org/10.1787/888933828296

Although nationally, Kazakhstan shows a good balance between male and female entrepreneurship, this does vary across the regions (Figure 6.5). Most regions are similar to the national average of 47% of individual entrepreneurs being women and 26% of incorporated enterprises owned by women. However, the proportions of women entrepreneurs range from 58% (Almaty City) to 33% (South Kazakhstan) for individual entrepreneurs and from 33% (Almaty City) to 19% (North Kazakhstan) for incorporated enterprises. This suggests that programmes to support women entrepreneurs are particularly needed in certain regions that are lagging behind, and should focus on identifying and responding to specific constraints in these regions.

Figure 6.5. Gender variations in business ownership by region, 2016

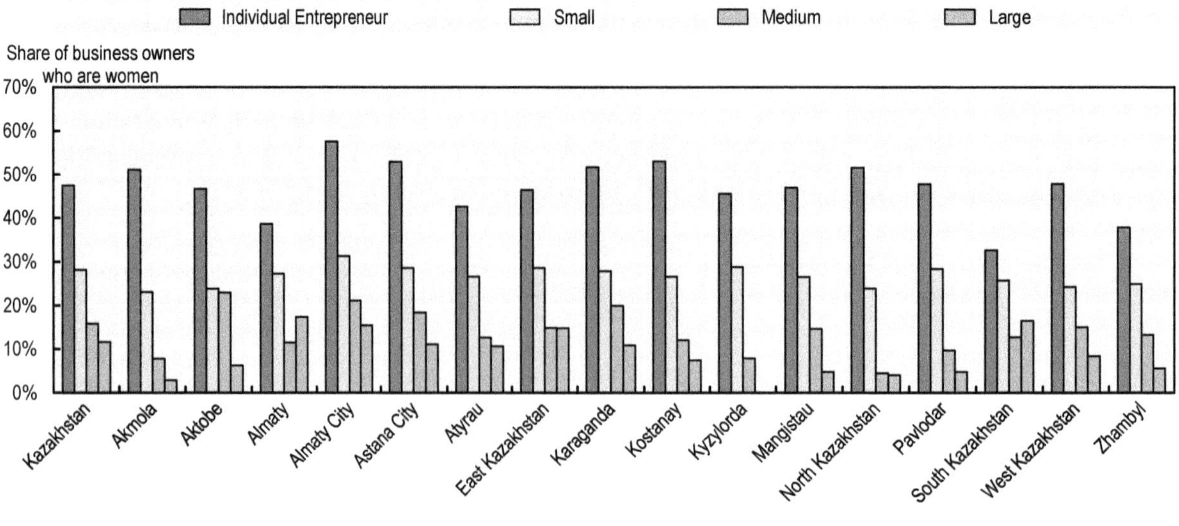

Source: Ministry of National Economy, Committee on Statistics.

StatLink http://dx.doi.org/10.1787/888933828315

The major obstacles to business vary between regions

The European Bank for Reconstruction and Development (EBRD) / World Bank Business Environment and Enterprise Performance Survey (BEEPS) for Kazakhstan shows substantial regional variation in business perceptions of obstacles to business such as corruption, informality, skills, taxation, access to finance and infrastructure. Table 6.2 highlights these differences across five macro-regions of the country. The Table shows that certain major obstacles to business appear with very high frequency in certain regions, notably corruption in the South, tax rates in the West, and access to electricity in the East. The fact that the most cited obstacles differ across the regions suggests the need for regionally-targeted strategies to address these regionally-focused obstacles. There are several other significant, but less marked, differences across the regions, which also merit regional actions, including particular concerns of businesses with skills in the North and West, tax rates in the East, and access to finance in the Centre, North and West.

Table 6.2. Regional variations in major obstacles to business in Kazakhstan, 2014

Per cent of businesses identifying the factor as a major constraint for their business

	All regions	Centre	East	North	South	West
Corruption	16.5	5.5	3.2	7.9	35.2	3.3
Practices of competitors in the informal sector	12.7	3.2	6.1	14.8	14.9	15.3
Inadequately educated workforce	11.2	12.3	14.4	17.3	2.1	19.2
Tax rates	9.4	10.1	14.9	8.1	3.3	24.8
Access to finance	9.4	12.8	6.9	12.3	5.2	12.1
Electricity	8.9	8.1	35.2	11.6	4.1	3.9
Access to land	3.6	3.2	1.1	4.0	5.0	0.9
Business licensing and permits	3.0	5.0	1.0	5.3	1.8	0.4
Transport	3.0	1.4	2.1	2.8	4.1	2.5
Customs and trade regulations	2.8	2.1		1.5	3.9	4.6
Courts	1.4	3.2		2.2	0.8	
Crime, theft and disorder	1.4		2.1	1.8	1.2	1.9
Political instability	1.3				3.2	0.7
Tax administration	0.7	0.4	1.0	0.1	1.5	0.1
Labour regulations	0.5			0.9	0.6	

Source: OECD calculations from data from EBRD-World Bank BEEPS V survey. Centre = Karaganda; East = East Kazakhstan; North = Astana City, Akmola, North Kazakhstan, Kostanay, Pavlodar; South = Almaty City, Kyzylorda, Zhambyl, South Kazakhstan, Almaty Region; West = Mangistau, Atyrau, Aktobe, West Kazakhstan.

Further evidence on regional obstacles to SME and entrepreneurship development is provided by an ADB-funded survey (Sange Research Centre, 2013), which focused on barriers to growth of businesses in the production sector (Table 6.3). This identifies a number of interesting region-specific issues. For example, non-competitive price is more frequently identified as a problem in Akmola, Almaty, East Kazakhstan, Kylzylorda and Pavlodar than other regions, suggesting a particular need for efficiency improvements or diversification strategies in these regions. Lack of technologies was more frequently seen as a constraint by production businesses in Astana City, Akmole, Almaty, West Kazakhstan, Karaganda, Kostanay, North Kazakhstan and South Kazakhstan, suggesting both a greater need and greater likely take up for technology development initiatives in these regions. Similarly, lack of qualified staff was a particular issue in West Kazakhstan, Kostanay, Pavlodar, and South Kazakhstan, and access to finance problems were particularly constraining in Atyrau, Zhambyl and West Kazakhstan.

Table 6.3. Regional variations in obstacles to business growth in Kazakhstan

	Expensive transportation	Lack of domestic demand	Lack of information about foreign market demand	Non-competitive price	Low quality	Lack of technologies	Lack of manpower	Lack of qualified staff	Underdevelopment of infrastructure	Lack of pledge for loans	High rates on loans	Lack of raw materials
Astana City	5.2	7.0	2.6	7.8	5.2	22.6	7.8	14.8	5.2	2.6	6.1	6.1
Almaty City	14.0	2.8	0.9	14.0	10.3	12.1	6.5	9.3	7.5	3.7	6.5	1.9
Akmola	4.7		0.9	19.6	5.6	27.1	0.9	8.4	15	1.9	1.9	13.1
Aktobe	9.8	2.4	9.8	9.8	7.3	29.3	4.9	9.8	9.8	2.4	2.4	
Almaty	3.8	5.1	2.5	15.2	7.6	29.1	1.3	11.4	3.8	3.8	6.3	6.3
Atyrau	5.2		3.0	8.9	3.0	14.1	0.7	17	11.9	5.9	15.6	12.6
East Kazakhstan	5.8	1.3	2.6	20.6	5.2	19.4	1.9	11.6	8.4	3.2	11.6	5.2
Zhambyl	2.1		3.5	14.2	4.3	14.9		14.9	8.5	9.2	12.8	12.8
West Kazakhstan	3.3			10.0	3.3	26.7	6.7	20.0	6.7		16.7	6.7
Karaganda	1.1		1.1	9.9	4.4	26.4	1.1	11.0	8.8	8.8	9.9	9.9
Kostanay	4.2	3.6	2.4	14.4	10.2	22.8	7.2	15.6	9.0		3.6	6.6
Kyzylorda	12.0	4.0	6.0	17.3	4.0	14.7	3.3	8.7	10.0	4.0	6.7	7.3
Mangistau	8.0	11.4	2.3	10.2	13.6	15.9	8.0	10.2	6.8	1.1		8.0
Pavlodar	2.0			26.5	6.1	10.2		18.4	16.3		8.2	2.0
North Kazakhstan	14.3		9.5	9.5	9.5	38.1		14.3				
South Kazakhstan	2.9	1.3	1.3	11.7	13.6	22.7	3.9	19.4	14.6	1.3	3.9	2.9

Source: Sange Research Centre (2013).

These regional differences imply a need for a good understanding of the different nature of key constraints in the different regions and prioritisation of actions that will address the problems in the relevant regions.

Policy tailoring and coordination in the regions

Regional authorities in Kazakhstan have significant economic development powers

Kazakhstan's territory is divided on a hierarchical basis into 14 regions (Oblasts), 176 districts (Raions) and more than 2 000 rural communities. The head of the regional government authority (the Akim) is appointed by and reports to the President. The heads of executives at lower levels are appointed and are responsible to the relevant regional government leader. This unified structure is supplemented by cities, which can be at any of these three levels. In particular, the two largest cities of Astana and Almaty have the same status as regions. For statistical and administrative purposes, therefore, the country is divided into 16 regions. All region, city and district administrations (Akimats) have equal powers regardless of the sizes of their populations, geographical areas or economies, although the representative and executive bodies of the cities of Almaty and Astana are assigned broader powers.

The overall budgets for each regional authority are determined centrally, based on the region's population size and its needs, and taking into account finance raised at a local level (certain payments stay within the region, in particular fines for non-compliance with regulations). The regional government leader (the Akim) determines a budget for the region, which should be ratified by the regional assembly (the Maslikhat). However, despite the equivalence of the powers of regions, districts and rural communities, almost all SME and entrepreneurship policy actions at subnational level are implemented by the regions and two major cities.

Regional government authorities have used financing opportunities presented by a variety of different government programmes (as well as their own funds) in order to support SME and entrepreneurship development projects. These include programmes such as the "100 steps" national development programme, and programmes for innovation. These programmes have financed business incubators as well as some SME and entrepreneurship financing instruments. However, the majority of the funding for SME and entrepreneurship policy actions in the regions comes from the national and regional contributions to the national BRM 2020 programme.

Arrangements are in place to co-ordinate national and regional policy efforts on SMEs and entrepreneurship

There are clear mechanisms to co-ordinate SME and entrepreneurship policy actions between the national and regional levels of government. The basic framework is set by the 2015 Entrepreneurial Code. This specifies the Entrepreneurship Development Department in the Ministry of National Economy as the body with overall responsibility for co-ordinating SME and entrepreneurship support in the regions. It also sets out the roles and responsibilities of local executive bodies in carrying out the implementation of SME and entrepreneurship support (including business development infrastructure, financial subsidies and provision of training and business development services to SMEs and entrepreneurs).

The resulting structure is a system of Regional Programme Coordinators, who are responsible for co-ordinating implementation of the BRM 2020 at the level of the regions, and Regional Co-ordinating Councils headed by the leaders of regional government authorities (Akims), which are responsible for determining the priorities of their regions, and approving BRM 2020 projects in their regions. The Regional Co-ordinating Councils are essentially consulting and advisory bodies on SME and entrepreneurship policies and programmes at the regional level, the memberships of which consist of government officials, development institutions, business organisations, second-tier banks, independent experts, and entrepreneurs. They are tasked with determining the priorities of their regions.

These mechanisms help to co-ordinate national and regional interventions for SME and entrepreneurship development while allowing for some regional flexibility, particularly with respect to the main SME and entrepreneurship programme in Kazakhstan, the BRM 2020. On the other hand, some central initiatives with significant regional impacts on SME and entrepreneurship development have been less strongly co-ordinated between central and regional government authorities. For example, the creation of Special Economic Zones (SEZs) was driven by presidential decree, and although the SEZs are implemented in close coordination with regional government authorities, it is not clear how the national choice of locations has been coordinated with regional desires, analysis, and plans. The programme for mono-industry towns was similarly decided centrally (including the definition of exactly which towns are included) and is not necessarily strongly coordinated with regionally-determined policies, for example on infrastructure and economic diversification.

Regional Co-ordinating Councils help to tailor the mix of national SME and entrepreneurship policy actions to regional priorities

In principle, the same BRM 2020 support actions should be available to SMEs and entrepreneurs in every region. However, the regional government authorities have a significant influence on the nature of the BRM 2020 actions actually pursued in their regions. Much of this influence comes through the decisions made by the Regional Coordinating Councils on which BRM 2020 projects to bid for and co-fund with regional government resources. Through this mechanism, the Councils can put greater funding emphasis on lines of action that meet their priorities, adjusting for example the relative funding for SME financing, developing management capabilities in SMEs or training new entrepreneurs. They can also influence the overall amount of funding drawn down to their regions by the scale of their bids and co-funding resources.

Alongside the BRM 2020, the regional government authorities can influence how certain national initiatives are implemented on the ground. For example, a presidential decree has led to the establishment of a network of Investor Support Centres in all regions in order to attract and support foreign direct investment. The actual activities of these centres is affected by the staffing and resources that the regions put in and by the remit that they ask the centres to carry out. In some regions, the Investor Support Centres have mainly concentrated on promotion activity to attract new foreign direct investment (FDI) rather than FDI aftercare or development of supply chains around foreign investors, but others have developed more aftercare and supply chain building activity where it reflects a regional priority.

There is a mismatch across regions between the scale of SME and entrepreneurship support and the size of the small business base

Although the current process of allocating BRM 2020 funding across the regions is involving the regions and allowing for some tailoring of SME and entrepreneurship programmes to regional priorities, it is resulting in significant differences in the scale and availability of policy support to SMEs and entrepreneurs across the regions. This can be seen in Figure 6.6, which shows the numbers of BRM 2020 subsidies to enterprises relative to the size of the small business base in each region. There is little relationship between the number of subsidies given to enterprises by BRM 2020 and the population of SMEs in each region, implying that SMEs and entrepreneurs in some regions are under-served. There is also an inconsistent density of business support infrastructures for entrepreneurship development, such as business incubators.

Figure 6.6. Relationship between the number of BRM 2020 subsidies and the SME population by region

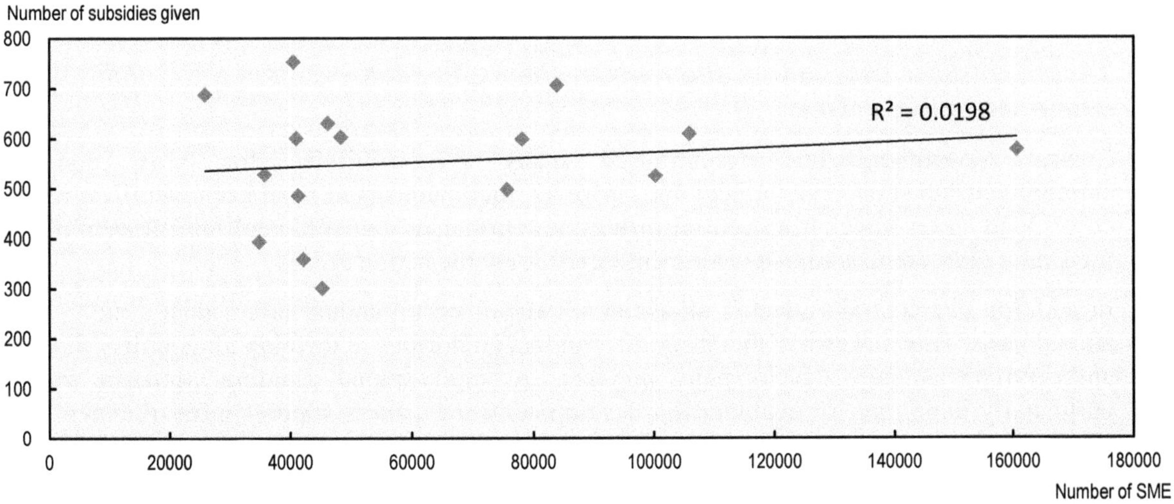

Source: Data provided by Damu Entrepreneurship Development Fund. Figures to January 2017.

StatLink http://dx.doi.org/10.1787/888933827821

This contrasts with "reactive" business development services, which are more driven by the demand expressed by enterprises for information, advice, and consultancy. For these programmes, monitoring data show that the number of consultations given corresponds much more closely with the population of potential clients (Figure 6.7).

Figure 6.7. Relationship between the number of business development services consultations and the SME population by region

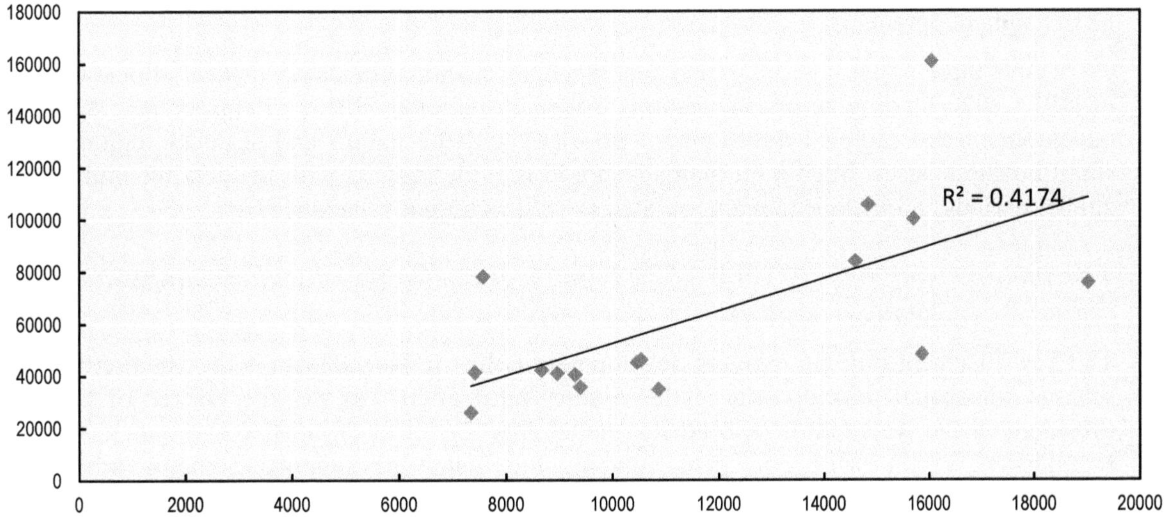

Source: OECD calculations from data extracted from http://business.gov.kz/ru/dkb2020/reports/nonfin-report.php 30/01/2017.

StatLink http://dx.doi.org/10.1787/888933828334

The differences in the scale and availability of BRM 2020 financial supports and business support infrastructures appear to reflect both different choices of Regional Coordinating Councils on how far to invest, and inertia in national funding allocations, which are partly based on past regional patterns of spending.

There is insufficient funding and outcome focus for some regional SME and entrepreneurship actions

Central government has decentralised many responsibilities for SME and entrepreneurship support to the regions. However, there appears to have been insufficient corresponding resources from central institutions (principally government ministries and the Damu Entrepreneurship Development Fund) for some action areas.

In addition, the central budget is allocated to regions on an annual rather than a multi-annual basis. This makes it difficult for the regional authorities to develop long term SME and entrepreneurship development projects. A multi-annual funding scenario is particularly important for enabling the development of business support infrastructures, which tend to have needs for both capital (e.g. buildings) and current (e.g. staff) expenditures that spread over several years, and for projects that focus on building the capabilities of SMEs and entrepreneurs with training and business development services. Regions have therefore often sought to focus more on drawing down financial subsidies for SMEs and entrepreneurs rather than building these other types of projects (Urinboyev, 2015).

Furthermore, although the regional government authorities are obliged to report on their use of national BRM 2020 programmes based on agreed Key Performance Indicators (KPIs), which could be a very valuable tool for policy design and policy learning at the regional level, the current approach appears to work rather bureaucratically. In particular, the KPIs collected are mainly at an output level (e.g. how many enterprises received training support) rather than an outcome one (whether their performance improved as a result) (Junusbekova, 2013). This focus is not optimal for steering policy intervention towards where it has the greatest impacts or to ensuring quality provision for beneficiary SMEs and entrepreneurs.

To resolve these issues, a more transparent mechanism should be developed for allocation of BRM 2020 funding across the regions, based on national SME and entrepreneurship development and regional development priorities and the nature and scale of regional small business bases. Such a mechanism should provide regions with budgets for multi-annual periods and include outcome-related as well as output-related KPIs.

The spatial component of BRM 2020 is not well co-ordinated with Kazakhstan's regional development strategy

The key document guiding regional development policy in Kazakhstan is the "predictive scheme for spatial development of the country until 2020" (as per the Decree of the President of the Republic of Kazakhstan dated July 21, 2011 № 118) (Government of Kazakhstan, 2011). This document contains the vision of supporting major urban agglomerations as growth poles to seed economic development in the macro-regions in which they are located. The document identifies five macro-regions covering all of Kazakhstan and five major agglomerations that can act as hubs for their development – Astana (covering the Northern macro-region), Ust-Kamenogorsk (covering the Central-East macro-region), Aktobe (covering the Western macro-region) and Almaty and Shymkent (covering the southern macro-region). The hubs represent strategic points relative to existing transport, infrastructure and other assets and are seen as strategic points for further public and private investments.

The BRM 2020 SME and entrepreneurship development programme includes a spatial component that provides dedicated support to lagging rural areas, small settlements and mono-industry towns. However, the aim of this spatial component does not match with the main growth pole thrust of the regional policy approach. Whereas the regional policy focuses on building growth centres, the spatial element of BRM 2020 focuses on helping the most lagging regions. For example, the objective of the BRM 2020 intervention in the mono-industry towns is expressed as the stabilisation and diversification of the local economy.

There is therefore a mismatch between the growth pole focus of the regional development strategy and the lagging area focus of the SME and entrepreneurship development strategy. Furthermore, a concentration of the spatial support on SMEs and entrepreneurship on lagging territories may make it difficult to achieve national SME and entrepreneurship development targets for substantial growth in SME value added as set out in the Kazakhstan 2030 and Kazakhstan 2050 vision documents. This type of substantial growth is more likely to be achieved by favouring innovative, high productivity and high growth potential businesses, which generally tend to be concentrated in larger cities. The recent OECD Territorial Review of Kazakhstan (OECD, 2017) identifies under-exploited potential benefits of agglomeration in Kazakhstan suggesting the need for a more strategic approach to regional development. SME and entrepreneurship policy could contribute to this effort.

Figure 6.8. Density of small incorporated enterprises against level of urban population

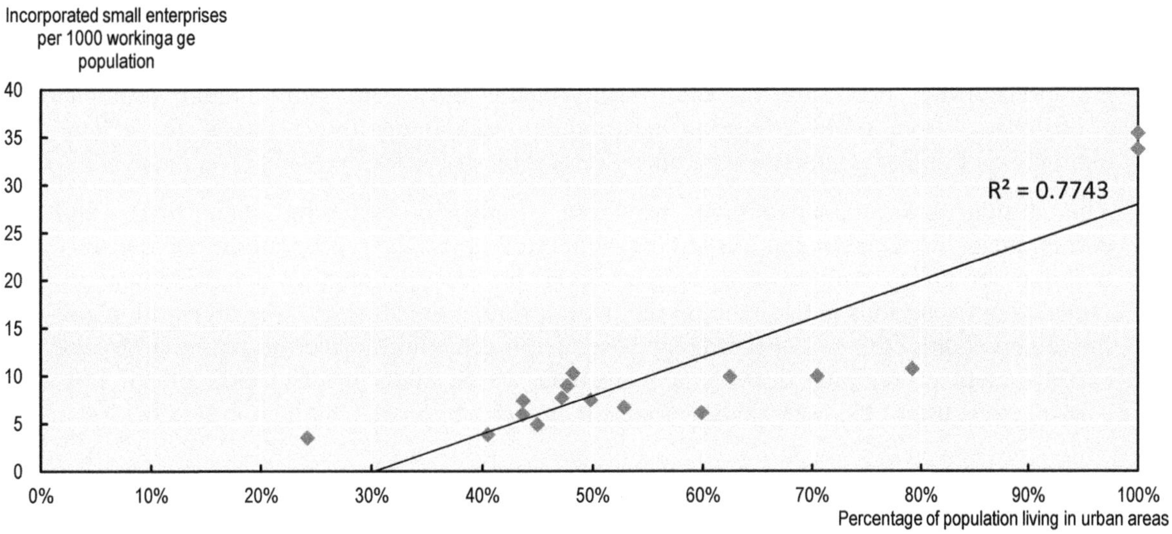

Source: OECD calculations from Ministry of National Economy, Committee on Statistics data. Figures for 2016.

StatLink http://dx.doi.org/10.1787/888933828353

An approach could be developed to marry the growth pole objectives of the regional development policy with the support for rural areas, small settlements and mono-industry towns currently prioritised by the BRM 2020 by adding a further adapted spatial element to BRM 2020. The approach would involve continuing to direct parts of the existing basic SME and entrepreneurship supports of BRM 2020 towards lagging areas whilst introducing a new high-level initiative to BRM 2020 offering targeted and dedicated support for high-growth potential enterprises in the five urban growth pole hubs. Analysis of the numbers of small incorporated enterprises (as opposed to independent entrepreneurs and non-incorporated enterprises) in Kazakhstan shows them to be concentrated in urban areas (Figure 6.8). Since this is the group most likely to include higher growth enterprises, this confirms the opportunity of concentrating a dedicated high-growth enterprise and innovative SME development programme in the large cities.

The development of integrated regional strategies would support regional tailoring and co-ordination of SME and entrepreneurship policy

Although each region in Kazakhstan produces a regional strategic plan, they appear to be short-term documents, updated on an annual basis, and relating mainly to budgetary planning and performance monitoring of the regional government authorities. They are not primarily a guide to designing longer-term, tailored and co-ordinated economic development actions according to a regional strategic vision (Junusbekova, 2013). Furthermore, the regional development planning approach in Kazakhstan has largely emphasised a top-down approach with little focus on adapting investment to the needs and priorities of regions by a bottom-up regional planning process (OECD, 2017).

The development of genuine medium-term integrated regional development strategies for each region of Kazakhstan would be a great help in the regional tailoring and national-regional co-ordination of economic development policies, including their SME and entrepreneurship development component. Such strategies should be based on an assessment of the distinct comparative advantages of each region and include key objectives and priorities for SME and entrepreneurship development, key programmes to be used to this end and KPIs to assess success. They should also show how SME and entrepreneurship measures in each region will draw on multi-annual financial contributions from BRM 2020 and contribute to achieving its objectives, as well as combine with regional support from other sectoral programmes.

The design and implementation of these strategies, including their SME and entrepreneurship components, could be supported through a programme of capacity building for policy making at a regional level, based on extending the existing work undertaken for regions in the national regional development strategy. The preparation and implementation of this regional strategy based approach could further be supported by the establishment of regional development agencies in Kazakhstan. The example of how Turkey made use of the regional development agencies approach is given in Box 6.1.

Box 6.1. Regional Development Agencies in Turkey

Approach

Turkey is historically a centralised state where Regional Development Agencies (RDAs) were established only in 2006. They were first mentioned in the 8th National Development Plan (2001-2005). In total, 26 regional development agencies have been established. They do not form another administrative tier, but rather are created as effective bodies for the management of funds from the central state budget and funds allocated from the budgets of regional authorities. They are governed by a Board of Directors, including representatives of public, private, and non-governmental organisations.

The RDAs have the following tasks:

- Prepare regional development plans and strategies;
- Design and implement support programmes for economic and social development; and
- Improve the regional investment climate and attract investors to the region.

The RDAs prepare regional development strategies based on comprehensive field research in their region involving all actors and related to regional needs. They also produce annual work plans in accordance with both national plans and local priorities. The RDAs all implement support programmes for SMEs and entrepreneurship as well as for the development of non-governmental organisations promoting social development projects, including operating a business development service provider.

Results

Evaluations have found the RDA programmes to be successful in creating economic and social impacts in the regions (for example related to increases in productivity, turnover and employment in supported SMEs compared to non-supported ones). Other RDA activities include investment promotion units working to improve the investment climate in regions, and policy units working with regional stakeholders to enhance regional innovation ecosystems.

Success factors

A key success factor has been defining appropriate regions – there is a need for a critical mass of people and economy as well as a functional economic area. In addition, appropriate levels of resources have been provided, not just for the preparation of the regional development plans, but also for maintaining the institutional capacity of the agencies themselves. All RDAs select and employ highly qualified staff in their operational units (General Secretariats). They carry out intensive field research in their regions to develop regional plans and support programmes. Another important success factor is that the Board of Directors of each RDA is drawn from regional leaders in the public and private sectors, leading to a high level of regional ownership of the RDA initiatives. They regularly meet once a month. This also helps to promote RDA activities and ensure that they are well known by the target groups.

Problems and responses

The RDAs are the result of a long-term process of discussion and development, related to the issues of decentralisation in a highly centralised country. Each RDA territory corresponds to several administrative regions, based on the need to create critical mass and to have a functional economic area for their actions. Since this was a major step for Turkey, initially only two RDAs were created and after evaluation of their activities and issues over two years the others were established taking account the lessons learnt from these pilots.

Relevance to Kazakhstan

This case shows how regional economic strategies can be developed in a centralised state without wholesale decentralisation to the regions and how they can support regionally tailored business development actions.

Source : Polat, Erkan et al (2011), Toktas et al (2013).

Local regulations

Legislation determining the regulation of businesses is centralised in Kazakhstan and sub-national governments have no powers to adjust it. However, the regional government authorities (the Akimats) have an important influence on the regulatory environment for SMEs and entrepreneurship through their role in implementing national legislation via their direct contacts with businesses in their regions. There appear to be some significant differences in how business regulations are interpreted across the regions, leading to an uneven quality of regional regulatory environment for SMEs and entrepreneurship. This is evident in differing perceptions across the regions of the degree to which businesses see regulations and corruption as a constraint for their development. As shown in Table 6.2 above, for example, the share of businesses identifying corruption as a major constraint for their business varied from 3.2% in the East to 35.2% in the South, and the share of businesses identifying business licensing and permits as a major constraint varied from 0.4% in the West to 5.3% in the North.

The decision to introduce one-stop shops for business support in the Enterprise Support Centres in the regions should assist in introducing a more consistent approach to business regulation across the regions. These one-stop shops will provide information to businesses on how to negotiate the regulations involved in setting up a business. However, it would be useful to extend their services to providing information and support on how to deal with regulations affecting existing businesses (for example gaining construction permits or access to utilities). They could also have a role in collecting data on the effectiveness and consistency of regulation. It is important to have an organisation in Kazakhstan with clear and unified responsibility for the implementation of regulations at regional level, covering not just new business start-ups but also existing businesses. Box 6.2 gives the example of a one-stop shop approach in Italy that achieves this.

Box 6.2. Single Counters – Italy

Approach

The Single Counters (Sportelli Unici) are local one-stop shop centres with the objective of providing all administrative authorisations necessary to either locate and start up a new business activity, or to expand, innovate, or restructure an existing business activity. They bring under one roof all procedures for issuing authorisations for business establishment, location, restructuring, enlargement, closure, transformation, and small-scale planning. The network was introduced within the framework of a wider government reform programme designed to streamline business administration. The first nine centres were established in 1999 and the network now covers the whole country, generally at commune level. They work on an electronic basis but also offer front offices for face-to-face and telephone contacts with businesses.

The Single Counters front offices are operated through cooperative agreements between municipal authorities and local chambers of commerce. Since the reforms also established the principle of silent assent, in most cases this approach enables entrepreneurs to complete necessary procedures through self-declarations. In situations where several government authorities need to review an application, it is possible for municipal authorities to convene a "service council" at the Single Counter office in order to expedite decision-making. Such a council involves representatives of all relevant departments in order to make a simultaneous decision.

Results

The Single Counters have increasingly allowed electronic submission of applications for business registration and construction permits. They have helped to decrease the time taken for businesses to complete the administrative procedures for start up from 23 days to 5.5 days between 2004 and 2016 and the time for registering property from 25 days to 16 in the same period (figures from http://www.doingbusiness.org). In addition, the unified network has provided assurance of a common level of service and approach across the whole country.

Success factors

The system works well because it is a unified system across the whole country, but at the same time there is strong out-reach to businesses through offices at local level that are managed by local operators.

Problems and responses

Initial development of the nationwide network was very slow because of the need to secure the agreement of municipalities and local chambers of commerce to participate in the initiative and to provide them with appropriate guidance. A presidential decree of 2010 improved the situation by giving clear specifications on what each Single Counter should offer and ensuring that all were connected to an electronic network.

Relevance to Kazakhstan

A network of Enterprise Support Centres now supports new businesses with administrative compliance in Kazakhstan. However, they do not cover the regulation of existing businesses. Furthermore, they do not offer a seamless connection to electronic business regulation facilities and self-declaration opportunities and do not involve cross-departmental accelerated decision making on complex cases. Extending the work of the Enterprise Support Centres through a network of local Single Counters for all business regulation along the lines of the Italian model would help to streamline government decision-making and assist businesses in dealing with some of the regulatory issues which are seen as local barriers to business in Kazakhstan (notably corruption and supply of utilities). In addition, a unified local Single Counter system would help to feed information to the business ombudsman on key bottlenecks experienced by small businesses in Kazakhstan with respect to regulatory compliance.

Source: http://www.impresainungiorno.gov.it/

The decision to create a business ombudsman function also offers a method to improve business regulation at the sub-national level, as long as the function has good regional connections to businesses. An important step has already been taken by linking the national business ombudsman with the network of the Chamber of Entrepreneurs. This will help bring to national attention the concerns of local SMEs and entrepreneurs with their treatment by government. These regional connections could be strengthened further by creating a formal network of business ombudsman representatives in each region. These regional representatives of the ombudsman would seek to define ways to improve regulatory compliance implementation with each regional government authority and the SMEs and entrepreneurs in the regions, as well as acting as a channel to deal with complaints from business about regulation.

References

Government of Kazakhstan (2011) Об утверждении Прогнозной схемы территориально-пространственного развития страны до 2020 года. Указ Президента Республики Казахстан от 21 июля 2011 года № 118 [On approval of the predictive scheme for spatial development of the country until 2020. Decree of the President of the Republic of Kazakhstan dated July 21, 2011 № 118]

Junusbekova, Gulsara (2013), Issues of Improving the System of Public Planning in the Republic of Kazakhstan, Public Policy and Administration 2013, Vol. 12, No 2, p. 190–196

OECD (2017), OECD Territorial Reviews: Kazakhstan, OECD Publishing, Paris, DOI http://dx.doi.org/10.1787/9789264269439-en

Polat, Erkan et al (2011), Emerging regional planning structures in Turkey: limits and challenges

Sange Research Centre (2013), "Kazakhstan: Improving Capacity to Support SME Development - SME Survey – A Needs Assessment", May, Asian Development Bank, Manila.

Totkas, Y., Sevinc, H. and Bozkurt, E. (2013) The Evolution of Regional Development Agencies: Turkey Case, Annales Universitatis Apulensis Series Oeconomica, 15.2, 670-681.

Urinboyev, Rustamjon (2015), Local Government Capacity in Post-Soviet Central Asia. Public Policy and Administration 2015, Vol. 14, No 3, p. 177-199.

Chapter 7. Promoting Linkages between Foreign Direct Investment and SMEs in Kazakhstan

This chapter examines how to make use of opportunities for small and medium-sized enterprise (SME) development through promoting linkages between domestic SMEs and foreign direct investment (FDI) establishments operating in Kazakhstan. It examines the opportunities in terms of the scale and nature of FDI, the types of linkages that the FDI can have in the domestic economy and the types of policy measures that could encourage linkages with SMEs. It examines the relevance of modifying existing FDI policy approaches to put more emphasis on the aftercare of the FDI projects that are attracted and of focusing FDI attraction efforts on FDI with linkage potential and steering it towards the locations with related value chain activities. It also examines proactive policy approaches to broker connections between FDI and SMEs and build SME capabilities to supply FDI in regional clusters, suggesting the creation of linkage development teams in each region. It also examines the scope for involving FDI establishments in the support of SME supply chain building and the relevance of strengthening supply chain finance.

Key messages and policy recommendations

Small and medium-sized enterprises (SMEs) can receive a strong boost to their technologies, market access, efficiency and growth by supplying foreign direct investments (FDI) hosted in their regional economies. However, policy actions may be required to create these linkages. In Kazakhstan, the development of linkages between inward FDI operations and domestic SMEs is still in its infancy. This partly reflects the concentration of much of Kazakhstan's inward FDI stock in extractive industries where there are relatively few upstream supply chain opportunities. It is also related to the limited numbers of domestic SMEs with capabilities for supplying FDI at internationally-competitive levels of technology, quality, price, flexibility and delivery performance. To address these issues, policy should focus on attracting the types of inward FDI that are more associated with local supply linkages, improving the capabilities of domestic SMEs to supply foreign investors and brokering the connections between FDI and SMEs.

The main operators in Kazakhstan's FDI policy approach are the national company Kazakh Invest JSC and the regional Investor Service Centres (ISCs). They have so far focused mainly on FDI attraction. They have pursued only limited aftercare activities with FDI operations, despite the potential to use aftercare to encourage foreign-owned operations to explore linkages with local SMEs. Furthermore, the FDI attraction effort is broad and has not been highly focused on targeting the types of FDI projects with the greatest potential SME linkage benefits or steering these projects towards the locations with the greatest potential for supporting regional supplier linkages.

Regional clusters have been mapped out in Kazakhstan in terms of key industry sector concentrations and assets. These clusters could provide an important focus for FDI policy and SME development policy. A common policy tool for FDI-SME linkage development is a database of potential suppliers. Such a database is in the course of establishment in Kazakhstan. The database should be developed in such a way as to make it easy for FDI operations to identify relevant potential SME suppliers in their regional cluster.

Furthermore, FDI attraction efforts should focus more strongly on bringing related FDI projects to regional clusters, i.e. bringing FDI projects to clusters where there is the best potential for developing supply chain linkages. FDI policy should also be extended to pay greater attention to the provision of aftercare to key FDI projects in regional clusters, with the aim of building relationships that encourage greater use of local SME suppliers. At the same time, policy should identify SMEs in the clusters with good potential for supplying FDI and channel available public support to them in areas such as consultancy, finance and training to help them increase their capacities to supply FDI.

In order to develop comprehensive and integrated approaches to FDI-SME linkage development, linkage building teams should be created in each region with the responsibility for providing FDI aftercare, brokering linkages between FDI and regional SMEs, and co-ordinating capacity building support for SMEs with potential to supply FDI. These teams could build on the work that the Kaznez Investor Support Centres already undertakes on FDI aftercare. The OECD Regional Competitiveness Programme detailed FDI-SME linkage building pilot actions that could be pursued in three regions of Kazakhstan working with specific FDI projects. These pilot action proposals can be used as a model for linkage team building and linkage development actions in each region of the country.

Policy should seek to engage foreign investors as far as possible in supporting the development of potential SME suppliers alongside the actions of the public sector. Supply chain finance also needs to be strengthened, although there are various alternatives to encourage it.

The key recommendations of the report on strengthening FDI-SME linkages in Kazakhstan are set out below.

Summary of key recommendations on linkages between FDI and SMEs

- Increase the focus of FDI policy on the potential for SME supply chain development by:
  - Seeking to steer appropriate FDI projects to regional clusters in which FDI-SME linkage building has high potential, based on existing regional cluster mapping; and
  - Expanding FDI aftercare activities, including regular contacts between the public sector and FDI establishments already hosted in Kazakhstan, with the aim of building relationships that would support local supply chain development.
- Develop an integrated set of policy measures to support FDI-SME linkages in each region. This should include activities to:
  - Create an easily accessible and usable database of potential SME suppliers to FDI in the regional clusters;
  - Create and develop regional linkage building teams to make contacts with FDI projects and SMEs within regional clusters and broker and support new linkages; and
  - Co-ordinate an integrated package of consultancy, finance, training and innovation support to selected SMEs with strong potential to supply FDI in regional clusters in order to upgrade their capacities to supply FDI and support them in winning supply contracts.
- Introduce supply chain finance initiatives through the Damu Enterprise Development Fund, such as initiatives to stimulate the factoring market.

Opportunities for linkages between SMEs and FDI in Kazakhstan

FDI inflows are significant, but concentrated in extractive sectors

FDI inflows to Kazakhstan in 2014 amounted to USD 9.6 billion, representing 19.7% of gross fixed capital formation; higher than the average for Commonwealth of Independent States (CIS) countries (7.3%) or transition economies (8.0%) (UNCTAD, 2015). The key countries of origin are the USA, France, the Netherlands, and the United Kingdom, while investment from China has started to become more significant (OECD, 2012).

However, more than 70% of the FDI attracted to Kazakhstan has been in natural resources extraction (OECD, 2012). Kazakhstan has the sixth largest reserve of natural resources in the world and the eleventh largest proven oil reserves. The Kashagan oil field under the Caspian Sea is estimated to represent the largest discovery worldwide in the past 30 years. Kazakhstan is also a source of gold, copper, cobalt, nickel and uranium, as well as iron and coal. Although there are opportunities to build supply chain linkages around FDI in the extractive industries, they can be more limited than in many other sectors because of relatively short supply chains, and because many of the requirements are extremely specialised and need the intervention of international contractors.

The government has a long-term strategy of seeking to diversify the FDI stock towards non-energy sectors, and this should provide more opportunities to develop local supply chains around FDI in the future. In particular, FDI managers see strong inward FDI opportunities in the industry and automotive sectors (Ernst and Young, 2014).

There is a range of potential types of linkages and benefits

Linkages between FDI and SMEs can have a range of benefits for the different parties involved:

- For the host country, linkages can support increased economic activity, import substitution, an improved balance of payments, and a stronger enterprise sector.
- For domestic SMEs, linkages can support better quality standards and competitiveness, market diversification, and possible transfer of technology.
- For multinational companies, there can be gains from transferring to domestic suppliers in the form of lower production costs, increased specialisation and flexibility and better adaptation to local markets.

Table 7.1 summarises the main types of FDI-SME linkages and the types of benefits that they can generate for SMEs. Some of the benefits will only appear over time. The main focus for SME and entrepreneurship policy in this framework tends to be on developing backward linkages – i.e. increasing the use of local suppliers and seeking to encourage technology transfers.

Table 7.1. Types and benefits of FDI-SME linkages

Type of linkage	Definition	Typical benefits
Backward linkages with suppliers	FDI purchases components, materials and services locally.	New market opportunities for local SMEs. Transfers of technology to local SMEs.
Forward linkages with customers	FDI outsources the distribution of its products to local distributors.	Leads to development of downstream relationships with local SMEs (e.g., franchising).
Competition effect	FDI sets new standards for local firms to compete with.	Raises productivity and quality of final goods and services produced by local SME competitors.
Linkages with technology partners	FDI initiates common projects with SME partners (e.g., joint ventures, licensing and strategic alliances)	Source of new technology and know-how for local SMEs partnering with FDI on technology development.
Demonstration effects, labour market mobility, other effects	FDI demonstrates new ways of doing things to local firms. Workers and managers in FDI take jobs in local SMEs or start new local businesses.	Stimulates innovation and human capital spillovers.

Source: OECD, based on OECD (2013) Local Strategies for FDI-SME Linkage Building in Kazakhstan, OECD LEED Programme Paper, OECD, Paris.

FDI-SME linkages do not necessarily occur naturally

To some extent linkages between FDI and SMEs will occur naturally – FDI will often look in its local host region for potential suppliers. However, there are also often barriers to the creation of FDI-SME linkages:

- A common reason for lack of local FDI-SME linkages is lack of a full value chain locally with which FDI can deal, or lack of knowledge among FDI about the existence of SMEs that could fill roles in their value chains;
- SMEs operating within the region of FDI operations with related value chains that they could potentially supply frequently lack information on the FDI supply opportunities and on how to approach and deal with FDI. Regional SMEs with relevant products and services may also lack the capabilities to meet the specific requirements of the FDI in the sense of quality, efficiency, flexibility and other standards required by FDI for their value chain partners;
- Lack of availability of supply chain finance can be a significant barrier for SMEs, which may have to wait to receive payment for work delivered to FDI projects but need to commit working and investment capital in advance of the payment; and
- Lack of appropriate management and workforce skills within SMEs within the value chains of local FDI can be a related barrier, which can hamper SMEs in developing the necessary practices and standards, and limit their productivity and innovation.

Each of these factors appear to be at play in Kazakhstan. In particular, a major barrier lies in limited capabilities in the domestic SME sector in terms of providing a sufficient level of sophistication to work with FDI, as manifested by low levels of productivity and product quality in many firms. In order to engage in business relationships with foreign investors, SMEs need to be competitive in price; meet safety, quality assurance and control requirements; provide timely delivery; be flexible and quick to change designs/product or service mix; be able to design parts and components; and assure long-term commitment (OECD, 2005; UNCTAD, 2011).

The regional level is appropriate to promote FDI-SME linkages

Policy actions are needed to address the various barriers to FDI-SME linkage development. Key actions that can be taken include coordinating FDI attraction efforts with regional cluster building, undertaking matchmaking between FDI establishments and SMEs, and offering targeted consultancy, training, finance and innovation support to SMEs with strong potential for supplying FDI.

National, regional and local policy actors and actions should be involved in this policy effort in both the domains of FDI policy and SME development policy. However, there is particular scope to develop FDI-SME linkage policy actions at the regional level. The regional level offers strong potential to identify appropriate FDI establishments and SMEs to work with, to develop face-to-face contacts to broker and build relationships, to engage FDI establishments in support of local potential suppliers, and to develop targeted SME development actions with selected firms or groups of firms. At this level, the actions of the various relevant national and regional bodies can also be integrated in regionally-tailored packages. There are also important regional clusters in Kazakhstan that provide potentially highly propitious environments for FDI-SME linkages. The effectiveness and efficiency of regional actions can be heightened by targeting these clusters.

Increasing the emphasis of FDI policy on aftercare and embedding

FDI promotion has not been closely targeted to regional supply chain development opportunities

The main responsibility for FDI policy in Kazakhstan lies with the national company Kazakh Invest JSC. It has largely focused on marketing and promotion of Kazakhstan to new FDI. Its approach to this task has developed over time. Its initial activities centred on the promotion of potential investment projects, in particular natural resource exploitation projects, to potential FDI. The existence of regional supply chains (or their potential creation) was not a major factor in those promotional activities.

More recently, the FDI promotion approach of Kaznex Invest has moved to identifying mobile and contestable investments and communicating value propositions to the investors focused on attracting them to locate in Kazakhstan rather than other countries. This has been reflected within Kaznex Invest in a change from orientation toward countries to a more sectoral approach. However, although there is a list of priority sectors for FDI promotion (and, indeed, a list of priority sectors for SME development) the choice of sectors for FDI promotion does not appear to be based directly on the ability to develop linkages in regional clusters.

Government FDI organisations have focused more on FDI attraction than aftercare and supply chain building

Kaznex Invest has mainly focused on FDI attraction

Kaznex Invest, the national investment promotion agency, has so far focused mainly on marketing and promotion and finding new investors. Kaznex Invest has not been strongly involved in the aftercare of FDI ventures already located in the country, except when they requested support for reinvestment and are considered new investors. It has also not operated a dedicated initiative to develop supply chains with existing investors.

Nonetheless, the remit of Kaznex Invest has recently been extended from marketing and promotion to include aftercare and embedding of FDI once it has located in the country. For example, Kaznex now shows on its website a comprehensive set of aftercare services for investors and the resolution of their problems. This offers a good opportunity to strengthen FDI-SME linkages.

The National Agency for the Development of Local Content has focused on extractive industries

In the past, Kazakhstan operated local content legislation that obliged subsoil users (individuals or legal entities that in accordance with the legislation have the right to conduct subsoil use operations) to comply with agreed levels of local content in their procurement processes and to procure goods and services using the prescribed tender process. Such obligations are contained in subsoil use contracts, concluded between the government and the subsoil user. Implementation of these agreements is monitored by the Ministry of Investment and Development and JSC National Agency for the Development of Local Content (NADLoC). Legislation on subsoil use includes providing conditional discounts to Kazakh producers of goods at a rate of 20%. However, after acceding to the World Trade Organisation (WTO) in 2015, Kazakhstan made a commitment to bring the legislation on local content rules into line with WTO rules by 2021 with respect to subsoil use contracts.

The emphasis of the work of NADLoC has therefore shifted towards monitoring the local content in subsoil use contracts and assisting domestic enterprises (of all sizes) to provide local content in competitive processes. In this effort it has worked with the National Chamber of Entrepreneurs and local support agencies in supporting SMEs to identify and obtain procurement opportunities. On the other hand, its operations have been essentially reactive, i.e. assisting SMEs seeking to supply FDI in extractive industries. It has not worked actively in promoting supply chains in regional clusters outside of extraction.

Regional Investor Support Centres have also mainly focused on FDI attraction

In 2013, under a national initiative, Investor Support Centres (ISCs) were established by each regional government authority (Akimat), funded from the regional government budgets and generally hosted by the region's Social Entrepreneurial Company. The role of the ISCs was insufficiently specified in the initial stages, including their relationship with Kaznex Invest, their role in promotion (in particular the degree to which they should promote the regions separately from the whole country, and the way in which Kaznex Invest should forward queries from potential investors), and their involvement in aftercare.

To date, the ISCs have tended to focus on untargeted promotion of their regions to potential inward FDI. Furthermore, the regional governments have provided only limited staff (generally only 2 people) to the ISCs to undertake their work. Kaznex Invest has sought to strengthen the FDI promotion activities by the ISCs at regional level by agreeing protocols on information exchange across the ISCs and with Kaznex Invest centrally to increase co-ordination and differentiation in the FDI promotion work and by providing training in FDI promotion to their staff.

The ISCs could potentially play important roles in FDI aftercare and supply chain development in the regions, working in collaboration with Kaznex Invest. This has been hampered to date by the lack of clear objectives set by Kaznex Invest and the Ministry of National Economy for the ISCs on FDI aftercare and supplier development and an ambiguity about the role of the ISCs and their relationship with national activities.

However, a number of the ISCs (notably Atyrau and Astana) have merged their FDI promotion operations with support for innovation in SMEs. This approach provides a strong potential platform for FDI-SME linkage building through the ISCs and could be extended to other regions. The approach could be reinforced by including FDI-SME linkage development in the definitions of the role expected from ISCs and the key performance indicators used in monitoring this objective.

Developing linkages in regional clusters

Regional clusters can provide a critical mass for FDI-SME linkage building actions

In general, relatively long and specialised supply chains are not highly developed in Kazakhstan. Therefore developing FDI-SME linkages will often require efforts to stimulate the creation of new supply chains. The most favourable environments are likely to be existing regional clusters where there is already some critical mass of SMEs capable of supplying FDI in particular sectors. Further mobile FDI ventures can be steered towards these regional clusters and complementary SME sector strengths in these clusters can be built locally.

The OECD Regional Competitiveness Project has identified potential regional clusters in Kazakhstan. Drawing on this analysis the government could agree and adopt a set of regional clusters. Actions taken to strengthen these clusters could then be delivered, including through targeted FDI promotion, SME development, including workforce training, and specific actions to promote FDI-SME linkages within the clusters.

A supplier database is required for regional clusters

An important common tool internationally for the support of FDI-SME linkages is an accessible supplier database showing the SMEs that could be potential suppliers to FDI. An initiative is underway in Kazakhstan to develop such a database. The database should include a facility to search for SME suppliers within regional clusters together with information on their products and services. Using such a database, foreign investors located in regional clusters could quickly identify which regional SMEs they could potentially set up supply contracts with.

Linkage facilitators and organisations can have an important role in clusters

Where there is already a possible source of supply in the regional cluster, it may be necessary for the SME to make improvements to its design, production capacity, quality, delivery or price to meet the FDI's requirements. Where there is not a source of supply, it may be possible to find an SME willing to diversify to meet this new market opportunity. However, organising this type of development will depend on good relationships with FDI and SMEs and the ability to connect to public support for developments required in the SME, including in terms of associated financing.

Clearly not all local SMEs are able or willing to be involved in linkages with FDI. Therefore any public support for FDI-SME linkages needs to be well targeted towards the smaller number of SMEs with FDI supply potential. In order to identify appropriate SMEs for linkage development support, it is important for the public SME development organisations to get to know their local SME sector very well, including detailed capabilities and intentions of relevant firms. In addition, it is important to work with existing FDI to obtain a good understanding of the FDI's supply requirements and securing the active support of key managers.

Individuals working as linkage facilitators within cluster organisations or inward investment organisations can play an important role in developing close links with the managers of local FDI subsidiaries and SMEs. Currently there is no institution performing this function in regional clusters and no individuals are playing the roles of linkage facilitator. However, the ISCs already have the task of FDI aftercare as well as to undertake general promotion of their respective regions to FDI and could be well placed to undertake the necessary analysis of relevant companies, undertake matchmaking work, and direct SME capability building support to relevant SMEs.

Integrated regional FDI-SME linkage building strategies should be developed

National, regional and local policy actors and actions in the domains of FDI policy and SME development policy can all be engaged in the effort to promote FDI-SME linkages.

However, there is particular scope to develop FDI-SME linkage policy actions at the regional level. The regional level offers strong potential to identify appropriate FDI establishments and SMEs to work with, to develop face-to-face contacts to broker and build relationships, to engage FDI establishments in support of local potential suppliers, and to develop targeted SME development actions with selected firms or groups of firms. At this level, the actions of the various relevant national and regional bodies can also be integrated in regionally-tailored packages.

Integrated regional FDI-SME linkage building strategies should be developed to support this effort, potentially focusing on regional clusters. These strategies should include a number of key features, in particular:

- *Clear responsibility and accountability* (public and private sector institutions that are capable of supporting the strategy and SME development in general). It should be made clear which institutions are responsible for FDI-SME linkages and which roles and responsibilities they have. Appropriate resources also need to be mobilised, including ensuring that staff are appropriately skilled for the tasks to be undertaken;
- *Adequate information/intelligence on FDI and SME activities and motivations* (so that actions take place on the basis of objective information and resources are prioritised). Supply chain development requires actions related to networking and making connections between companies. This should be based on a good understanding of what opportunities exist. This may include, for example, a comprehensive regional supplier database including individual SME capabilities as quantitative information, and clear understanding of the intentions and timetables of FDI as more qualitative intelligence;
- *Engagement of SMEs* (so that the SME sector is actively involved in the programme). SMEs are frequently suspicious of state-run programmes and therefore some action has to be taken to "sell" any new programme to them and to show to them that it has tangible benefits;
- *Engagement of FDI* (so that FDI makes its own contribution). FDI needs also to be convinced of the benefits of participation in any programme. While local content legislation could be a short-term stimulus for some, for successful supply chain development FDI operations will need to find real benefits from linkages; and
- *Policy coordination* (so that actions of different government bodies reinforce each other). Actions to develop linkages need to be coordinated not only with SME policy but also with regional policy and with policies related to attraction and aftercare of FDI.

Box 7.1 offers an example of an integrated local approach to developing SME suppliers around a new FDI project in the United Kingdom.

Box 7.1 Strategy to involve regional SME suppliers in the Hitachi Rail FDI project, United Kingdom

Approach

Hitachi Rail undertook a major FDI project in the North East of the United Kingdom in 2011. It involved investment of GBP 70 million in a new factory in the city of Durham in order to upgrade intercity express trains. The factory was expected to create 500 jobs directly and to deal with orders worth some GBP 4.5 billion over 30 years. The city council and local business associations decided to develop a strategy to seek to maximise the supplies provided from within the region. They were also involved in making the initial case for attracting the project to their region based on the availability of potential suppliers.

Activities

In order to help create supply opportunities for SMEs in the region, the city council and local business associations performed the following linked activities:

- The city council made a special collation of an existing company database to find relevant potential suppliers for the new FDI project;
- The association of local engineering firms organised engineering forums and an annual exhibition event including opportunities to "meet the buyer";
- The city council organised specific supplier engagement events for the FDI project, including events on a sectoral basis. Some 1 800 people from over 1 000 companies attended the events with the FDI project;
- The city council organised a website to keep SMEs informed and to ensure that SMEs helped to keep the database up to date; and
- The city council maintained a strategic account manager for the project to offer aftercare and support in developing linkages with local companies.

Success factors

One of the keys to the success of this initiative was coordination between the local government authority and business representative organisations. The business associations played a critical role in engaging SMEs and providing information on potential suppliers. It was also important to appoint a strategic account manager in the local government authority to work with the FDI project and keep the FDI management in touch with local suppliers and opportunities.

Relevance to Kazakhstan

This example illustrates a proactive strategy for building supplier linkages around a new FDI project. The approach included appointing a local government representative to work on aftercare relationships with the FDI venture, developing a supplier database and brokering linkages between the FDI and potential suppliers through meet the buyer events. In the United Kingdom, the potential suppliers usually had the existing capabilities to meet the needs of the FDI project. In case of Kazakhstan, the aftercare and matchmaking work is likely to need to be complemented with capacity building support for selected potential SME suppliers focused on supporting their investment, innovation, management capacity upgrading and workforce training.

Three existing regional pilot actions in Kazakhstan offer inspiration

During 2012 to 2016, the OECD undertook analytical and capacity-building work with the Kazakhstan government authorities and financial support from the European Union to propose regional FDI-SME linkage actions in the regions of Atyrau, East Kazakhstan and Kyzylorda (see Box 7.2). The work highlighted the need for each region to identify FDI operations willing to increase their purchases from local SMEs, identify SMEs with potential to supply these FDI operations, and offer targeted and proactive business development advice and investment support to the SMEs to help them meet the requirements of FDI contracts.

The work offers guidance on the types of integrated actions that could be undertaken in each region of Kazakhstan to develop a systematic approach to promoting FDI-SME linkages.

Box 7.2 OECD FDI-SME linkages regional pilot actions in Kazakhstan

Approach

As part of the OECD Regional Competitiveness Project undertaken in collaboration with the European Commission and the government of Kazakhstan in 2012-16, outline regional FDI-SME linkage strategies were developed for the Kazakhstan regions of Atyrau, East Kazakhstan and Kyzylorda. They included recommendations for the establishment of linkage building teams within the respective regional government authorities to collate information on local FDI and potential local SME suppliers and outlined some pilot actions with specific FDI partners that would help the linkage building teams to gain credibility and experience with FDI.

Activities

For each region a strategy was proposed involving the following components:

- Form a linkage strategy team with adequate skills and resources;
- Undertake preparatory actions including collecting information on the SME sector and existing FDI, organising finance, SME support, communications and skills provision and planning monitoring and evaluation;
- A set of developmental actions including developing a transparent system that gives comprehensive SME support and formalises networking and contacts with FDI; and
- A set of pilot actions with specific FDI establishments in the region to develop networking with the FDI establishment and the SME sector, demonstrate the potential and needs of supplying FDI to SMEs and give experience to the linkage building team.

Results

In East Kazakhstan, the FDI-SME linkages pilot is now embedded in work to develop local dairy co-operatives to ensure that they can make deliveries of adequate size and quality for the foreign-owned Metro supermarket group, which operates various stores in the region. This included developing a working group on dairy cooperatives, working with KazAgro on financing and development of dairy cooperatives, and working with the Ministry of Agriculture on relevant legal reforms.

In Kyzylorda, the Business Support Centres of the National Chamber of Entrepreneurs have supported the development of capabilities in potential SME suppliers to FDI, including improvements to their industrial property. In addition, the region's ISC worked with a foreign-owned feed mill in Kyzylorda city to promote the use of local supply opportunities. The regional government authority also supported visits by the National Agency for the Development of Local Content and its work with local investments.

In Atyrau, the linkage building work has related to unifying and supporting national business support programmes for SMEs, supporting business start-ups through the Atyrau school of Young Entrepreneurs, and running a forum on local content development bringing together the relevant public and private sector actors in FDI-SME linkage building.

Problems and responses

These pilots have highlighted a lack of detailed regional information on FDI establishments and potential SME suppliers that could be candidates for linkage building support. Developing this intelligence would need to be one of the first priorities of any regional FDI-SME linkage team. In addition, appropriate resources would need to be allocated to the analysis, contacts with FDI and SMEs and the delivery of support actions to SMEs.

Relevance to Kazakhstan

The project developed specific proposals for initiatives that could be taken to develop FDI-SME linkages at regional level and to develop regional capacities to support FDI-SME linkages. These types of initiatives can be further developed in the pilot regions and spread to other regions in Kazakhstan.

Source:
http://www.oecd.org/cfe/leed/fdi-smelinkagestrategiesinkazakhstan.htm.
http://www.oecd.org/globalrelations/centralasiacompetitivenessinitiative.htm.
OECD (2013) Local Strategies for FDI-SME Linkage Building in Kazakhstan, OECD LEED Programme, Paris.

Engaging FDI in SME development support

There is scope for involving FDI in supporting SMEs to access FDI supply chains

In responding to local content legislation, FDI ventures have often listed and certified selected companies as suppliers. In some cases, they have also offered supplier credit to assist firms to engage. However, the typical FDI establishment in Kazakhstan has not worked more proactively to help potential suppliers to build their capacities to engage in supply chains.

It is not uncommon, however, for FDI establishments in Kazakhstan and other countries to become strongly involved in supply chain development and partner with government in preparing and delivering supplier chain development programmes. Box 7.3 presents the example of Chevron, which was actively involved in supporting local start-ups in the Atyrau region of Kazakhstan. Box 7.4 provides another example, focusing on a programme involving BP and other FDI in Azerbaijan, which focused more on building linkages with existing SMEs.

These models highlight the potential for public authorities in Kazakhstan to engage FDI operations themselves more strongly in supply chain development with SMEs.

Box 7.3 FDI-supported business incubator, Atyrau, Kazakhstan

Through Tengizchevroil, Chevron supported a small business development programme in Atyrau which ran over to 12 years up until 2009. A major objective of the programme was to increase the participation of local SMEs in the Tengizchevroil supply chain. One part of the programme was a business incubator initiative supported by the company and the United Nations Development Programme. Over its life, the incubator supported 174 start-ups and small business by providing advice and loan funding of approximately USD 7 million (KZT 840 million). Close to 2 000 new jobs were created. However, only 6 of the start-ups joined Tengizchevroil's supply chain. Furthermore, these businesses were largely service suppliers, providing printing and electrical services, for example. The one manufacturer, TauKen LLP, was a raw materials production and processing firm providing broken stone.

This experience illustrates both that FDI operations can make important investments in building a local supplier base and the difficulties of developing new suppliers for FDI through start-up support.

Box 7.4 FDI-supported Enterprise Development and Training Programme, Azerbaijan

Approach

BP launched the Enterprise Development and Training Programme (EDTP) in Azerbaijan in June 2007 to build a sustainable local supply chain and underpin the company's license to operate in the Caspian region. It offers targeted training and development services for SMEs, working with an independent local contractor (AZERMS LLC-Azerbaijan Enterprise Risk Management Services) and some 15-20 other FDI operations in the oil and gas sector (co-venturers).

EDTP is a hands-on outreach programme to SMEs located in Baku and Sumgait, the two largest cities of Azerbaijan. An SME is eligible to participate in the programme if it is an existing enterprise with ongoing business registered in Azerbaijan and provides products or services of interest to the oil and gas industry. Participating SMEs are chosen through market research and self-enrolment. The cost of the programme is covered by BP and co-venturers.

The assistance provided comprises a 4-step process that analyses companies' technical and commercial gaps, designs a customised upgrade plan, provides targeted technical assistance to implement the plan, and then follows up and monitors the progress. The support is in three main areas: marketing and sales;

compliance with buyer requirements for quality, safety and the environment; and training and education.

Those SMEs that successfully complete the EDTP are prepared and qualified to participate in BP supply tenders in Azerbaijan. They are also expected to be well positioned to meet the opportunities offered by the oil and gas industry across the wider Caspian and Black Sea regions and beyond.

Activities

The process through which SME development services are delivered is highly interactive. This interaction is very important for the success of the programme. If an SME meets the eligibility requirements, it undergoes a preliminary gap analysis, which is actually a business assessment, by the EDTP team. During this stage, the company is mainly required to demonstrate its willingness and commitment to development, and show that it is ready to work with the EDTP team and fulfil the requirements for becoming a competitive supplier.

After agreeing on the way forward, a service agreement is signed between the SME and the EDTP. Once the agreement is signed, a detailed gap analysis is performed, looking at both technical and commercial areas for improvement. Then the EDTP team meets with the SME and works with them to develop an action plan based on the results of the gap analysis. At this stage, the EDTP team works closely with owners, general managers, senior management, and staff of the SME to ensure that the approaches taken are suitable for the company. The action plan elaborates the quality management requirements, actions to meet international standards and requirements for technical upgrades as well as staff training needs.

To work on the technical issues, the EDTP arranges one-on-one visits and meetings with an industry expert to provide assessments and recommendations. These specialised consultants provide highly technical insight and guidance to SMEs. They also advise on international quality certification requirements.

It is the SME's responsibility to implement the actions. The EDTP team mainly facilitates and guides, and works closely with the SME to ensure the full and effective implementation of the action plan. SMEs that implement their action plans are required to maintain performance records and meet all the requirements set in the action plan. An SME graduates from the EDTP when the action plan is successfully implemented. SMEs find this approach very useful as it helps them build capacities and internalise the whole process of developing their management and technical capacities.

Success factors

Specific success factors behind the EDTP that are relevant in considering how to develop similar programmes elsewhere include:

- FDI is involved in and committed to the linkage programme and has ownership as potential customers. This is particularly the case with the leadership of BP. There is also a critical mass of FDI and a pool of local SMEs looking for new clients and new markets;
- A dedicated and qualified implementation team has been critical. In the case of EDTP, the AZERMS team had clear tasks, responsibilities, and

business processes at the beginning. During implementation stage, they continuously monitored the progress and learned from mistakes;

- The skills and competencies of the consultants to the SMEs are also important. The EDTP team uses professional certified consultants with experiences in related activities. Its human resources structures include a core local staff and additional foreign experts for high-complexity sectors and some specific development needs. The core consultants follow a continuous professional development programme; and
- Other components of the local supplier development efforts of BP and its co-venturers complement the EDTP. One of them is the Supplier Finance Facility (SFF). This has provided access to USD 15 million of financing to BP's local contractors. BP and its co-venturers funded USD 6 million and the IFC and Micro-Finance Bank of Azerbaijan (MFBA) contributed USD 6 million and USD 3 million, respectively.

Problems and responses

It can be difficult to engage SMEs in such a programme, at least at the beginning. The EDTP team started with organising introductory workshops and tried to reach SMEs through various channels such as the chambers, unions, government departments responsible for SME supports. However, the team realised that none of these approaches were sufficiently effective. They therefore decided to identify and visit companies one-by-one, sit with them and discuss their growth and competitiveness problems.

Results

From 2007-2011, the EDTP yielded the following outcomes:

- More than 1 000 companies took part in trainings and preliminary assessments;
- Detailed gap analyses were performed and action plans were produced for 360 SMEs;
- More than 100 companies completed the programme successfully;
- More than half of the graduate companies won contracts with BP and its co-venturers; and
- Local companies secured additional contracts valued at more than USD 184 million, of which USD 125 million was with BP in Azerbaijan.

Relevance to Kazakhstan

This programme shows how an FDI company can put in place a programme to rapidly upgrade the capabilities of local SMEs and assist them to enter its supply chain. This type of initiative could be stimulated by the government in Kazakhstan with relevant FDI companies. Furthermore, the programme achieved good results in the extractive industries sector, which is a sector in which Kazakhstan has strong FDI inflows and specialisation.

Source: Interviews with BP and the EDTP team by the OECD and material supplied by BP.

Developing supply chain finance

Supply chain finance should be strengthened

One of the common challenges to supply chain development can be a lack of investment and working capital among potential SME suppliers to enable them to upgrade their products and processes and to deliver output in advance of payment. In Kazakhstan, financial markets are still underdeveloped and there are still shortages of supply chain finance. New initiatives should therefore be considered to strengthen supply chain finance.

The need to strengthen supply chain finance in Kazakhstan is clear, but the best mechanism to supply it requires further examination of the various alternatives. A potential model to develop supply chain finance is illustrated by a public development bank supported electronic factoring platform in Mexico, as outlined in Box 7.5.

Box 7.5 NAFIN Reverse Factoring Programme, Mexico

Approach

National Financiera (Nafin) is a public development bank in Mexico. It created a reverse factoring initiative in the early 2000s called Productive Chains (Cadenas Productivas). This involved large enterprises (often FDI) initiating contact with the public development bank to offer online low cost factoring services through commercial financial institutions to support SMEs to enter their supply chains.

Activities

The programme worked by creating 'chains' between 'Big Buyers' with low credit risk and SME suppliers with needs for financing receivables. Participating SMEs had to be registered with Nafin and have an account with a bank that had a relationship with the supplier's Big Buyer. Following a factoring transaction, funds were transferred directly to the supplier's bank account, and the bank (the factor) became the creditor (i.e. the Buyer repays the bank directly). The factor collected the loan amount directly from the Buyer (in 30 to 90 days). Nafin provided low cost funds to the banks to cover these transactions.

Nafin required that all factoring services it brokered were offered by the commercial banks without additional collateral or service fees, at a maximum interest rate of seven percentage points above Nafin's bank rate (five percentage points, on average), which is about eight percentage points below commercial bank rates.

The sale of receivables from the Buyer to the factor and the transfer of funds from the factor to the supplier were managed on an electronic platform operated by Nafin. Over 98% of all services were provided electronically, which reduces time and labour costs required and improves security.

Success factors

The electronic factoring platform was critical to the success of the programme. Nafin covered the costs of establishing and running the platform and all the legal work, such as document transfers, preparing and signing documents, etc. The electronic platform also allowed all commercial banks to participate in the programme, which gave national reach, via the Internet, to regional banks and developed a competition among banks for factoring services. Nafin covered its cost with the interest that lenders paid for Nafin's refinancing capital and its service fees. Furthermore, all the factoring was undertaken on a non-recourse basis, which enabled small firms to increase their cash holdings and improve their balance sheets.

An additional advantage of the electronic platform is that it reduced opportunities for fraud. Since only large buyers were able to enter new receivables, sellers could not submit fraudulent receivables. Moreover, since the bank was paid directly by the buyer, suppliers could embezzle the proceeds.

Problems and responses

The success of this type of initiative depends on having the infrastructure and institutions to work electronically on factoring. For example, the programme depended on legal and regulatory support offered in Mexican Electronic Signature and Security laws and on high levels of internet connection by SMEs. These may be bottlenecks in Kazakhstan, meaning that any pilot system would have to grow slowly.

Results

This programme gave a critical stimulus to creating a significant factoring market in Mexico and helped SMEs to participate in FDI value chains. Many SMEs participating in the Nafin programme reported that they had no access to external financing before receiving financing from Nafin and most previously depended on internal funds and credit from their own suppliers. In addition, suppliers stated that Nafin financing was preferable to bank financing, since banks were slow to make credit decisions, would offer less credit and charged higher rates.

Between 2001 and mid-2004 Nafin established Productive Chains with 190 Big Buyers (about 45% in the private sector) and more than 70 000 SMEs (out of a total of approximately150 000 participating suppliers). About 20 domestic lenders participated, including banks and independent finance companies. Some 11 million transactions were brokered at a rate of about 4 000 operations per day. In addition to the factoring services, Nafin capitalised on its information on the sales and payment history of small sellers to offer contract financing. This provided financing of up to 50% of confirmed contract orders from buyers with Nafin supply chains, with no fees or collateral, and a fixed rate.

Relevance to Kazakhstan

This programme highlights how the use of an electronic platform can create new financial services for SMEs and penetrate to large numbers of banks across the country including in rural areas.

Source: Klapper (2006), The Role of Factoring for SME Finance. Access Finance December 2006 Issue No. 15. World Bank Group, Washington.

References

Ernst and Young (2014), EY's attractiveness survey Kazakhstan 2014: The brand paves the way.

Klapper, L. (2006), The Role of Factoring for SME Finance. Access Finance December 2006 Issue No. 15. World Bank Group, Washington.

OECD (2013), Local Strategies for FDI-SME Linkage Building in Kazakhstan: Final Report May 2013 (unpublished).

OECD (2012), OECD Investment Policy Reviews: Kazakhstan 2012, OECD Publishing, Paris, http://dx.doi.org/10.1787/9789264121812-en

OECD (2005) Encouraging Linkages between Small and Medium-sized Companies and Multinational Enterprises -An Overview of Good Policy Practices by the OECD Investment Committee, OECD, Paris.

UNCTAD (2015), World Investment Report. United Nations, New York.

UNCTAD (2011) How to Create and Benefit from FDI-SME Linkages, United Nations, New York.

ORGANISATION FOR ECONOMIC CO-OPERATION AND DEVELOPMENT

The OECD is a unique forum where governments work together to address the economic, social and environmental challenges of globalisation. The OECD is also at the forefront of efforts to understand and to help governments respond to new developments and concerns, such as corporate governance, the information economy and the challenges of an ageing population. The Organisation provides a setting where governments can compare policy experiences, seek answers to common problems, identify good practice and work to co-ordinate domestic and international policies.

The OECD member countries are: Australia, Austria, Belgium, Canada, Chile, the Czech Republic, Denmark, Estonia, Finland, France, Germany, Greece, Hungary, Iceland, Ireland, Israel, Italy, Japan, Korea, Latvia, Lithuania, Luxembourg, Mexico, the Netherlands, New Zealand, Norway, Poland, Portugal, the Slovak Republic, Slovenia, Spain, Sweden, Switzerland, Turkey, the United Kingdom and the United States. The European Union takes part in the work of the OECD.

OECD Publishing disseminates widely the results of the Organisation's statistics gathering and research on economic, social and environmental issues, as well as the conventions, guidelines and standards agreed by its members.

OECD PUBLISHING, 2, rue André-Pascal, 75775 PARIS CEDEX 16
(85 2018 13 1 P) ISBN 978-92-64-30144-3 – 2018

www.ingramcontent.com/pod-product-compliance
Ingram Content Group UK Ltd.
Pitfield, Milton Keynes, MK11 3LW, UK
UKHW051500290926
15471UKWH00008B/1319

9 789264 301443